Careers in Education & Training

Careers in Education & Training

Editor

Michael Shally-Jensen, Ph.D.

SALEM PRESS

A Division of EBSCO Information Services, Inc.

Ipswich, Massachusetts

GREY HOUSE PUBLISHING

Publisher's Cataloging-In-Publication Data
(Prepared by The Donohue Group, Inc.)

Names: Shally-Jensen, Michael, editor.
Title: Careers in education & training / editor, Michael Shally-Jensen, Ph.D.
Other Titles: Careers in education and training | Careers in--
Description: [First edition]. | Ipswich, Massachusetts : Salem Press, a division of EBSCO Information Services, Inc. ; [Amenia, New York] : Grey House Publishing, [2016] | Includes bibliographical references and index. | Identifiers: ISBN 978-1-68217-150-9 (hardcover)
Subjects: LCSH: Education--Vocational guidance--United States. | Training--Vocational guidance--United States. | Teaching--Vocational guidance--United States.
Classification: LCC LB1775.2 .C374 2016 | DDC 370.2373--dc23

First Printing

CONTENTS

PUBLISHER'S NOTE

Careers in Education & Training contains twenty-four alphabetically arranged chapters describing specific fields of interest in this field. Merging scholarship with occupational development, this single comprehensive guidebook provides students interested in careers in the fields of education and training with the necessary insight into potential careers, and provides instruction on what job seekers can expect in terms of training, advancement, earnings, job prospects, working conditions, relevant associations, and more. *Careers in Education & Training* is specifically designed for a high school and undergraduate audience and is edited to align with secondary or high school curriculum standards.

Scope of Coverage

Understanding the wide net of jobs in the areas of education and training is important for anyone preparing for a career within those fields. *Careers in Education & Training* comprises twenty-four lengthy chapters on a broad range of occupations including jobs such as archivist and curator, curriculum specialist, and principal, as well as in-demand jobs including reading specialist, ESL teacher, administrator, and media specialist. This excellent reference also presents possible career paths and occupations within high-growth and emerging fields in this field.

Careers in Education & Training is enhanced with numerous charts and tables, including projections from the US Bureau of Labor Statistics, and median annual salaries or wages for those occupations profiled. Each chapter also notes those skills that can be applied across broad occupation categories. Interesting enhancements, like **Fun Facts**, **Famous Firsts**, and dozens of photos, add depth to the discussion. A highlight of most chapters is **Conversation With** – a two-page interview with a professional working in a related job. The respondents share their personal career paths, detail potential for career advancement, offer advice for students, and include a "try this" for those interested in embarking on a career in their profession.

Essay Length and Format

Each chapter ranges in length from 3,500 to 4,500 words and begins with a Snapshot of the occupation that includes career clusters, interests, earnings and employment outlook. This is followed by these major categories:

- **Overview** includes detailed discussions on: Sphere of Work; Work Environment; Occupation Interest; A Day in the Life. Also included here is a Profile that outlines working conditions, educational needs, and physical abilities. You will also find the occupation's Holland Interest Score, which matches up character and personality traits with specific jobs.

- **Occupational Specialties** lists specific jobs that are related in some way, like software developer, librarian, multimedia artist and animator, and chief science officer. Duties and Responsibilities are also included.
- **Work Environment** details the physical, human, and technological environment of the occupation profiled.
- **Education, Training, and Advancement** outlines how to prepare for this field while in high school, and what college courses to take, including licenses and certifications needed. A section is devoted to the Adult Job Seeker, and there is a list of skills and abilities needed to succeed in the job profiled.
- **Earnings and Advancements** offers specific salary ranges, and includes a chart of metropolitan areas that have the highest concentration of the profession.
- **Employment and Outlook** discusses employment trends, and projects growth to 2020. This section also lists related occupations.
- **Selected Schools** list those prominent learning institutions that offer specific courses in the profiles occupations.
- **More Information** includes associations that the reader can contact for more information.

Special Features

Several features continue to distinguish this reference series from other career-oriented reference works. The back matter includes:
- Appendix A: Guide to Holland Code. This discusses John Holland's theory that people and work environments can be classified into six different groups: Realistic; Investigative; Artistic; Social; Enterprising; and Conventional. See if the job you want is right for you!
- Appendix B: General Bibliography. This is a collection of suggested readings, organized into major categories.
- Subject Index: Includes people, concepts, technologies, terms, principles, and all specific occupations discussed in the occupational profile chapters.

Acknowledgments

Thanks to editor Michael Shally-Jensen, who played a principal role in shaping this work with current, comprehensive, and valuable material. Thanks are also due to Allison Blake, who took the lead in developing "Conversations With," with help from Vanessa Park, and to the professionals who communicated their work experience through interview questionnaires. Their frank and honest responses provide immeasurable value to *Careers in Education & Training*. The contributions of all are gratefully acknowledged.

EDITOR'S INTRODUCTION

Introduction

For those who enjoy working with children, youth, or even adult learners, a career in teaching may be just the thing. Educating the next generation of workers and professionals to take their place in the global economy has long been a national priority. Noting that there have been some declines in student performance in core subject areas, including science and math, policymakers across the United States have called for solutions that give students an edge. Today's students have embraced technology like no other generation has. To keep up with the trends of the 21st century, policies have been enacted to put more teachers in schools and to support the use of technology in the classroom—and beyond. Across all education levels and over a variety of platforms, teachers engage students in learning every day.

Teachers give students the knowledge and skills to succeed in school and to prepare them for life after graduation. The size of the teaching force, in fact, has expanded greatly in recent years. The U.S. Census Bureau indicates that preK-thru-12 teachers form the largest occupational group in the nation, and it continues to grow. There have been dramatic increases in the number of pre-kindergarten teachers, bilingual/English-as-a-Second-Language (ESL) teachers, and those teaching elementary enrichment classes (i.e., single subjects like art, music, physical education, computer science, or mathematics). Another major growth area has been that of special education, linked to changes in the Individuals with Disabilities Education Act.

Teaching as a career, then, is expected to present many job opportunities in the coming years. According to the U.S. Bureau of Labor Statistics (BLS), between 2014 and 2024 nearly 1.9 million job openings will arise for teachers of preschool through postsecondary school. The great majority of teaching positions have been and likely will continue to be in public school settings, but charter schools and private schools remain important employers as well. Most of the new hires in the next years will be recent college graduates, but a significant number are expected to be somewhat older yet inexperienced beginning teachers (including those switching careers from other occupations). And, while the teaching force has traditionally been substantially populated by women and is expected to continue to be so, the opposite is true in terms of the race or ethnicity of teachers: minorities have been entering teaching at higher rates than whites in recent decades, and that trend seems likely to continue.

At the college level, there has been an increase in the use of part-time adjunct professors, which has brought about a variety of changes and opportunities in that field. Furthermore, teaching is not limited to schools and colleges. Many businesses and organizations make use of instructors or trainers to keep their employees up to date on the latest developments in technology, business improvement, and human relations. In short, teaching is a broad field that presents good opportunities for a wide range of career seekers.

Varieties of Teaching

Preschool and K-12 Teachers. This is by far the largest group in the teaching profession. Employment of teachers in preschools and kindergartens and elementary, middle, and high schools totaled about 3.6 million workers in 2014, according to BLS. The largest number were in elementary schools, where about 37 percent of teachers in this group worked. BLS expects most of these occupations to have average employment growth over the next ten years.

In this group are also career/technical education teachers in high schools and middle schools; yet far fewer of these teachers (roughly 25,000) will be needed by school districts over the next ten years than, for example, elementary school teachers (380,000).

The same can generally be said of occupations such as librarian, school counselor, or sports coach: those who do this work will certainly be needed in the coming years, but demand for them will be somewhat lower than that for regular classroom teachers.

Postsecondary Teachers. Teachers in this group (usually known as professors or instructors) work in community colleges, universities, technical and trade schools, and other institutions of higher learning. They instruct students in a variety of disciplines, including business, engineering, and culinary arts. Most of them have master's degrees or Ph.D.s. Nearly 1.9 million postsecondary teachers were employed in 2014, according to BLS. In general, these occupations are expected to grow faster than the average in the next ten years, creating more than half a million job openings.

The fastest growth (19 percent increase) is expected to be in the area of health sciences, including nursing instructors and teachers. (Obviously, however, this is a specialized subject demanding years of training and experience; it is not for the beginning teacher!) By comparison, employment of vocational education teachers, which also had high employment, is expected to have average growth (7 percent).

Special Education and Literacy Teachers. This is another strong area. Special education teachers work with students who have disabilities or special learning needs, while literacy, or ESL, teachers work with those needing instruction in practical English. Another group of teachers, tutors or teaching assistants, work with students who want remedial help.

According to BLS, there were 876,800 special education and other teachers in 2014. All special education and literacy occupations are expected to experience average (7 percent) or slightly above average (9 percent) growth over the next ten years.

Teaching-Related Occupations. This group includes school counselors and administrators along with librarians and coaches and those who work in nonschool settings such as businesses and nonprofit organizations. BLS does not have detailed data on this group as a group, but the picture for the individual occupations mentioned here is close to the average for all occupations, as far as expected growth is concerned. The one exception may be librarian, with future growth only around 2 percent (but growth, nonetheless).

Teachers' Pay

Naturally, teachers' wages vary based on factors such as grade level and geographic location. Among K-12 teachers, according to BLS, annual wages were highest, in 2015, for secondary, or high school, teachers at $57,200. Other K-12 teachers earned wages in the $50,000 range, with the exception of preschool teachers—who earned about half that amount ($28,570).

Also in 2015, postsecondary teachers earned about $10,000 more per year than K-12 school teachers ($64,450 compared with $54,890). Yet, nearly every teaching occupation earned more than the median annual wage for all occupations in May 2015: $36,200. Vocational education teachers had the lowest annual wage ($49,470) of all postsecondary teachers, while law professors earned the highest average wage ($105,250). Ironically, self-improvement teachers, who work outside the schools, had the highest employment along with a high projected growth rate (15 percent)—yet also had the lowest wage ($36,680) of any educators.

Teacher Qualifications

The teaching profession demands a number of skills, educational accomplishments, and other qualifications of its members (and its would-be members). Although the specifics of each job tend to vary by subject and grade level, teaching generally comes with three requirements: communication skills, a bachelor's degree, and a teacher's license.

Communication and Other Skills. Communication skills, both written and oral, are crucial for teachers. At all education levels, teachers must be able to express information in a clear and engaging manner and be open to listening to and responding to students' questions. Teachers also write reports, give feedback on assignments, and interact with different types of people—including parents, colleagues, and students. They need to be accommodating yet authoritative with students, and patient and resourceful with regard to the school environment and the many expectations of the job. One key to successful teaching is the ability to engage students at the personal level and find learning strategies that work for each individual.

Organizational skills are also important. Teachers must manage numerous different components throughout the day: curricula and lesson plans, student assignments and tests, teacher meetings and committees, and professional development goals, to name a few. Solid recordkeeping, along with good people skills, helps keep teachers on track and the workweek go more smoothly.

Education Requirements. Most teaching jobs require at least a bachelor's degree. For example, K-12 teachers in most states need a bachelor's degree. Prospective teachers take education courses to learn different instructional techniques and communication styles appropriate to their students' level. Those planning to teach kindergarten and elementary school, for example, may need to take a course in child psychology. Those specializing in science or math, obviously, would do well to study those subjects—although that is not a requirement in all cases.

There are two teaching occupations that generally require less than a bachelor's degree for entry: preschool teachers (associate's degree) and what is called nonvocational self-improvement teachers (high school diploma). In the case of postsecondary teachers, or those who teach at professional schools or at colleges or universities, a master's or doctoral degree is usually required.

Other Qualifications. To work in public schools, teachers usually need certification or a license. This may mean completing a teacher education program and passing tests that demonstrate subject-matter and instructional knowledge.

Teacher education programs prepare teaching candidates to work in the occupation. These programs often include internships—commonly known as student teaching— that require teacher candidates to work with a mentor teacher and gain experience in the classroom.

Most states also require teachers to pass a background check and to complete continuing education classes or seminars in order to maintain their certification or license. National Board certification is a voluntary credentialing option that may allow teachers to bypass continuing education in some states, but it does not replace each state's individual requirements. Some states have alternative teacher certification or reciprocity agreements with other states to encourage people to enter or continue in the occupation.

Rewards and Challenges of Teaching

As with many professions, teaching comes with its own set of rewards and challenges. It can be gratifying, for example, to see students excel, but it can also be difficult to keep students orderly, interested, and on track with the lesson plan.

For most teachers, helping students to learn is the best part of the job. Sharing ideas and information with students and knowing that they have grasped a subject is regarded as a satisfying, even exciting, experience. Teachers also can learn about and bond with their students personally as they help them to make the most of their school years. In doing so they often become not just teachers but mentors and role models for students. In some cases, they may even become friends, in some respects, who remain in touch after the student graduates.

Teachers also have the benefit of working with other teachers and professionals who value education as much as they do. People working together in a school often serve as a support network for one another, sharing ideas, friendship, and advice.

Such sharing may be needed because, typically, each new day brings new surprises, challenges, and rewards. Another advantage of teaching is that the school year usually lasts 10 months, allowing teachers time to travel, relax, or earn additional income during their breaks.

On the negative side, teachers often remark that classroom management is one of their biggest challenges. Keeping students interested and engaged in a lesson requires a good deal of energy and devotion, particularly when students have varied learning styles and absorb the material at different rates. Keeping the classroom under control can be stressful for teachers when bored or discouraged students disrupt lessons. Long hours at school and bringing the workload home at night to do grading or prepare new materials add to the stresses of the job. Likewise discouraging, it is often noted, are the various federal and state educational requirements that must be satisfied. Education standards that use test scores to measure student performance, for example, may limit how much time teachers can spend on a topic. Another point of frustration is limited school funding or budget cuts that can affect the quality of education in a school district and in the classroom.

—M. Shally-Jensen, Ph.D.

Sources

Ingersoll, Richard and Lisa Merrill. *Seven Trends: The Transformation of the Teaching Force*. Philadelphia: Consortium for Policy Research in Education, 2013.

Thompson, Scott. "Trends in Teaching Jobs," *Chron*. Houston: Houston Chronicle, n.d.

Vilorio, Dennis. "Teaching for a Living," *Career Outlook*. Washington, DC: Bureau of Labor Statistics, 2016.

Archivist & Curator

Snapshot

Career Cluster(s): Arts; Education & Training

Interests: History, culture, art, preserving documents, organizing information, research, communication

Earnings (Yearly Average): $50,250

Employment & Outlook: Average Growth Expected

OVERVIEW

Sphere of Work

Archivists and curators are preservationists of human culture and history and the natural world. They collect, appraise, organize, and preserve documents, artwork, specimens, ephemera, films, and many other objects for historical and educational purposes. Archivists usually handle documents and records that are of historical value. Curators are more likely  to manage cultural or biological items, such as artwork or nature collections.

Work Environment

Archivists work in libraries, government depositories, universities, and historical museums, while curators are more often employed in art museums, zoos, nature centers, and other cultural or scientific institutions. Each typically divides the workweek between independent projects and interaction with other staff and outsiders, such as dealers, researchers, and the public.

Profile

Working Conditions: Work Indoors
Physical Strength: Light Work
Education Needs: Master's Degree, Doctoral Degree
Licensure/Certification: Usually Not Required
Opportunities For Experience: Internship, Apprenticeship, Volunteer Work, Part Time Work
Holland Interest Score*: AES, IRS

* See Appendix A

Occupation Interest

People interested in archivist or curator positions value the contributions of humans or the natural world and realize their importance in research. They are scholars who possess good organizational skills and a knack for handling irreplaceable items that are often fragile and extremely valuable. They need to be both detail-oriented and aware of larger cultural, scientific, and/or historical contexts. Other important traits include critical thinking, leadership ability, oral and written communication skills, and a high level of integrity.

A Day in the Life—Duties and Responsibilities

Archivists and curators build on their institution's collections by purchasing items or receiving them as gifts, often the result of bequests. A collection donated by a celebrated author might consist of boxes of unpublished manuscripts and drafts, personal correspondence, publishing contracts, and other printed matter. A collection obtained from a philatelist might include rare postal stamps, philatelic books and journals, microscopes, antique magnifying glasses, and other materials.

The archivist or curator is usually responsible for deciding what items to keep based on physical condition, financial, historical, and cultural value, and relevance to the institution's mission or purpose. While assessing each item, he or she authenticates its provenance (date and origin) and researches the item for any additional relevant information. The archivist or curator also determines how best to preserve and store items. For example, special cabinets may have to be ordered or an item may be given to a conservator for repairs.

Next, the archivist or curator catalogues or classifies items in a database so scholars can access the information. These databases also allow archivists or curators to keep track of their collections, provide reference service, and plan exhibits. Many different classification systems are used, although the most common one in the United States is the Library of Congress Classification System. Some items may be given a taxonomic classification as well as a call number.

Curators and archivists have other tasks in addition to their preservation work. Curators and archivists often write articles, grant proposals, and annual reports. Depending on their work environment, they may give tours and presentations to the public. Curators and archivists may also take care of other administrative duties or oversee assistants who handle some of these responsibilities, or they may do everything themselves.

Duties and Responsibilities

- Analyzing and appraising the value of documents, such as government records, minutes, meetings, letters and charters of institutions
- Selecting and editing documents for publication and display
- Preparing budgets, maintaining inventories, representing the institution at meetings and soliciting financial support
- Planning and designing exhibits
- Writing for technical publications
- Setting up educational displays at a museum

OCCUPATION SPECIALTIES

Museum Technicians

Museum Technicians prepare specimens for museum collections and exhibits. They preserve and restore specimens by reassembling fragmented pieces and creating substitute pieces.

Art Conservators

Art Conservators coordinate the examination, repair and conservation of art objects.

Historic-Site Administrators

Historic-Site Administrators manage the overall operations of an historic structure or site.

Museum Registrars

Museum Registrars maintain records of the condition and location of objects in museum collections and oversee the movement of objects to other locations.

WORK ENVIRONMENT

Physical Environment

Archivists and curators tend to work at least part of the time in climate-controlled storage facilities. They may have to wear white gloves or masks to protect items from human contamination. They sometimes deal with dust, mold, and insect infestations. Fieldwork may include visits to off-site locations such as auctions, schools, and private residences.

Relevant Skills and Abilities

Communication Skills
- Speaking effectively
- Writing concisely

Organization & Management Skills
- Coordinating tasks
- Making decisions
- Managing people/groups
- Paying attention to and handling details

Research & Planning Skills
- Analyzing information
- Creating ideas
- Developing evaluation strategies
- Using logical reasoning

Technical Skills
- Performing scientific, mathematical and technical work

Human Environment

Archivists and curators usually report to a director and may supervise assistants, volunteers, or interns. In some cases, the curator is the director and reports to a board of administrators. Archivists and curators also interact with clerical staff and fellow preservation professionals, such as librarians, conservators, or museum technicians. They also work with researchers and other members of the public who use their facilities.

Technological Environment

Archivists and curators rely heavily on computers for research, database management, file sharing, and communication. They also use a variety of digitization equipment for preservation purposes, including digital photography and video cameras. Microscopes are often used for detail work. In many cases, they must be familiar with radio-frequency identifications (RFIDs) and other inventory control and anti-theft systems.

EDUCATION, TRAINING, AND ADVANCEMENT

High School/Secondary

Archivist and curator positions require advanced education. A strong college preparatory program with electives in the areas of professional interest will provide the best foundation for postsecondary studies. History courses are especially important for aspiring archivists and curators. Students interested in becoming a curator of art should take art history and appreciation courses. Botany, zoology, and other natural sciences are important for curators of natural history. Students should also consider volunteering or working part-time in a library, museum, or other similar institution.

Suggested High School Subjects
- Algebra
- Arts
- Biology
- Chemistry
- College Preparatory
- Composition
- English
- Foreign Languages
- History
- Humanities
- Literature
- Social Studies

Famous First

The first museum devoted exclusively to American political memorabilia was the Museum of American Political Life, established in 1989 at the University of Hartford. The museum was designed to display political posters, buttons, banners, textiles, medals, and a host of other paraphernalia—nearly 70,000 items in all—amassed by insurance executive J. Doyle Dewitt. In 2003, however, the building in which the collection was housed was converted to other purposes. In 2016 there were plans afoot to auction off the collection, even as supporters sought to keep it together and possibly display it elsewhere.

College/Postsecondary

A bachelor's degree in history, art history, botany, political sciencé, or other relevant discipline, with additional coursework in archival or museum studies, is the minimum requirement; however, most positions require a master's degree or doctorate in the specialized discipline or a master's degree in library science, archival studies, or museum studies. Business and public administration courses may also be useful. An internship or other work experience in a related institution is typically required for employment. Continuing education courses are expected as part of ongoing professional training.

Related College Majors
- American (U.S.) History
- Art History, Criticism & Conservation
- Art, General
- Historic Preservation/Conservation & Architectural History
- History
- Library Science/Librarianship
- Museology/Museum Studies
- Public History & Archival Administration

Adult Job Seekers

Adults who have experience working at a relevant institution, researching a particular type of collection, or writing grant proposals or fundraising have an advantage over inexperienced graduates, as maturity and experience are often desired in addition to education.

Advancement is highly dependent upon the size of the institution. In larger institutions, advancement usually takes the form of increasing responsibility, such as a supervisory or directorial position. In government positions, one can move into higher pay grades with proper experience and education. Consulting is also an option for experienced professionals.

Professional Certification and Licensure

Licensing is typically not necessary for archivists and curators, although some employers may require certification by a professional organization, such as the Academy of Certified Archivists (ACA). A master's degree and archival experience are necessary before one can take the ACA written exam for certification. Those interested in becoming certified should consult credible professional associations within the field and follow professional debate as to the relevancy and value of any certification program.

Additional Requirements

Physical strength is needed to lift heavy boxes or other items, and good eyesight is needed for detail work. Membership in professional archivist or curator associations may provide access to networking opportunities and professional development programs.

Fun Fact

The word "archivist" can conjure up images of a lonely desk in a dusty corner, but think again. Paramount Studios had an official archivist (Richard Arnold) for the show "Star Trek." According to Arnold, the words "Beam me up, Scotty," were never spoken on the TV show.

Source: http://articles.latimes.com

EARNINGS AND ADVANCEMENT

Earnings of archivists and curators vary greatly according to the individual's education and experience, the employer, geographic location and job specialty. The size and funds of a museum may also affect earnings. Salaries in the Federal government are generally higher than those in private organizations. Salaries of curators in large, well-funded museums may be several times higher than those in small ones.

Median annual earnings of archivists were $50,250 in 2015. The lowest ten percent earned less than $30,430, and the highest ten percent earned more than $86,040. Median annual earnings of curators were $51,520 in 2015. The lowest ten percent earned less than $28,440, and the highest ten percent earned more than $91,710.

Archivists and curators may receive paid vacations, holidays, and sick days; life and health insurance; and retirement benefits. These are usually paid by the employer.

Metropolitan Areas with the Highest Employment Level in this Occupation

Metropolitan area	Employment	Employment per thousand jobs	Annual mean wage
New York-Jersey City-White Plains, NY-NJ	540	0.08	$56,180
Los Angeles-Long Beach-Glendale, CA	320	0.08	$48,820
Washington-Arlington-Alexandria, DC-VA-MD-WV	320	0.13	$76,640
Boston-Cambridge-Newton, MA	180	0.10	$68,090
Seattle-Bellevue-Everett, WA	130	0.09	$62,840
Houston-The Woodlands-Sugar Land, TX	110	0.04	$63,840
Philadelphia, PA	100	0.11	$46,050
Baltimore-Columbia-Towson, MD	80	0.06	$47,440
Providence-Warwick, RI-MA	70	0.12	$61,480
Pittsburgh, PA	60	0.05	$37,960

Source: Bureau of Labor Statistics

EMPLOYMENT AND OUTLOOK

There were approximately 30,000 archivists and curators employed nationally in 2014. They were employed in museums and historical sites; federal, state, and local governments; and public and private educational institutions, mainly college and university libraries. Employment of archivists and curators is expected to grow as fast as the average for all occupations through the year 2024, which means employment is projected to increase 5 percent to 9 percent. Demand is expected to increase as public and private organizations emphasize establishing archives and organizing records, especially electronically. Museum and zoo attendance has been on the rise and is expected to continue increasing, which will generate demand for curators.

Employment Trend, Projected 2014–24

Archivists, curators, and museum workers: 7%

Total, all occupations: 7%

Librarians, curators, and archivists: 4%

Note: "All Occupations" includes all occupations in the U.S. Economy. Source: U.S. Bureau of Labor Statistics, Employment Projections Program

Related Occupations
- Anthropologist
- Librarian
- Media Specialist
- Research Assistant

Conversation With . . .
SAMANTHA NORLING

Archivist, Indianapolis Museum of Art
Indianapolis, Indiana
Archivist, 4 years

1. **What was your individual career path in terms of education/training, entry-level job, or other significant opportunity?**

My interest in archives took root while I was pursuing a bachelor's degree in American studies and interned at two museums in visitor services. After graduating, I cataloged artifacts part-time at the Scottish Rite of Freemasonry Museum and Library in Washington DC. While researching graduate programs in museum studies, my supervisor (a professional archivist) suggested that I keep library science in mind, which is a common academic path into archival work—many archivist job postings require a library science degree, often with an archives management concentration.

Ultimately, I selected a dual graduate program in public history and library science. Before moving to Indianapolis to begin grad school, I secured a part-time job as Project Archivist at the Indiana Historical Society, which I held throughout graduate school thanks to a work-study partnership between my school and the society. Each summer, I returned to DC for archival internships: first at the Library of Congress, and then at the Association of American Medical Colleges. This practical experience in a variety of settings, along with additional educational opportunities such as conferences, workshops, and webinars, made me a strong applicant for professional positions when I left school. I was offered my current job at the Indianapolis Museum of Art three months after graduating.

2. **What are the most important skills and/or qualities for someone in your profession?**

Attention to detail and strong organizational skills are necessary when arranging and describing sometimes overwhelmingly large collections of documents, photographs, or other materials. The ability to conduct research effectively is also important, as archivists are often asked to assist others in their research projects, which can reach outside the institution where you work. And strong communication and people skills are a must because, contrary to the popular image of the archivist sitting alone among stacks of books, collaboration with colleagues and interacting with the public are common.

3. What do you wish you had known going into this profession?

I cannot stress how important mentorship was in my career path, and that has been true for many early-career archivists that I know. Professors, supervisors, and connections made at conferences can really point students in the right direction and help you establish yourself in the profession before graduating and entering the job market.

4. Are there many job opportunities in your profession? In what specific areas?

There are many job opportunities in the archives profession, in a wide variety of organizations: museums, historical societies, public and university libraries, non-profits, city, state and national government, businesses, and more. However, there's a lot of competition for jobs among recent graduates, so it's important to enter the market with both practical experience and theoretical knowledge. It is common for recent graduates to work at least one temporary, grant-funded position (part- or full-time) for a year or longer before securing a permanent position. Taking courses in born-digital preservation and related topics could help give you an edge in the job market. (Born-digital records are those that were originally produced in a digital format, rather than converted from, for instance, print.)

5. How do you see your profession changing in the next five years? What role will technology play in those changes, and what skills will be required?

It's an exciting time as archivists face the challenges that born-digital records present and best practices evolve to meet those needs. Because of the digital nature of many records collected by archives today, technology in many forms is becoming more central to archival work. Knowledge of a wide variety of digital file formats, along with the systems and tools to help ingest and preserve those files long-term, will likely be a requirement for archivists in the not-so-distant future.

6. What do you enjoy most about your job? What do you enjoy least about your job?

I love when I get the chance to collaborate with colleagues in other departments of the museum. Creating exhibitions, selecting and implementing a new digital asset management system for the museum, and creating an online portal allowing the public to access our digitized collections are examples of cross-departmental projects I've worked on.

My least favorite part of the job is that I often work alone because I'm the only archivist in my institution. This is known as a "lone arranger" in the profession, and is somewhat common, though the majority of archivists work with other archivists on a daily basis.

7. Can you suggest a valuable "try this" for students considering a career in your profession?

Visit a local archives (believe me, there are many in every city!) and talk the archivists. If possible, go with a research need in mind, perhaps a collection that the archives hold that you would like to look through. Students should find an opportunity to conduct primary source research in an archives for an assignment— most colleges and universities have special collections and university archives right on campus.

MORE INFORMATION

Academy of Certified Archivists (ACA)
1450 Western Avenue, Suite 101
Albany, NY 12203
518.694.8471
ww.certifiedarchivists.org

American Association for State and Local History
1717 Church Street
Nashville, TN 37203-2991
615.320.3203
www.aaslh.org

American Association of Museums
Attn
Bookstore
1575 Eye Street NW, Suite 400
Washington, DC 20005
202.289.1818
www.aam-us.org

American Institute for Conservation of Historic & Artistic Works (AIC)
1156 15th Street NW, Suite 320
Washington, DC 20005
202.452.9545
www.conservation-us.org

Association for Art Museum Curators (AAMC)
174 East 80th Street
New York, NY 10075
646.405.8065
www.artcurators.org

Association of Moving Image Archivists (AMIA)
1313 North Vine Street
Hollywood, CA 90028
323.463.1500
www.amianet.org

National Association of Government Archives and Records Administrators (NAGARA)
1450 Western Avenue, Suite 101
Albany, NY 12203
518.694.8472
www.nagara.org

National Council on Public History
327 Cavanaugh Hall - IUPUI
425 University Boulevard
Indianapolis, IN 46202
317.274.2716
www.ncph.org

National Trust for Historic Preservation
1785 Massachusetts Avenue, NW
Washington, DC 20036-2117
202.588.6000
www.nthp.org

Organization of American Historians
112 N. Bryan Avenue, P.O. Box 5457
Bloomington, IN 47408-5457
812.855.7311
www.oah.org

Society for History in the Federal Government
P.O. Box 14139
Benjamin Franklin Station
Washington, DC 20044
www.shfg.org

Society of American Archivists (SAA)
17 North State Street, Suite 1425
Chicago, IL 60602-3315
866.722.7858
www2.archivists.org

Sally Driscoll/Editor

Career & Technical Education Teacher

Snapshot

Career Cluster: Education & Training; Human Services
Interests: Teaching, working with students, public speaking
Earnings (Yearly Average): $55,120
Employment & Outlook: Average Growth Expected

OVERVIEW

Sphere of Work

Career and technical education teachers teach career-related technical skills to middle and high school students. They also provide education to college-aged students or adults at vocational and technical schools. Career and technical instructors teach courses in a wide variety of fields, including automotive repair, computer science, and the culinary arts. The work of these teachers focuses on specific real-world skills, as opposed to broader theories. Their job is to equip students with practical, hands-on, career-related skills to be used in the field.

Work Environment

Career and technical education teachers work in schools. As many schools are closed in the summer months, many teachers do not work during this period. However, some teachers may work year round. In addition to classroom work, career and technical education instructors spend a significant amount of time working outside of the classroom, preparing lesson plans, grading assignments, and carrying out various administrative tasks.

Profile

Working Conditions: Work Indoors
Physical Strength: Light Work
Education Needs: Junior/
Technical/Community College,
Bachelor's Degree
Licensure/Certification: Required
Physical Abilities Not Required: No
Heavy Labor
Opportunities For Experience:
Internship, Military Service, Part-Time
Work
Holland Interest Score*: SEC

* See Appendix A

Occupation Interest

Career and technical education teachers must have the patience and desire to impart knowledge to students. Individuals who are interested in entering the field must be willing to work with both adults and students. Many career and technical educators transition to the role after working in fields closely related to the subjects they teach.

A Day in the Life—Duties and Responsibilities

The workday of a career and technical education teacher begins each morning at school, but his or her work begins long before that. Like other teachers, career and technical education teachers prepare lesson plans for their classes, which vary in length, frequency, and format based on the employing institution. Class planning takes up a large portion of an instructor's time.

In addition to preparing lesson plans, instructors must make time to advise students outside of class and grade assignments. Teachers of younger students may also meet regularly with parents. Career and technical courses are designed to be hands on, and instructors must spend time organizing their classrooms or workshops to ensure they are safe and accessible for students. Teachers must also establish rules or guidelines for the use of equipment, machinery, or technology and enforce those rules in class. During free periods, instructors may reorganize their classrooms, meet with students, retool lesson plans, or grade assignments.

The workday of a career and technical teacher typically extends beyond regular school hours. Some teachers may teach classes during the summer months or in the evenings. Additionally, career and technical teachers may attend conferences or other professional-development events and work with other teachers to construct or improve lesson plans.

Duties and Responsibilities

- Developing practical and technical programs of study
- Presenting information and demonstrating skills in a classroom setting
- Testing and evaluating students
- Working with advisory committees from business and industry
- Recruiting participants

WORK ENVIRONMENT

Physical Environment

The physical environment in which career and technical education teachers work varies based on each particular instructor's specialty. A teacher specializing in automotive repair will likely work in a garage-like environment, while an instructor specializing in information technology (IT) will typically work in a computer lab.

Human Environment

Career and technical education teachers interact regularly with students and are responsible for running their classrooms and guiding students through hands-on instruction. They must be aware of their students' safety at all times. Teachers communicate on a regular basis with colleagues and school administrators and may also hold conferences with parents.

Relevant Skills and Abilities

Communication Skills
- Speaking effectively
- Writing concisely

Interpersonal/Social Skills
- Cooperating with others
- Motivating others
- Teaching others
- Working as a member of a team

Organization & Management Skills
- Coordinating tasks
- Managing people/groups
- Paying attention to and handling details

Research & Planning Skills
- Creating ideas
- Developing evaluation strategies

Technological Environment

The technological environment of career and technical education teachers is dependent on the courses they teach. An IT class will rely heavily on computer technology, while a culinary arts or automotive repair class will rely on machine technology, hand tools, and appliances. It is important for teachers to issue specific instructions regarding the proper use of classroom equipment.

EDUCATION, TRAINING, AND ADVANCEMENT

High School/Secondary

Most technical careers require a solid understanding of mathematics and science, and aspiring career and technical education teachers are encouraged to explore coursework in both areas. Decisions regarding course specialization are field dependent. For example, a chef uses principles of chemistry, as do those who work in health and medicine. A mechanic uses principles of physics and engineering, as do those who work in robotics. Individuals interested in teaching should also develop their verbal and written communication skills.

Suggested High School Subjects
- Agricultural Education
- Applied Communication
- Applied Math
- Applied Physics
- Arts
- Building Trades & Carpentry
- Business
- Business & Computer Technology
- Child Growth & Development
- College Preparatory
- Composition
- English
- Family & Consumer Sciences
- First Aid Training
- Health Science Technology
- Industrial Arts
- Literature
- Mathematics
- Psychology
- Science
- Speech
- Trade/Industrial Education

Famous First

The first vocational high school for girls was the Trade School for Girls, opened in Boston in 1904. Subjects taught were sewing, advanced sewing, dressmaking, millinery (hatmaking), costume design, domestic science, and machine operation. The school was racially mixed and, besides providing day classes for fulltime students, offered evening classes for adults. The building used was previously owned by a Catholic diocese, and when the property was purchased by the school the chapel was converted to a gymnasium.

College/Postsecondary

Postsecondary training for most career and technical education teachers is tailored to their respective fields. An aspiring culinary arts instructor will typically study the culinary arts but also take courses in education, while an aspiring automotive repair instructor will learn the trade as well as how to communicate his or her understanding of the trade in a classroom setting. Regardless of specialization, an associate's or bachelor's degree is required for most positions, though some teachers may instead accumulate knowledge and experience through hands-on work in the field.

Related College Majors
- Agricultural Teacher Education
- Bilingual/Bicultural Education
- Business Teacher Education (Vocational)
- Education Administration & Supervision, General
- Elementary/Pre-Elementary/Early Childhood/Kindergarten Education
- Family & Consumer Science Education
- Health Teacher Education
- Marketing Operations Teacher Education (Vocational)
- Secondary/Jr. High/Middle School Teacher Education
- Technology Teacher Education/Industrial Arts Teacher Education
- Trade & Industrial Teacher Education (Vocational)
- Vocational Education Teacher

Adult Job Seekers

The field of career and technical education may be a good fit for adults who have already spent time learning and practicing a trade or skill and would like to pass their knowledge on to students. Many adults who aspire to become career and technical education teachers later in life already have significant training and practical experience, which may make them capable teachers.

Professional Certification and Licensure

Certification and licensure are required for career and technical education teachers, although the specific requirements vary from state to state. Some states require every teacher to hold a bachelor's degree, while others require a number of years of experience followed by a period of supervised student teaching. Organizations such as the National Center for Alternative Certification provide helpful tools for those who lack training in education but have technical skills suited to the field of career and technical education.

Additional Requirements

Career and technical education teachers must be patient with their students and capable of communicating assignments and instructions in a manner easy for students to follow. They must be able to plan detailed lessons but also improvise when students do not understand.

Fun Fact

It used to be known as voke ed and, in some schools, had a separate track that was not academically rigorous. Now it's known as Career & Technical Education, and its students are on the fast track to success. According to the Georgetown University Center on Education and the Workforce, 43 percent of of young workers with this certification earn more than those with an associate degree and 27 percent earn more than those with a bachelor's degree!
Source: www.cte.osceola.k12.fl.us/cte_facts.shtml

EARNINGS AND ADVANCEMENT

Earnings depend on the individual's education, experience, and specialty area, and the type, size, and geographic location of the employer. Career and technical education teachers have lower salaries in rural areas. Advancement into administrative positions in departments of education, colleges and universities and corporate training departments is possible, though such positions may require advanced degrees.

Median annual earnings of career and technical education teachers were $55,120 in 2013. The lowest ten percent earned less than $38,560, and the highest ten percent earned more than $81,680.

Career and technical education teachers may receive paid vacations, holidays, and sick days; life and health insurance; and retirement benefits. These are usually paid by the employer.

Metropolitan Areas with the Highest Employment Level in this Occupation

Metropolitan area	Employment	Employment per thousand jobs	Hourly mean wage
Houston-Sugar Land-Baytown, TX	1,860	0.67	$55,570
Dallas-Plano-Irving, TX	1,700	0.79	$52,420
New York-White Plains-Wayne, NY-NJ	1,370	0.26	$82,800
Charlotte-Gastonia-Rock Hill, NC-SC	1,310	1.50	$49,990
Richmond, VA	1,100	1.81	$58,170
Philadelphia, PA	1,080	0.59	$69,650
Miami-Miami Beach-Kendall, FL	1,010	0.99	$54,540
Washington-Arlington-Alexandria, DC-VA-MD-WV	1,010	0.43	$72,320
Los Angeles-Long Beach-Glendale, CA	990	0.25	$79,510
Atlanta-Sandy Springs-Marietta, GA	880	0.38	$55,990

Source: Bureau of Labor Statistics

EMPLOYMENT AND OUTLOOK

There were approximately 240,000 career and technical education teachers employed nationally in 2012. Employment is expected to grow about as fast as the average for all occupations through the year 2022, which means employment is projected to increase 5 percent to 12 percent. Job growth due to increasing student enrollments will be tempered by more of a focus on traditional academic subjects.

Employment Trend, Projected 2010–20

Vocational Education Teachers, Postsecondary: 12%

Total, All Occupations: 11%

Career/Technical Education Teachers: 9%

Career/Technical Education Teachers, Middle school: 5%

Career/Technical Education Teachers, Secondary School: 5%

Note: "All Occupations" includes all occupations in the U.S. Economy. Source: U.S. Bureau of Labor Statistics, Employment Projections Program

Related Occupations
- College Faculty Member
- Farm & Home Management Advisor
- Secondary & Middle School Teacher
- Special Education Teacher
- Vocational Rehabilitation Counselor

Related Military Occupations
- Personnel Specialist
- Training Specialist & Instructor

Conversation With . . .
CHARLOTTE GRAY

Career & Tech Lead Teacher, Family & Consumer Sciences
Holt High School, Wentzville, Missouri
Teacher, 27 years

1. What was your individual career path in terms of education/training, entry-level job, or other significant opportunity?

After high school, I attended Patricia Stevens Career College in St. Louis and graduated with a diploma in fashion merchandising and a minor in public relations. Back then, it was known as a finishing school for girls. Today, I would compare the program to Career and Technical Education (CTE). During college, I worked in retail sales, shipping, and bookkeeping for a small family-owned business and found it was not exactly what I wanted to do for the rest of my life. I enrolled at the University of Missouri and somehow found my way to the Home Economics Education program. I really enjoyed the course work and had a great advisor who saw the potential in me to be a teacher. After graduating, I got a teaching position and worked for several years. I became involved with the Association for Career and Technical Education (ACTE) and during a national conference, a professor from The Ohio State University asked me if I'd be interested in attending their master's program as a graduate assistant. I said yes. So, I quit my teaching job and went back to college. I finished my master's and returned to teaching and never looked back. I currently teach courses in child development and culinary arts in a high school. The goal of Family and Consumer Science (FACS) courses is to equip students to survive and thrive in daily life and to show them how to apply their knowledge and skills in real-world situations.

2. What are the most important skills and/or qualities for someone in your profession?

Leadership is important. You must be organized, flexible, patient, and good at multi-tasking. You have to enjoy hands-on, project-based teaching. You have to be creative, dependable, self-motivated, a critical thinker, a team player, a good listener, and have strong written and verbal communication skills.

3. What do you wish you had known going into this profession?

That there would be constant changes in the education system that you have no control over. I wish I had realized the number of hours you have to spend planning and preparing lessons to be an exemplary teacher. And in a small school, you might teach six or seven different classes, all of which you have to prep for daily. Finally, I wish I had known how to motivate the unmotivated.

4. **Are there many job opportunities in your profession? In what specific areas?**

The need for FACS teachers continues to grow nationwide, and this specialty is on most states' critical needs list. Many teachers are retiring, so jobs are becoming available yearly. A FACS education major has many opportunities outside of teaching because of the wide variety of course work required: child development, family living, consumer economics, foods and nutrition, clothing and textiles, living environments, interpersonal relationships, human sexuality, parenting, family financial management, consumer purchasing, and resource management. Some of the fields FACS majors could end up in include culinary arts, dietetics, interior design, youth services, apparel design and community health services.

5. **How do you see your profession changing in the next five years? What role will technology play in those changes, and what skills will be required?**

Schools are more career-focused than ever. It's hard to know what technological advances are coming, particularly in the classes covered by Careers in Technical Education and FACS, but the challenge for teachers and schools will be to keep up with the technology.

6. **What do you enjoy most about your job? What do you enjoy least about your job?**

I am passionate about what I teach and worry about children who have relied heavily on convenience in their lives. The best part of my job is seeing students use what they have learned in my classroom in their everyday lives, from realizing the importance of nutrition to learning to get the desired response from a preschooler using positive statements.

I don't enjoy the politics behind education today, and disagree with the emphasis placed on everyone going to a four-year college. There's not enough emphasis on how to live a healthy life, financially and nutritionally, nor on healthy relationships. Some days I just want to spend time exploring ideas with students, but there never seems to be time because of all the mandates and testing.

7. **Can you suggest a valuable "try this" for students considering a career in your profession?**

Work as an aide for the FACS teachers in your school. Take as many FACS or CTE classes as will fit in your schedule. Get involved with Family, Career and Community Leaders of America (fccla.com). Take a class working with young children where you actually get to assist with teaching. Offer to help at after-school programs.

SELECTED SCHOOLS

Many colleges and universities have bachelor's degree programs in education and related subjects; some offer a focus on career/technical education. The student may also gain initial grounding in the field at a technical or community college. Consult with your school guidance counselor or research post-secondary programs in your area. The web site of the Association for Career and Technical Education (see below) has a section on "Postsecondary Education Resources" and other tools and resources.

MORE INFORMATION

American Association for Adult and Continuing Education
10111 Martin Luther King Jr. Hwy.
Suite 200C
Bowie, MD 20720
301.459.6261
www.aaace.org

American Association for Employment in Education
3040 Riverside Drive, Suite 125
Columbus, OH 43221
614.485.1111
www.aaee.org

American Association of Colleges for Teacher Education
1307 New York Avenue, NW
Suite 300
Washington, DC 20005-4701
202.293.2450
www.aacte.org

American Federation of Teachers
Public Affairs Department
555 New Jersey Avenue, NW
Washington, DC 20001
202.879.4400
www.aft.org

Association for Career and Technical Education
1410 King Street
Alexandria, VA 22314
800.826.9972
www.acteonline.org

National Association of State Directors of Career Technical Education Consortium
8484 Georgia Avenue, Suite 320
Silver Spring, MD 20910
www.careertech.org

National Education Association
1201 16th Street, NW
Washington, DC 20036-3290
202.833.4000
www.nea.org

Molly Hagan/Editor

College Faculty Member

Snapshot

Career Cluster(s): Education & Training

Interests: Teaching, research, writing, public speaking, helping others, communicating with others

Earnings (Yearly Average): $72,470

Employment & Outlook: Faster Than Average Growth Expected

OVERVIEW

Sphere of Work

A college faculty member is a professional instructor who teaches courses at a postsecondary institution. He or she has a master's or doctorate degree in a specific academic discipline and is considered qualified to teach within that discipline only. Faculty members design their own courses, plan discussion topics and reading and writing assignments, and plan and coordinate test and examination schedules. As they conduct their classes, faculty members lecture students, grade papers and exams, and advise students on their major fields of study. A college faculty member

will typically research and write scholarly books and articles on their particular field of expertise and, occasionally, present their individual works at relevant conferences.

Work Environment

A member of a college faculty typically manages his or her classes individually (although at larger universities, many professors delegate grading papers and exams or running student discussion groups to graduate students). Outside of the classroom, however, they often collaborate with fellow professors in writing and editing scholarly books and articles. Furthermore, as part of the faculty, they will meet frequently with their department colleagues to discuss departmental policies and other school news. A college faculty member's workload is therefore diverse, although not physically strenuous.

Profile

Working Conditions: Work Indoors
Physical Strength: Light Work
Education Needs: Master's Degree, Doctoral Degree
Licensure/Certification: Usually Not Required
Opportunities For Experience: Military Service, Part Time Work
Holland Interest Score*: ESI

* See Appendix A

Occupation Interest

Most people pursue careers in postsecondary institutions because they love to study a particular subject and share their insights with others. Aspiring college faculty members should also be interested in helping to shape young minds. College faculty members are, by nature, intellectuals willing to spend long hours researching, writing on, and teaching the many elements of their particular discipline.

College faculty members (often called professors) come from a wide range of backgrounds and demonstrate an equally broad range of perspectives, experience, and teaching styles. They are considered experts in their fields, having completed many years of study at the undergraduate and postgraduate levels.

A Day in the Life—Duties and Responsibilities

A member of a college faculty is primarily a teacher, using his or her past studies, research, and professional experience on a particular subject to help others learn more about it. He or she will select the required texts and articles for the course, design a course syllabus (an overview of the topics for discussion and required reading and homework for each scheduled class), prepare lectures and discussions for each class, lead effective class discussion, and issue and grade tests and student work. Depending on the nature and level of the course, the faculty member may simply lecture a class or provide a "seminar" approach in which students are expected to actively participate.

In addition to their responsibilities to the courses they teach, faculty members will also pursue their own projects, researching and writing scholarly works on topics within their discipline. Occasionally, when these works are published, professors will present these scholarly documents at regional, national, and international conferences. This individual research can help the faculty members continue to work at their respective colleges and even receive tenure (an agreement that the professor may stay on the faculty indefinitely).

College faculty members must also work with other members of their respective departments to shape departmental policies, activities, and courses. Periodically, these individuals may be selected to serve as department chairs, the senior-most position of a department's faculty.

Duties and Responsibilities

- **Preparing and delivering lectures**
- **Compiling, administering and grading papers and examinations**
- **Supervising laboratory assignments, field work and independent study**
- **Directing research of others working for advanced degrees**
- **Advising students on academic and vocational curricula**
- **Participating in conferences**
- **Serving on faculty committees**
- **Conducting research and publishing findings in professional journals**
- **Providing consulting services to government and industry**

WORK ENVIRONMENT

Physical Environment

A college faculty member works at buildings that are situated on a university campus. Their physical environment includes classrooms, lecture halls, laboratories, and seminar rooms. They will also perform some of their duties in their offices, such as advising students, meeting with peers, and grading and preparing for classes.

Faculty members who teach engineering, chemistry, and other scientific or vocational courses work in a lab environment and are required to follow certain safety procedures. Faculty may be exposed to some dangerous equipment or chemicals and are responsible for educating students as to their proper handling.

Relevant Skills and Abilities

Communication Skills
- Expressing thoughts and ideas
- Persuading others
- Speaking effectively
- Writing concisely

Interpersonal/Social Skills
- Cooperating with others

Organization & Management Skills
- Coordinating tasks
- Making decisions
- Organizing information or materials

Research & Planning Skills
- Analyzing information
- Gathering information
- Using logical reasoning

Human Environment

While professors at smaller colleges and universities tend to manage their classes alone, faculty members at larger institutions will often call upon graduate students to assist them in preparing syllabi, grading papers, and lecturing. Professors also meet frequently with one another on departmental matters and collaborate on research projects.

Technological Environment

Faculty members typically use basic office technology and tools to aid them with lecturing, compiling research, organizing class materials, and in communicating with students. Professors working in scientific fields may use a number of other technologies that are relevant to their fields, such as particle accelerators, spectrometers, and engineering equipment.

EDUCATION, TRAINING, AND ADVANCEMENT

High School/Secondary

In addition to taking courses in the intellectual discipline in which they are interested, high school students who wish to become college faculty members are encouraged to take classes and participate in clubs that help them develop their research and communications skills, such as debate teams, writing courses, and extracurricular clubs that focus on the field in which they are interested.

Suggested High School Subjects
- Algebra
- Arts
- Audio-Visual
- Biology
- Bookkeeping
- Business
- Business & Computer Technology
- Business Math
- Chemistry
- College Preparatory
- Composition
- Computer Science
- Earth Science
- Economics
- English
- Entrepreneurship
- Foreign Languages
- Geography
- History
- Humanities
- Literature
- Mathematics
- Merchandising
- Physics
- Science
- Social Studies

- Sociology
- Speech
- Statistics

Famous First

The first professor of climatology to be appointed at a college was Robert DeCourcy Ward, who was appointed by Harvard University in 1910. Although on the cutting edge of climate science at the time, Ward was also a strong advocate of eugenics and immigration restriction.

College/Postsecondary

College faculty members develop their knowledge and experience over a period of many years at the undergraduate and postgraduate levels. Postsecondary students should continue to study all aspects of their chosen discipline at the undergraduate level. Many students choose to obtain an internship in their chosen field, studying this discipline outside of the college setting. Additionally, college professors are strongly encouraged to pursue master's and doctorate degrees in their chosen field, taking a wide range of courses at the graduate level and writing an extensive independent study known as a dissertation.

Related College Majors
- For this occupation, related college majors will vary, based on the area of faculty expertise.

Adult Job Seekers

College faculty positions are often difficult to obtain due to the large number of individuals with advanced degrees seeking jobs in higher education. Many adults who plan to become a full member of a faculty may start out as "adjunct" professors, teaching at an institution on a part-time basis. Many other people will attend conferences and similar events to meet and share their independent work with tenured professors and university officials to help secure a faculty position.

Professional Certification and Licensure

For most full-time college faculty members, a master's and doctorate degree are required. Some institutions are willing to allow people to join without a doctorate, provided that those candidates have extensive experience and expertise in their fields.

Additional Requirements

College faculty members find satisfaction in researching, learning, and sharing knowledge with others. They must be self-motivated and able to motivate others as well. In addition, they should be willing to handle multiple tasks, such as managing multiple classes, working with students, and conducting their own individual research.

Fun Fact

What's the stereotypical college professor? According to College Review, there are eight of them: The Tweed, The Activist, The Hippie, The Adjunct, The Coach, The World's Most Interesting Man, The Writer and, finally, The Double Life.
Source: www.collegeview.com

EARNINGS AND ADVANCEMENT

Earnings of college faculty members depend largely on the academic qualifications, academic specialty, academic rank and experience of each individual, and the type of institution. Generally, professors of medicine, dentistry, engineering and law receive higher salaries than professors in other fields. Faculty in four-year schools earned higher salaries, on the average, than those in two-year schools.

Full-time college faculty members usually work on a nine-month contract. Median annual earnings of college faculty members were $72,470 in 2015. The lowest ten percent earned less than about $35,000, and the highest ten percent earned more than about $140,00.

Many faculty have additional earnings from research, consulting, writing and other employment opportunities.

College faculty members may receive paid vacations, holidays, and sick days; life and health insurance; and retirement benefits. These are usually paid by the employer.

Metropolitan Areas with the Highest Employment Level in this Occupation

Metropolitan area	Employment	Employment per thousand jobs	Annual mean wage
Washington-Arlington-Alexandria, DC-VA-MD-WV	2,030	0.84	$64,990
Miami-Miami Beach-Kendall, FL	2,010	1.84	$64,680
Atlanta-Sandy Springs-Roswell, GA	2,010	0.81	$64,150
Omaha-Council Bluffs, NE-IA	1,310	2.76	$52,090
Orlando-Kissimmee-Sanford, FL	1,290	1.15	$64,650
Tallahassee, FL	1,240	7.78	$66,430
Warren-Troy-Farmington Hills, MI	1,230	1.05	$46,200
Fresno, CA	1,180	3.46	$66,590
New Orleans-Metairie, LA	1,170	2.10	n/d
Phoenix-Mesa-Scottsdale, AZ	1,060	0.56	$61,010

Source: Bureau of Labor Statistics

EMPLOYMENT AND OUTLOOK

There were approximately 1.3 million college and university faculty members employed nationally in 2014. Employment is expected to grow faster than the average for all occupations through the year 2024, which means employment is projected to increase 10 percent to 15 percent. This is due to the projected growth in college and university enrollment over the next decade from the expected increase in the population of 18 to 24 year olds.

Employment Trend, Projected 2014–24

Postsecondary teachers: 13%

Education, training, and library occupations: 8%

Total, all occupations: 7%

Note: "All Occupations" includes all occupations in the U.S. Economy. Source: U.S. Bureau of Labor Statistics, Employment Projections Program

Related Occupations
- Anthropologist
- Astronomer
- Biological Scientist
- Career & Technical Education Teacher
- Education Administrator
- Physicist
- Secondary & Middle School Teacher
- Social Scientist

Related Military Occupations
- Teacher & Instructor

Conversation With . . .
CHRISTINE EVANS

Graduate Program Director/Associate Professor of Practice
Simmons College, Boston, Massachusetts
Education, 34 years; College faculty, 25 years

1. What was your individual career path in terms of education/training, entry-level job, or other significant opportunity?

I started out as a teacher and now am a program director for a graduate program at Simmons College. As a child, I used to play school with my siblings and neighbors—and I was always the teacher. My parents even set up old desks and a chalkboard in the basement. Later, I thought nursing would be my path and was admitted to an undergrad program, but I was discouraged by the fact that the clinical experience wouldn't occur until my junior year. My advisor suggested an internship at a school for children with autism and other developmental disabilities. I was hooked. I changed my major and got my degree in education. When I graduated, I got a job at The New England Center for Children (NECC) in Southborough, Massachusetts, which is a leader in autism research and teaching. I worked there for 10 years as a teacher and family service specialist, and got my master's degree in special education. In 1992, NECC and Simmons College in Boston partnered together to offer a Master of Science in Education with licensure in Severe Disabilities and I was asked to direct it.

2. What are the most important skills and/or qualities for someone in your profession?

You have to be dedicated and willing to mentor students. That means providing support and guidance to maximize their potential as a new teacher. You have to keep current with research in order to model best practices. Strong leadership and communication skills are a must. You have to stay true to your beliefs and not get too caught up with the politics of education. Always remember the student is the priority.

3. What do you wish you had known going into this profession?

How complex teaching would become in terms of licensure requirements, addressing social and emotional issues in the classroom, and meeting the needs of diverse types of learners and their families. I really didn't understand how society views classroom teachers. I thought it was a very honorable profession. On the other hand, if you tell someone you're a professor, they're impressed, but it's really not that glamorous.

4. Are there many job opportunities in your profession? In what specific areas?

Experience counts. Being a teaching assistant (TA), adjunct, or supervisor all give you an edge, as does field experience and published research. For a job to open up on a college faculty, usually somebody has to retire or the department has to expand. College professors don't always retire at 62; many stay on much longer than that. Also, there's a misconception that because you're a professor and work at a higher level, you get paid more than a classroom teacher. Most college professors, to make a respectable salary, supplement their income with consulting, publishing, speaking engagements, grants and that kind of thing.

5. How do you see your profession changing in the next five years? What role will technology play in those changes, and what skills will be required?

Technology has been a game changer. Online learning, hybrid learning, and distance learning can attract students all over the world. Simmons also offers its special education degree to U.S. students in Abu Dhabi, Qatar, London and India who work in NECC partner programs and do their practicum onsite. And there's no need for textbooks or handouts anymore; they're all accessible online. This generation of students is often more comfortable having discussions online. Teachers need to be tech savvy for many reasons. There are applications for learners with communication, social and emotional issues as well as academic issues.

6. What do you enjoy most about your job? What do you enjoy least about your job?

The best part of my job is supervising practicum students and seeing them begin to really understand and evolve. I love to mentor students and provide useful feedback. For me, the real payoff is hearing from students after they've graduated about how their training prepared them for the real world. I travel to the different countries where Simmons has programs, and I enjoy seeing how special education has evolved there. When I started going to Abu Dhabi, it was like going back in time 30 years. The whole concept of inclusion was very foreign.

One of the hardest parts of my job is counseling students out of the program when they're not cut out for teaching. Smart students don't always translate into good teachers. Special education demands teachers who instinctively know how to make accommodations to best serve children. It's not always immediately intuitive, but by the end of the program, it should be.

7. Can you suggest a valuable "try this" for students considering a career in your profession?

The best advice I would give to anyone who wants a career in higher education is to stay connected to what's going on in the classroom. Get experience with a position that requires you to be a leader.

MORE INFORMATION

Academic Keys, LLC
P.O. Box 162
Storrs, CT 06268
860.429.0218
www.academickeys.com

American Association for Employment in Education
3040 Riverside Drive, Suite 125
Columbus, OH 43221
614.485.1111
www.aaee.org

American Federation of Teachers
Public Affairs Department
555 New Jersey Avenue, NW
Washington, DC 20001
202.879.4400
www.aft.org

National Teaching and Learning Forum
2203 Regent Street
Madison, WI 53726
www.ntlf.com

Preparing Future Faculty
One Dupont Circle NW, Suite 230
Washington, DC 20036-1173
202.223.3791
www.preparing-faculty.org

Michael Auerbach/Editor

Curriculum Specialist

Snapshot

Career Cluster(s): Education

Interests: Teaching, leadership, communication, research

Earnings (Yearly Average): $62,270

Employment & Outlook: Average growth expected

OVERVIEW

Sphere of Work

Curriculum specialists are educational administrators responsible for creating, evaluating, and refining a school's curriculum. Curriculum specialists conduct research, mentor and train teachers to implement new educational tools or policies, and observe students and teachers to evaluate an institution's educational effectiveness. Curriculum specialists are also responsible for setting guidelines for student advancement and are typically tasked with determining when new textbooks, classroom

activities, or technological teaching tools should be integrated into a organization's curriculum. Nearly 40 percent of curriculum specialists work in elementary or secondary schools, while 16 percent work for colleges or universities. The remaining 44 percent work are divided between positions in federal or state government and private companies.

Work Environment

Curriculum specialists typically work in office environments and usually work full time. Unlike teachers, curriculum specialists typically work year round and, while school is not in session, work on strategies for changing the curriculum and meet with teachers and administrators to implement changes before the start of the next school session. While school is in session, curriculum specialists observe teachers, students, and classes to evaluate the effectiveness of the school or company's curriculum and also provide mentoring and training for the school's educational staff.

Profile

Working Conditions: Work Indoors
Physical Strength: Light Work
Education Needs: Bachelor's Degree, Master's Degree
Licensure/Certification: Required in some school districts
Opportunities For Experience: Internship, Student Teaching
Holland Interest Score*: SIE

* See Appendix A

Occupation Interest

Curriculum specialists are typically former teachers who underwent additional training to become curriculum specialists. Professionals in the field spend much of their work time meeting with teachers or other administrators and should have skill and interest in interpersonal communication. As curriculum specialists are administrators, entrants to the field should also have an interest in taking a leadership role, which may include serving as a mentor to teachers or junior administrators.

A Day in the Life—Duties and Responsibilities

While school is in session, curriculum specialists may begin work before the start of daily classes, meeting with teachers to discuss any current or future changes to the curriculum. During the day, a curriculum specialist may spend time studying test scores or other metrics used to evaluate student and teacher performance. Curriculum specialists are also responsible for helping a school to adjust to and comply with state or federal changes to educational policy. On a less regular basis, curriculum specialists may meet with student or parent groups or may attend professional development conferences to learn about new developments in the field.

When class is not in session, curriculum specialists may spend time conducting research. This may include examining tests and evaluations from the end of the previous session, attending conferences, meeting with administrators or government officials, or researching new textbooks and other learning materials. Often, curriculum specialists are asked to take part in an organization's budget and financial planning and a specialist may therefore spend time writing or revising grant proposals or conducting budget reviews of the school's curriculum spending.

Duties and Responsibilities

- Observing teaching staff to evaluate performance and adherence to curriculum guidelines
- Meeting with students and teachers to discuss curriculum changes or to receive input on current policies
- Researching and evaluating new educational materials or techniques
- Creating training materials and conducting training sessions
- Prepare budget proposals for new educational materials or participate in writing grants to obtain curriculum funding
- Learning about and implementing any changes to state or federal educational policies

OCCUPATION SPECIALTIES

Director of Learning Commons

A director of learning commons works at a college or university and oversees tutoring services offered through the university. The individual may be responsible for overseeing a staff of tutors and for communicating with teachers about the supplementary needs of students.

Corporate Training Specialist

A corporate curriculum specialist creates and evaluates training materials used by a corporation to train employees.

Educational Materials Manager

An educational materials manager works for a publisher helping to oversee the creation of textbooks and other educational materials and ensuring that the publisher's materials meet state and federal guidelines.

Government Curriculum Specialist

A government curriculum specialist works with the Department of Education and/or state education administrators to manage the implementation of government educational standards in educational materials and school programs.

WORK ENVIRONMENT

Relevant Skills and Abilities

Communication Skills
- Speaking effectively
- Clear and effective writing

Interpersonal/Social Skills
- Being able to work in a team environment
- Communicating with a wide variety of individuals

Organization & Management Skills
- Managing staff
- Conducting performance evaluations
- Training staff to adjust to changes in policies or standards

Research & Planning Skills
- Researching new technologies and materials
- Evaluating current institutional effectiveness

Technical Skills
- Using word processing, digital communication, and spreadsheet software
- Understanding technical and governmental policies and guidelines
- Basic knowledge of budget management

Physical Environment

Curriculum specialists typically work in an office environment, whether they work in a school or for a corporation or governmental organization. Some curriculum specialists may be required to divide their time between more than one location, though most are employed by a single school. Curriculum specialists might also be required to attend conferences on professional development or government standards and travel may therefore be a necessary part of the job for many professionals in the field.

Human Environment

Curriculum specialists are part of a school or organization's administrative staff and often function as mentors and managers of teachers and support staff. Professionals in the field spend time every day in meetings or working closely with students and/or teachers. Depending on the subfield, curriculum specialists may also need to work closely with government or public officials to align school curriculum with state/federal standards. In addition to attending and conducting meetings and training sessions, curriculum specialists are also typically asked to communicate through email and telephone and should therefore be comfortable with digital communication.

Technological Environment

Curriculum specialists often use word processing software to create manuals, memos, and other documents to communicate with teachers, students, and administrators. Depending on the details of the position, curriculum specialists might also use desktop publishing software or graphics/photo software to create training or educational materials. Most modern educational environments use personal computers, smart devices, and may also use other kinds of digital educational aides, like smart boards, projectors, and audiovisual equipment. There are also specific software programs designed to help teachers or curriculum specialists design teaching materials and some positions may require specialists to learn how to use these programs.

EDUCATION, TRAINING, AND ADVANCEMENT

High School/Secondary

Individuals interested in becoming curriculum specialists should begin by pursuing a career in education. Most curriculum specialists become teachers before transitioning to the field and so benefit from a well-rounded basic education including reading, writing, science, mathematics, and history. As curriculum specialists are typically required to have advanced degrees, high school students should take classes aimed at entering college to pursue a degree in education with the goal of obtaining a post-college degree upon the completion of their Bachelor's level education.

Suggested High School Subjects
- College Preparatory
- Language Arts
- Mathematics
- Science
- Social Studies
- World Languages
- History
- Introduction to Business
- Introduction to Computers

Famous First

In 1892, the National Education Association (NEA) formed the Committee of Ten, a group of educators and educational administrators, who attempted to create the first standardized curriculum for American high school students. The Committee of Ten's recommendations helped to standardize the typically educational structure in the U.S., with eight years of elementary school followed by four years of high school, and recommended a set of classes including physics, chemistry, classical studies, mathematics, and English that became part of a basic core curriculum for the entire nation.

College/Postsecondary

In most cases, curriculum specialists are required to have a Master's degree, and many educational institutions offer master's programs specifically designed for educational administrators and/or curriculum specialists. Many curriculum specialists first earn bachelor's degrees in education before becoming curriculum specialists, though individuals with bachelor's degrees in other subjects, such as mathematics, history, or English, who go on to obtain teaching certification at the state level may also be eligible for curriculum specialist graduate programs. Curriculum specialist Master's programs are typically considered Masters of Education (M.Ed.) degrees. According to the Bureau of Labor Statistics (BLS) more than 70 percent of those working as curriculum specialists have Master's degrees in education, education administration, or specifically in curriculum design.

Related College Majors
- Education
- Early Childhood Administration
- Elementary Education
- Interdisciplinary Studies
- General Studies
- Speech and Communications
- Special Education
- Science Education

Adult Job Seekers

Individuals who have completed the requisite training will typically need on-the-job experience in a related field before being eligible for a curriculum specialist position. Many curriculum specialists work as teachers or principals before applying for a position as a curriculum specialist. Student teachers may also apply for internship training for curriculum specialist positions. Individuals with requisite education and job experience can also apply directly for open positions.

Professional Certification and Licensure

Some colleges and teacher training institutions offer certification programs specifically designed for teachers or educational administrators looking to transition to curriculum management, though certification is not required in all states or for all positions. Some curriculum specialist positions may also require individuals to pass a state administered teacher's licensing examination or to have completed an educational administration certification program before applying for a position as a curriculum specialist. Requirements for teaching certification and licensing vary by state and educational level. Some curriculum specialist positions require applicants to have prior teaching experience or to have worked for a certain amount of time as an educational administrator before being eligible for a curriculum specialist position.

Additional Requirements

First and foremost, curriculum specialists need to be familiar with all aspects of teaching and educational administration. A working knowledge of state and federal educational standards and guidelines is also essential for the profession. Curriculum specialists should also have familiarity with word processing, spreadsheet preparation, budget management, and digital communication, as these are tasks frequently used by professionals in the field. In addition, curriculum specialists must be adept at communication and able to comfortably interact with a variety of individuals including students, teachers, teaching support staff, and administrators.

EARNINGS AND ADVANCEMENT

Salaries for curriculum specialists vary according to region and compensation for professionals in the field can vary significantly between positions. The BLS estimates a median income of $62,270 annually in 2015, with a range of $33,000 to $93,000 reported by the U.S. Department of Labor. Corporate positions may offer higher average compensation than similar positions in public education. Government curriculum specialists earn incomes at the higher end of the spectrum, with an average of $70,190 reported by the BLS. Entry level positions may pay salaries at the lower end of the scale. In addition to salary, most curriculum specialist positions offer benefits and vacation.

Metropolitan Areas with the Highest Employment Level in this Occupation

Metropolitan area	Employment	Employment per thousand jobs	Hourly mean wage
New York-Jersey City-White Plains, NY-NJ	6,000	0.93	$33.39
Washington-Arlington-Alexandria, DC-VA-MD-WV	5,380	2.23	$37.30
Los Angeles-Long Beach-Glendale, CA	4,010	0.98	$33.58
Houston-The Woodlands-Sugar Land, TX	3,050	1.04	$33.35
Phoenix-Mesa-Scottsdale, AZ	2,980	1.59	$27.98
Atlanta-Sandy Springs-Roswell, GA	2,960	1.19	$28.00
Chicago-Naperville-Arlington Heights, IL	2,580	0.72	$29.56
Dallas-Plano-Irving, TX	2,500	1.07	$32.86
Baltimore-Columbia-Towson, MD	2,440	1.85	$33.08
Boston-Cambridge-Newton, MA	2,370	1.34	$32.09

Source: Bureau of Labor Statistics

EMPLOYMENT AND OUTLOOK

The BLS reported 151,100 individuals employed as curriculum specialists in 2014 and estimates 7 percent growth between 2014 and 2024, which is considered average across all occupations. Changes in federal and state educational policies can stimulate growth in the field, and may increase demand for curriculum specialists at both the educational institution and governmental levels. Recent changes in educational policy initiated by programs such as the No Child Left Behind and the Core Curriculum Standards program have created a need for curriculum specialists in government and educational institutions. However, budget cutbacks at the state level have limited the growth of curriculum specialist positions in state government.

Employment Trend, Projected 2014–24

Education, Library, & Training: 8%

Total, all occupations: 7%

Curriculum specialist: 7%

Note: "All Occupations" includes all occupations in the U.S. Economy. Source: U.S. Bureau of Labor Statistics, Employment Projections Program

Related Occupations
- Elementary, Middle, and High School Principles
- High School Teachers
- Kindergarten and Elementary School Teachers
- Librarians
- Middle School Teachers
- Postsecondary Teachers
- Preschool Teachers
- School and Career Counselors
- Special Education Teachers
- Teacher Assistants

Related Military Occupations
- Military Curriculum Developer

Conversation With . . .
MEG BOWEN

Director of Elementary Curriculum & Instruction
Orange County (Florida) Public Schools
Education, 28 years
Curriculum Development, 8 months

1. What was your individual career path in terms of education/training, entry-level job, or other significant opportunity?

In college, I started as an English major but I was dating someone whose mother was a school librarian and she talked to me about going into education. I earned my undergraduate degree from the University of North Carolina at Charlotte in early childhood education. I soon got a job teaching kindergarten, then first grade, which I did for three years in North Carolina. After that, I taught kindergarten in Virginia. Through a grant program, we went to Canada and looked at multi-age teaching programs that we then implemented, so we had our students for two years. During that time, I earned a master's in reading from James Madison University in Virginia.

After I graduated, I became a middle school reading specialist in the Frederick County (Md) Public Schools, then went into administration in elementary language arts at the school district level and worked on professional development. I went on to become an assistant principal for four years, then principal at a K-8 school. During this time, I earned my education leadership certification. We then moved to Florida and I took a position as an assistant principal in Osceola County for four years before moving over to Orange County as a senior administrator for language arts and social studies. Several months ago, I was promoted to director.

Basically, my job is to take Florida state standards—which are similar to Common Core—and make them understandable to teachers by creating resources for them. We don't write lesson plans, but we create unit plans by grouping standards together in a meaningful way. We also provide tons of resources, mostly digital – high school students use devices; even the books are in electronic form. We also train the math and reading coaches that are in most schools.

In addition, we make videos so parents can support their children and understand expectations because school is very different than when they were students. Because we have a large English as a Second Language population in Florida, we collaborate with the multi-lingual services department to ensure resources are also available in other languages.

2. What are the most important skills and/or qualities for someone in your profession?

For curriculum development, you need a thorough, thorough knowledge of standards such as Common Core. You've also got to have a lot of people skills. At the level of director, you're dealing with many different stakeholders who have partnerships with the district, so you need to be diplomatic, tactful, establish boundaries, and able to communicate. You must organize and prioritize.

3. What do you wish you had known going into this profession?

I've been surprised by the degree to which schools are involved in all aspects of students' lives, including monitoring the physical and mental well-being of students. We are seeing more mental health issues in children and not a lot of community resources for those families.

Also, I underestimated the impact poverty can have on students' performance in school. We do everything we can to counteract that, but it's a tough battle. Students living in poverty tend to move more often, which can mean changing schools and having to rebuild relationships each time. I wish there were more resources to help students living in poverty.

4. Are there many job opportunities in your profession? In what specific areas?

There are, but the path is through a position such as reading coach. You'll need to start in a classroom, then be a literacy or math coach. In most school districts, there's a district-level coach, and that would lead you into a position such as mine. But you've got to be a good teacher at heart.

5. How do you see your profession changing in the next five years, what role will technology play in those changes, and what skills will be required?

Schools are going all digital. You must be current on all apps being used in education. The personal classroom will be tied to digital access and a student's particular needs. For example, content can be personalized based on a student's response to online assessments and assignments. That means students in the same classroom can access texts on the same topic but differentiated by reading level.

6. What do you enjoy most about your job? What do you enjoy least about your job?

I most enjoy creating and delivering professional development materials, and working with administrators, coaches, teachers and students. I still get to work with students in schools, even in my current role as director. I least enjoy the state department of education reporting requirements.

7. Can you suggest a valuable "try this" for students considering a career in your profession?

Often, high school kids can volunteer with younger students. Also, most states have a website that lets people post lesson plans and get feedback; in Florida, it's called CPALMS. It's a good way to find out: Do you really like writing curriculum?

MORE INFORMATION

American Association for Teaching and Curriculum (AATC)
www.aatchome.org

American Association for the Advancement of Curriculum Studies (AAACS)
www.aaacs.org

Association of American Colleges & Universities
1818 R Street NW
Washington, DC 20009
www.aacu.org

Association for Supervision and Curriculum Development (ASCD)
1703 North Beauregard St.
Alexandria, VA 22311-1714
www.ascd.org

Education Writer's Association (EWA)
3516 Connecticut Avenue NW
Washington, DC 20008
www.ewa.org

International Association for the Advancement of Curriculum Studies
www.iaacs.ca

National Education Association (NEA)
1201 16th Street, NW
Washington, DC 20036-3290
www.nea.org

Micah Issitt/Editor

Education Administrator

Snapshot

Career Cluster(s): Education & Training
Interests: Being a leader, making decisions, solving problems, working with students
Earnings (Yearly Average): $76,930
Employment & Outlook: Average Growth Expected

OVERVIEW

Sphere of Work

Education administrators occupy positions such as that of school principal, school superintendent, college dean or provost, academic director, guidance director, athletic director, and special education director. Primary and secondary schools, both public and private, as well as colleges and universities, hire education administrators to plan and coordinate all areas of school operation, including academics, management of faculty and staff, facilities maintenance and construction, and financial administration. Education administrators are trained in

educational leadership and decision making. They are responsible for ensuring the smooth and successful functioning of schools and education programs.

Work Environment

Education administrators spend their workdays in a wide variety of public and private educational settings, including preschools, elementary schools, secondary schools, school district central offices, colleges, and universities. Administrators such as principals and deans may have a fixed office where they perform their administrative duties. Other education administrators, such as assistant principals, may work in a more hands-on capacity throughout their workday, visiting classrooms and supervising lunch and recess activities. Given the diverse demands of the education administration profession, education administrators may need to work days, evenings, weekends, and on-call hours to meet school or program needs.

Profile

Working Conditions: Work Indoors
Physical Strength: Light Work
Education Needs: Master's Degree, Doctoral Degree
Licensure/Certification: Required
Opportunities For Experience: Internship, Military Service
Holland Interest Score*: ESA

* See Appendix A

Occupation Interest

Education administrators tend to be intelligent and charismatic, able to quickly assess situations, find resources, demonstrate caring, and solve problems. Those most successful at the job of education administration display leadership, responsibility, effective time management, knowledge of human behavior, initiative, and concern for individuals and society. Communication skills are essential for success in this profession. Education administrators should enjoy spending time with a wide range of people from diverse cultural, social, and educational backgrounds.

A Day in the Life—Duties and Responsibilities

The education administrator's specific daily occupational duties and responsibilities vary by job specialization and school or program size. In larger educational settings, there are usually many specialized education administrators, while in a smaller program or preschool, one administrator may handle responsibilities across multiple disciplines.

Education administrators who oversee academics and operations in elementary, middle, and high schools have a great deal of interaction with and influence over students, teachers, staff, and the wider community. They develop and enforce student guidelines and policies on attendance, truancy, dress, speech, and behavior. They are charged with ensuring that school facilities and equipment are safe for student use and comply with relevant laws and regulations. They are also responsible for creating and maintaining budget plans with the input of school staff, families, and community.

Department heads and other education administrators meet with teachers to set and revise the curriculum in response to trends in education theory and changes in government education standards. To ensure high-quality education for their students, education administrators must also perform annual teaching evaluations and assessment, meeting with teachers to discuss their performance and goals. As part of the effort to achieve educational excellence, education administrators may lead professional development and continuing education activities for school staff. Depending on their specific role, they may also meet with parents to discuss student behavior, performance, and academic goals.

In postsecondary institutions, education administrators may specialize in academic departments, admissions, residential or campus life, financial aid, or athletics. As they gain experience, these education administrators may attain higher positions, such as director, dean, or provost, with greater responsibility and prestige. Many postsecondary education administrators influence school policies, budgets, and curriculum, as do their counterparts in primary and secondary education; however, college and university administrators generally have less direct contact with students and student families.

In addition, all education administrators are responsible for completing required documentation, such as accident, incident, or grievance reports, on a daily basis. They must also communicate the school's goals, activities, and performance to community stakeholders through press releases and all-community school events.

Duties and Responsibilities

- Providing leadership and day-to-day management of educational activities
- Formulating and evaluating educational programs and policies
- Directing the preparation and presentation of school budgets
- Determining bond requirements
- Interpreting school programs and policies
- Supervising the examination, appointment, training and promotion of administrative and teaching personnel
- Addressing community and civic groups to inform and enlist support
- Handling relations with parents, prospective students and others outside of education

OCCUPATION SPECIALTIES

School Superintendents

School Superintendents direct and coordinate activities concerned with the administration of city, county or other school systems in accordance with board of education standards.

Principals

Principals direct and coordinate the educational, administrative, and counseling activities of elementary, junior high or high schools.

Vocational Training Directors

Vocational Training Directors supervise and coordinate vocational training programs according to board of education policies and state education code.

Education Supervisors

Education Supervisors develop program curriculum, evaluate teaching techniques, and supervise and assist in the hiring and in-service training of teachers.

WORK ENVIRONMENT

Relevant Skills and Abilities

Communication Skills
- Expressing thoughts and ideas
- Speaking effectively
- Writing concisely

Interpersonal/Social Skills
- Cooperating with others
- Working as a member of a team

Organization & Management Skills
- Coordinating tasks
- Making decisions
- Managing people/groups

Research & Planning Skills
- Using logical reasoning

Technical Skills
- Performing scientific, mathematical and technical work

Physical Environment

Education administrators work in different environments depending on their specialization and place of employment. They typically spend their workdays in the central offices of various public and private educational institutions, which may include preschools, elementary schools, secondary schools, school districts, colleges, and universities.

Human Environment

Education administrators interact with a wide variety of people and should be comfortable meeting with colleagues, staff, teachers, students, student families, community stakeholders, and members of the press.

Technological Environment

Education administrators must be comfortable using computers to access student records, develop budget spreadsheets, and contact staff and student families. Education administrators tend to use cell phones to ensure availability in case of student or school-related emergencies.

EDUCATION, TRAINING, AND ADVANCEMENT

High School/Secondary

High school students interested in pursuing a career as an education administrator should prepare themselves by developing good study habits. High school–level study of foreign languages, education, sociology, and psychology can provide a strong foundation for college-level study in the field. Interested high school students should secure internships or part-time work opportunities that expose them to diverse groups, education programs, and leadership opportunities.

Suggested High School Subjects
- Accounting
- Bookkeeping
- Child Growth & Development
- College Preparatory
- Composition
- Economics
- English
- Government
- Literature
- Political Science
- Psychology
- Social Studies
- Sociology
- Speech

Famous First

The first citywide superintendent of schools was Roswell Willson Haskins of Buffalo, NY, who was appointed superintendent in 1836. He resigned before the end of the school year, however, owing to restrictions hampering his work.

College/Postsecondary

A master's degree in education administration or a related subject is the minimum educational requirement for education administrators. Postsecondary students interested in becoming education administrators should earn a bachelor's degree in education or a related field. These programs typically offer courses in education, counseling, psychology, and foreign languages. Postsecondary students can gain work experience and potential advantage in their future job searches by securing internships or part-time employment as teachers or education program coordinators.

Related College Majors
- Business Administration & Management, General
- Education Administration & Supervision, General
- Secondary/Junior High/Middle School Teacher Education

Adult Job Seekers

Adults seeking employment as education administrators should have, at a minimum, a master's degree. Some schools and districts require their education administrators to hold a doctoral degree and second-language proficiency. Because of their in-depth knowledge of the field, many teachers and professors are able to assume positions in education administration later in their careers. Adult job seekers should educate themselves about the educational and professional license requirements of their home states and the organizations where they seek employment.

Qualified adult job seekers may benefit from joining professional education associations, such as the National Association of Elementary School Principals and the National Association of Secondary School Principals, which generally offer job-finding workshops and maintain lists of available jobs.

Professional Certification and Licensure

No licensure is required for education administrators at the postsecondary level; however, those at the preschool to secondary school level must obtain proper state licensure prior to beginning professional practice. Licensure and certification options and designations for education administration vary by state. For instance, the New York Department of Education requires that education administrators, depending on their job title and specifications, earn one of the following certifications: School Administrator and Supervisor, School District Administrator, School Building Leader, or School District Leader. Other states require School Business Administrator or new School District Business Leader certificates. State education administrator licensure or certification generally requires an advanced degree in education administration or leadership and three to five years of teaching and administrative experience.

Additional Requirements

Successful education administrators will be knowledgeable about the profession's requirements, responsibilities, and opportunities. They must demonstrate high levels of integrity and ethics, as professionals in this role oversee large budgets, supervise staff, interact with students, and have access to personal information. Membership in professional education associations is encouraged among all education administrators as a means of building professional community and networking.

Fun Fact

A number of school districts pay their superintendents based on corporate models used for CEOs; a few even call them CEOs. In 2015, the highest paid public school employee in New York, superintendent of Hewlett-Woodmore schools, was paid $625,214.

Sources: www.foxbusiness.com and http://eagnews.org

EARNINGS AND ADVANCEMENT

Earnings depend on the size and geographic location of the employer and the employee's training, experience and level of supervision. In 2015, elementary and secondary school administrators had median annual earnings of $90,410; postsecondary school administrators had median annual earnings of $88,580; and preschool and childcare center administrators had median annual earnings of $45,670.

Education administrators may receive paid vacations, holidays, and sick days; life and health insurance; retirement benefits; and sabbatical leaves. These are usually paid by the employer.

Metropolitan Areas with the Highest Employment Level in this Occupation

Metropolitan area	Employment	Employment per thousand jobs	Annual mean wage
Washington-Arlington-Alexandria, DC-VA-MD-WV	1,810	0.75	$98,350
Chicago-Naperville-Arlington Heights, IL	1,310	0.37	$81,230
Los Angeles-Long Beach-Glendale, CA	1,140	0.28	$117,640
Baltimore-Columbia-Towson, MD	1,120	0.85	$94,180
New York-Jersey City-White Plains, NY-NJ	1,070	0.16	$97,670
Minneapolis-St. Paul-Bloomington, MN-WI	930	0.50	$86,370
Silver Spring-Frederick-Rockville, MD	520	0.90	$98,830
Boston-Cambridge-Newton, MA	500	0.28	$83,670
Seattle-Bellevue-Everett, WA	480	0.31	$78,660
San Diego-Carlsbad, CA	430	0.32	$100,820

Source: Bureau of Labor Statistics

EMPLOYMENT AND OUTLOOK

There were approximately 450,000 education administrators employed nationally in 2014. Employment is expected to grow about as fast as the average for all occupations through the year 2024, which means employment is projected to increase 7 percent to 10 percent. Employment will increase as school enrollments grow and as services to students are expanded. Many job openings will result from the need to replace education administrators who retire or leave the profession.

Employment Trend, Projected 2014–24

Education administrators, postsecondary: 8%

Total, all occupations: 7%

Management occupations: 6%

Note: "All Occupations" includes all occupations in the U.S. Economy. Source: U.S. Bureau of Labor Statistics, Employment Projections Program

Related Occupations
- College Faculty Member
- Elementary School Teacher
- General Manager & Top Executive
- Principal
- Secondary & Middle School Teacher

Related Military Occupations
- Teacher & Instructor
- Training & Education Director

Conversation With . . .
GONZALO SALAZAR

Superintendent
Los Fresnos Consolidated Independent School
Los Fresnos, Texas
School superintendent, 11 Years

1. What was your individual career path in terms of education/training, entry-level job, or other significant opportunity?

I've been working in schools for a large portion of my adult life. While I was working on my undergraduate degree and teaching credentials, I worked in the Child Nutrition Department for the school district in my home town as a warehouse employee and was responsible for delivering canned and frozen goods to the school kitchens. After graduating, my first job was teaching grade 4 in a neighboring district. I was assigned to a fourth grade bilingual class, working with students who were acquiring English as a second language. I did that for about four years and kept working towards a master's degree. I came to Los Fresnos as an assistant principal. Two years later, I was hired as principal of an elementary school, which I did for two more years. The superintendent called me in one day and asked me to open a new elementary campus in an area of the district experiencing a lot of growth. I served as principal there and continued to work towards a superintendent's certificate. The next position I had in the district was that of interim superintendent and, six months later, I was named superintendent of schools.

2. What are the most important skills and/or qualities for someone in your profession?

You have to be grounded in your values and morals and know your non-negotiables. Your decisions must be based on district goals, which inevitably will keep you focused on what's good for students. You deal with people from all walks of life, so you have to have empathy and understand others. The job requires knowledge of various aspects of district operations. I pride myself on matters of instruction and student performance, but I also deal with architects, lawyers, engineers and insurance experts. In one meeting, we're discussing rooftop HVAC units and in the next, we're discussing personnel issues.

3. What do you wish you had known going into this profession?

With every passing day I realize how much I still have to learn. In my first year, I wished I had known more about bond issues. Later, I wished I had known more about politics, and also about educating the entire child. I didn't have any formal training in child bereavement. When children lose a sibling or a parent, there's a grieving process that goes on for their entire academic life. There's also so much to learn about the mental health issues that plague some children.

4. Are there many job opportunities in your profession? In what specific areas?

There are many, many opportunities. Unfortunately, there's a lot of turnover in this profession.

5. How do you see your profession changing in the next five years? What role will technology play in those changes, and what skills will be required?

I see resources becoming scarcer. A superintendent needs to be financially conservative and understand his or her fiduciary responsibility. Technology will continue to play a bigger role in the delivery of instruction, which will require improvements to the infrastructure. I've seen districts try to give each student an iPad, for example, and that's just not sustainable. However, if we invest in infrastructure and use the technology that kids bring and couple that with a fair amount of technology that we can afford, we'll be able to meet the needs moving forward.

6. What do you enjoy most about your job? What do you enjoy least about your job?

I enjoy making a difference and the rewards of seeing struggling students succeed. My favorite event is graduation, standing next to the principal who occasionally whispers to me things such as, "If you knew what that child dealt with, he lost his dad or lost his mom but was able to persevere," or "This student had to work to help sustain his family and still graduated in the top 10 percent." The success stories are incredible. And I enjoy seeing schools in the most impoverished areas have the same level of success as the schools in the brick veneer area of our district. It fills my cup.

Time away from family is one of the things I enjoy the least. As a superintendent there are many demands on your time. Sometimes making an event means missing a celebration at home.

7. Can you suggest a valuable "try this" for students considering a career in your profession?

Take every opportunity to participate in student organizations and serve in leadership roles. Embrace opportunities to work with a diverse group of people. You want to develop people skills by working alongside people who don't necessarily look like you or think the same way you do. Get involved in the type of decision making that helps improve conditions for others. I would encourage students to realize you're not always the smartest person in the room; be willing to listen to the ideas of others.

MORE INFORMATION

American Association of School Administrators
801 N. Quincy Street, Suite 700
Arlington, VA 82203-1730
703.528.0700
www.aasa.org

American Federation of School Administrators
1101 17th Street, NW, Suite 408
Washington, DC 20036
202.986.4209
www.admin.org

National Association of Elementary School Principals
Educational Products Department
1615 Duke Street
Alexandria, VA 22314
800.386.2377
www.naesp.org

National Association of Secondary School Principals
1904 Association Drive
Reston, VA 20191-1537
703.860.0200
www.nassp.org

National Association of Student Affairs Administrators in Higher Education
111 K Street NE, 10th Floor
Washington, DC 20002
202.265.7500
www.naspa.org

National Education Association
1201 16th Street, NW
Washington, DC 20036-3290
202.833.4000
www.nea.org

Urban Superintendents Association of America
P.O. Box 1248
Chesapeake, VA 23327-1248
757.436.1032
www.usaa.org

Simone Isadora Flynn/Editor

Elementary School Teacher

Snapshot

Career Cluster(s): Education & Training

Interests: Teaching, working with students, communicating with others

Earnings (Yearly Average): $54,890

Employment & Outlook: Average Growth Expected

OVERVIEW

Sphere of Work

An elementary school teacher works with and instructs students enrolled in grades one through six or eight. Elementary school teachers generally teach various academic subjects to one group of students throughout the nine-month school year; however, some teachers specialize in one specific subject (such as math or art), which they teach to numerous groups of elementary school students. In addition to academic instruction, teachers provide methods of discipline and enforce rules in the classroom.

Work Environment

Elementary school teachers usually work by themselves in one classroom and supervise up to thirty students. They are responsible for providing a safe and healthy developmental learning environment for pupils. Often, teachers work with and supervise a teacher aide, who assists with classroom activities and administrative tasks. Public elementary school teachers typically spend 36.5 hours per week in the classroom, with additional hours (approximately 9.5 per week) spent directing extracurricular programs, grading papers, completing reports, and attending meetings. Private school teachers may work longer hours.

Profile

Working Conditions: Work Indoors, Work both Indoors and Outdoors
Physical Strength: Light Work
Education Needs: Bachelor's Degree, Master's Degree
Licensure/Certification: Required
Opportunities For Experience: Volunteer Work, Part Time Work
Holland Interest Score*: SEC

* See Appendix A

Occupation Interest

Above all else, an individual interested in becoming an elementary school teacher should enjoy working with children and developing their critical thinking skills. He or she should also be highly proficient in all general academic areas, including mathematics, science, English, and social studies. A prospective elementary school teacher must have a passion for leading and instructing medium-sized groups and should be skilled in public speaking. He or she should also be open to learning and understanding new pedagogical methods and instructional materials, then adapting them to the needs of the students.

A Day in the Life—Duties and Responsibilities

An elementary school teacher spends much of the workday helping, instructing, and disciplining a classroom of young children. Elementary school teachers use daily presentations, lectures, creative activities, group work, and individual lessons to aid students in the application of core subjects such as science, mathematics, and English, and sometimes foreign languages. Teachers may occasionally schedule off-site field trips for their students in order to supplement the basic teachings of a specific subject. Teachers are usually required to accompany a group of students to other locations outside of the classroom, including the cafeteria, library, outdoor recess area, sports or physical education location, and bus loading areas. Teachers receive a lunch break, during which they can retreat to a teacher's room or lounge to eat, rest, and meet with other faculty members.

Elementary school teachers are also responsible for disciplining students and maintaining order in their classrooms. Therefore, teachers must establish strict rules and boundaries within the classroom and enforce those rules effectively and consistently from day to day.

In addition to active instruction, elementary school teachers must spend time coaching sports or leading extracurricular activities (usually in the afternoons following school), preparing lesson plans, evaluating student homework, attending teacher workshops, and completing any other school-related administrative work. Many of these tasks are done at home after school hours. Teachers are also required to discuss student academic progress and/or behavioral issues with parents; they may communicate via phone or e-mail, or may meet with the parents in person.

Duties and Responsibilities

- **Preparing bulletin boards**
- **Preparing appropriate lesson plans**
- **Keeping records and making reports**
- **Correcting papers and tests**
- **Supervising outdoor and indoor play activities**
- **Evaluating student performance**
- **Counseling pupils when academic and adjustment problems arise**
- **Meeting with parents**
- **Supervising field trips**
- **Preparing report cards**
- **Attending faculty meetings**

OCCUPATION SPECIALTIES

Kindergarten Teachers

Kindergarten Teachers teach elemental natural and social science, personal hygiene, music, art and literature to children from four to six years old to promote their physical, mental and social development.

WORK ENVIRONMENT

Relevant Skills and Abilities

Communication Skills
- Speaking effectively
- Writing concisely

Interpersonal/Social Skills
- Being patient
- Cooperating with others
- Counseling others
- Teaching others

Organization & Management Skills
- Coordinating tasks
- Making decisions
- Managing people/groups
- Performing duties which change frequently

Unclassified Skills
- Having a good sense of humor

Work Environment Skills
- Working indoors

Physical Environment

Most of an elementary school teacher's work is performed in the classroom of a public or private educational institution. Teachers are on their feet for the majority of the day and usually work in temperature-controlled, well-ventilated spaces. Teachers may supervise student recesses or other outdoor activities.

Human Environment

Elementary school teachers work and interact with dozens of students ranging from about six to twelve years old. They communicate with other faculty members, school personnel such as superintendents and principals, and administrative staff members. Some teachers work closely with teacher aides, who direct students and assist teachers with various tasks. Elementary school teachers must be comfortable working with students and families from diverse backgrounds.

Technological Environment

The technical landscape is always changing for elementary school teachers; however, they should be prepared to use media equipment such as CD players, DVD players, projectors, the Internet, and e-mail.

EDUCATION, TRAINING, AND ADVANCEMENT

High School/Secondary

High school students looking to become elementary school teachers should take a wide variety of courses, including the arts, mathematics, the sciences, social studies, psychology, geography, composition, literature, child development, music, history, technology, foreign languages, and public speaking. High school students may benefit from participating in extracurricular clubs and activities, particularly those in which they are able to take on a leadership position. These activities can help students become comfortable with and proficient in speaking in front of large groups.

Suggested High School Subjects
- Arts
- Audio-Visual
- Biology
- Child Care
- Child Growth & Development
- College Preparatory
- Composition
- Crafts
- English
- Geography
- Instrumental & Vocal Music
- Keyboarding
- Literature

- Mathematics
- Psychology
- Science
- Social Studies
- Sociology
- Speech
- Theatre & Drama

Famous First

The first blackboards for use in schools were introduced in 1714 by Christopher Dock of Skippack, PA. Dock, a Mennonite who emigrated from Germany, was also the author of the first book on teaching methodology to be published in America. He emphasized character building and, in the case of infractions by students, discussion over physical punishment.

College/Postsecondary

Prospective elementary school teachers should earn a bachelor's degree in education from a college or university program accredited by the National Council for Accreditation of Teacher Education and the Teacher Education Accreditation Council. Elementary school teachers are not required to graduate from an accredited program; however, those who do may have an easier time fulfilling teacher licensure requirements. A postsecondary program in education offers courses designed specifically for a career in the classroom, including the psychology of learning, methods of teaching, social foundations of education, technology in the classroom, and philosophy of education.

Undergraduate programs in teaching also usually offer a student-teaching internship, where college students can gain experience in the classroom during the school year, either by assisting a teacher as a teacher aide or by teaching select subjects themselves. Teachers in some states are required to complete a master's degree in education. Students interested becoming elementary school teachers should check the requirements of their home state.

Related College Majors
- Agricultural Teacher Education
- Art Teacher Education
- Bilingual/Bicultural Education
- Computer Teacher Education
- Education Administration & Supervision, General
- Education of the Blind & Visual Handicapped
- Education of the Deaf & Hearing Impaired
- Education of the Specific Learning Disabled
- Education of the Speech Impaired
- Elementary/Pre-Elementary/Early Childhood/Kindergarten Teacher Education
- English Teacher Education
- Foreign Languages Teacher Education
- Health & Physical Education, General
- Health Teacher Education
- Mathematics Teacher Education
- Music Teacher Education
- Physical Education Teaching & Coaching
- Science Teacher Education, General
- Secondary/Junior High/Middle School Teacher Education
- Special Education, General
- Speech Teacher Education

Adult Job Seekers

Adults seeking to become teachers can gain valuable teaching experience by working as teacher aides, camp counselors, private or small-group tutors, parks and recreation guides, assistant coaches or sports instructors, as well as working in the Peace Corps. Prospective teachers can also participate in job shadowing experiences, volunteer to work in local schools or athletic systems, lead community groups, or work in a daycare facility.

Many states support professional development schools, which offer one-year programs to those who already have a bachelor's degree. These development schools act as liaisons between universities and elementary schools, allowing postgraduate students to gain teaching experience under the guidance of faculty members.

Professional Certification and Licensure

Elementary school teachers who wish to teach at a public school or institution must be licensed by the State Board of Education or a licensure advisory committee. Elementary school teachers working at private institutions may not be required to obtain a license. The requirements for licensure vary by state; in general, elementary school teachers must hold a bachelor's degree and complete an approved teacher-training program in order to obtain a teaching license. Continuing education is typically required for licensure renewal.

Additional Requirements

Ultimately, an elementary school teacher plays a pivotal role in the academic, social, and emotional development of young children. What students learn in the classroom during their early years tends to influence not only their academic careers, but also the ways in which they view and think about the world in general.

Fun Fact

Surveys show that in the United States, teachers are second only to people in the military when it comes to the job that contributes most to society's well-being.
Source: http://articles.chicagotribune.com

EARNINGS AND ADVANCEMENT

Earnings of elementary school teachers depend on the employee's education and teaching experience, and the type, size and geographic location of the school system. Those who work in larger metropolitan areas usually receive higher wages than those who work in more isolated, rural areas. Elementary school teachers in private schools generally earn less than public elementary school teachers.

Median annual earnings of elementary school teachers were $54,890 in 2015. The lowest ten percent earned less than $36,190, and the highest ten percent earned more than $85,550.

The school calendar often allows elementary school teachers to receive vacation days on national and state holidays and receive winter and summer vacations. Most employers offer life and health insurance and retirement benefits. These are usually paid by the employer.

Metropolitan Areas with the Highest Employment Level in this Occupation

Metropolitan area	Employment	Employment per thousand jobs	Annual mean wage
New York-Jersey City-White Plains, NY-NJ	61,200	9.45	$71,190
Houston-The Woodlands-Sugar Land, TX	34,280	11.70	$57,530
Los Angeles-Long Beach-Glendale, CA	31,020	7.56	$73,430
Atlanta-Sandy Springs-Roswell, GA	28,950	11.67	$54,190
Chicago-Naperville-Arlington Heights, IL	27,730	7.76	$64,000
Dallas-Plano-Irving, TX	24,490	10.51	$54,270
Washington-Arlington-Alexandria, DC-VA-MD-WV	23,620	9.77	$70,210
Minneapolis-St. Paul-Bloomington, MN-WI	17,550	9.33	$63,600
Riverside-San Bernardino-Ontario, CA	16,690	12.73	$75,950
Phoenix-Mesa-Scottsdale, AZ	15,900	8.48	$42,600

Source: Bureau of Labor Statistics

EMPLOYMENT AND OUTLOOK

There were over 1.5 million elementary school teachers employed nationally in 2014. Employment is expected to grow about as fast as the average for all occupations through the year 2024, which means employment is projected to increase about 6 percent. Most job openings will occur as a result of the expected retirement of a large number of teachers.

The supply of elementary school teachers is likely to increase in response to growing student enrollment, improved job opportunities, more teacher involvement in school policy, greater public interest in education and higher salaries. Job prospects are greater in central cities and rural areas. However, job growth could be limited by state and local government budget deficits.

Employment Trend, Projected 2014–24

Total, all occupations: 7%

Preschool, primary, secondary, and special education school teachers: 6%

Elementary school teachers: 6%

Note: "All Occupations" includes all occupations in the U.S. Economy. Source: U.S. Bureau of Labor Statistics, Employment Projections Program

Related Occupations
- Education Administrator
- Preschool Teacher
- Principal
- Secondary & Middle School Teacher
- Special Education Teacher
- Teacher Assistant

Conversation With . . .
SHEA RUST

Second Grade Teacher
Riverdale Elementary School, Riverdale, Maryland
Teacher, 3 years

1. What was your individual career path in terms of education/training, entry-level job, or other significant opportunity?

I knew being a teacher was a lot of work because I watched my mom, a teacher, at her desk for long hours in the evenings while I was growing up. So I didn't really think about teaching until I was in my sophomore year at St. Mary's College and was required to do a project where we went out into the community to help. I did a placement each week in an elementary school. I loved working with little kids. I was an English major and decided to minor in Education Studies.

I went on to earn a master's in teaching at St. Mary's.

Now I teach second graders, mostly Hispanic, English as a Second Language (ESL) students. I teach reading, language arts, math and science. The most rewarding part of my job is seeing and hearing the progress of students who are learning English. I also love the relationships I build with the students. Being able to listen and talk with younger kids gives you a different, fun perspective on life. I know I make a difference every day. That's really rewarding.

2. What are the most important skills and/or qualities for someone in your profession?

The number one thing is flexibility, and rolling with the punches every day whether it's because lunch is delayed or the students didn't understand the lesson and I have to go back and re-teach. Also, especially with younger children, you must be patient. You have to make things simple for them, and make subjective things concrete for them. Literally, you have to teach them to stick the top of the marker on the bottom of it. They need very clear directions.

3. What do you wish you had known going into this profession?

There are so many things that are not child- or teaching-related that are mandatory, stemming from policy, that teachers are expected to do. For instance, in Maryland, every year we have to participate in SOL's, which stands for Student Learning Objectives, a research project we do on our students for math and science.

I also didn't realize how much of my own money I would spend—more than $300 a year—on classroom supplies, materials, and things I think will help my students.

4. Are there many job opportunities in your profession? In what specific areas?

I can only speak to Maryland, but every one of my classmates or friends who wanted to get a teaching job has been able to secure one. Special education teachers are especially in demand.

5. How do you see your profession changing in the next five years? What role will technology play in those changes, and what skills will be required?

Technology is going to be what changes the profession. I see classrooms where teachers put lessons on Google and students go ahead and work on them on their own. In my school, every third- and fifth-grader has a Chromebook. This will trickle down to the lower grades. As a teacher, I work with a smart board and an interactive projector. Say you have a Venn diagram up with different statements below. The kids can drag the statements onto the screen where they belong. And you can see the kids' writing on the board. In addition are online quizzes kids can take with their smartphones.

6. What do you enjoy most about your job? What do you enjoy least about your job?

I enjoy working with the kids. They're so cute and fun; every day I have a fun story. Seeing someone actually learn how to read, and seeing the change you're making, is really, really rewarding.

The least rewarding is when the administration wants you to do something related to a policy or test that has changed—and they seem to change every year—that you don't think is furthering the kids' learning.

7. Can you suggest a valuable "try this" for students considering a career in your profession?

Do a summer camp program. Or, some high schools arrange placements for students in an elementary school. I really recommend you do that to find out if you like working with children, because if you don't, you'll be miserable. Sometimes it's frustrating to realize how little younger children know. We have lessons in my class on how to sneeze and how to wash your hands.

MORE INFORMATION

**American Association for
Employment in Education**
3040 Riverside Drive, Suite 125
Columbus, OH 43221
614.485.1111
www.aaee.org

**American Association of Colleges
for Teacher Education**
1307 New York Avenue NW
Suite 300
Washington, DC 20005-4701
202.293.2450
www.aacte.org

American Federation of Teachers
Public Affairs Department
555 New Jersey Avenue NW
Washington, DC 20001
202.879.4400
www.aft.org

**National Association for the
Education of Young Children**
1313 L Street NW, Suite 500
Washington, DC 20005
800.424.2460
www.naeyc.org

**National Board for Professional
Teaching Standards**
1525 Wilson Boulevard, Suite 500
Arlington, VA 22209
800.228.3224
www.nbpts.org

**National Council for
Accreditation of Teacher
Education**
2010 Massachusetts Avenue, NW
Suite 500
Washington, DC 20036-1023
202.466.7496
www.ncate.org

**National Council of Teachers of
Mathematics**
1906 Association Drive
Reston, VA 20191-1502
703.620.9840
www.nctm.org

National Education Association
1201 16th Street, NW
Washington, DC 20036-3290
202.833.4000
www.nea.org

**U.S. Department of Education
National Center for Education
Statistics**
1990 K Street NW
Washington, DC 2006
202.502.7300
nces.ed.gov

Briana Nadeau/Editor

ESL Teacher

Snapshot

Career Cluster(s): Education, Adult Education

Interests: Language, teaching, immigration, sociology, interpersonal communication

Earnings (Yearly Average): $50,280

Employment & Outlook: Average growth expected

OVERVIEW

Sphere of Work

ESL (English as a Second Language) teachers, also known as Teachers of English for Speakers of Other Languages (TESOL), are English teachers specializing in teaching English to non-English speakers. ESL teachers may teach English to children or adults, though most

ESL classes are aimed at adult immigrants. ESL teachers may work independently or for an educational institution, and the duties required of an ESL teacher may differ according to the particularities of their employment. Often ESL teachers are also responsible for assessing the educational needs of students and tailoring materials and/

or class presentations to meet the specific needs of their students. Approximately 57 percent of ESL teachers work for elementary or secondary schools or junior colleges. ESL teachers are also employed by colleges universities, private instruction companies and social assistance and outreach organizations.

Work Environment

Most ESL teachers work in office environments inside educational institutions such as elementary and secondary schools, junior colleges, colleges and universities. Some ESL positions may require the instructor to travel to different destinations. Many organizations offering ESL classes offer classes at night or on weekends when the classes students, often working adults, are better able to attend. ESL instructors may therefore be required to work off hours or to work late.

Profile

Working Conditions: Work Indoors
Physical Strength: Light Work
Education Needs: Bachelor's Degree, Master's Degree
Licensure/Certification: Required
Opportunities For Experience: On-Job Training, Part-Time Work, Internship, Teaching Assistant Positions
Holland Interest Score*: SAE

* See Appendix A

Occupation Interest

ESL instruction combines education with social service as many ESL students are immigrants struggling to learn English to better assimilate or function in United States society. Those seeking to become ESL teachers should have a strong interest in teaching and a secondary interest in social outreach and human services. ESL teachers also benefit from experience and/or interest with one or more non-English languages. Individuals interested should also be comfortable in social environments as ESL teaching typically involves face-to-face interaction with students. Individuals who are self-motivated and artistic have an advantage in the ESL field when working on planning and executing lessons for students.

A Day in the Life—Duties and Responsibilities

There are a variety of different types of ESL classes offered through private organizations and educational institutions and the typical duties required of an ESL teacher will differ depending on the type of educational program. Some schools and organizations offer intensive programs that may last 10 weeks or longer, while other programs are organized to fit within a typical school semester or other session. Most ESL programs begin with teacher evaluations where the ESL teacher meets with and evaluates the speaking ability and educational needs of each student. Once classes begin, a typical day may involve delivering a class presentation, collecting and discussing assignments, completing class projects, or a variety of other educational activities.

Throughout a typical ESL session, the ESL teacher is responsible for monitoring student progress and, if needed, altering the curriculum to address the needs of students. ESL teachers may use a variety of commercially available textbooks and learning aides but must also often tailor educational materials and programs for the needs of their specific students. In general, ESL programs tend to focus on providing students with information that provides immediate aide in finding employment, navigating their environment, and preparing forcitizenship examinations.

Duties and Responsibilities

- Prepare lesson plans, classroom activities, and lecture materials
- Deliver lectures, presentations, or other classroom activities
- Assign and grade homework and other assignments.
- Prepare, deliver, and evaluate tests to monitor student progress
- Adhere to educational or state/federal guidelines for ESL education
- Evaluate the needs of new and continuing students
- Provide guidance for students in meeting class objectives
- Attend professional meetings or continuing education sessions to learn about new techniques and materials in the field

OCCUPATION SPECIALTIES

ESL Program Coordinator

ESL coordinators are managers or administrators who typically oversee a staff of ESL teachers. Coordinators are also typically responsible for ensuring that the school/organization's educational program continues to meet changing state and/or federal requirements for ESL instruction.

TEFL Teacher

TEFL (Teaching English as a Foreign Language) teachers are employed by schools and private language learning centers around the world to teach English to students in nations where English is not the primary language. TEFL teachers typically have some familiarity or fluency in the native language of the nation in which they teach.

TOEFL Test Preparation Teacher

The Test of English as a Foreign Language (TOEFL) is a standardized test offered to students seeking to enroll in English-speaking universities. TOEFL Test Preparation Teachers specialize in instructing students in the most useful information needed to pass the TOEFL examination, offered through the Educational Testing Service.

USCIS Test Preparation Teacher

USCIS test preparation teachers specialize in teaching the linguistic requirements needed to help students pass citizenship examinations given by the U.S. Citizenship and Immigration Services department (USCIS). USCIS instructors are familiar with USCIS testing requirements and can therefore better help students prepare for the test directly.

WORK ENVIRONMENT

Physical Environment

ESL teachers typically work in office environments, whether located in a school or college, or in a private educational organization. While some educational programs conduct field trips with students, most of an ESL teacher's work can be completed within an office or in the home. On a less regular basis, ESL teachers may be asked to attend conferences or meetings to learn about new developments in the English education field. Because ESL classes tend to be held in mornings and evenings, part time ESL positions are common in many areas.

Relevant Skills and Abilities

Communication Skills
- Communicating clearly across cultural/linguistic barriers
- Writing simply and effectively

Interpersonal/Social Skills
- Being able to work in a group environment
- Being able to handle frequent interactions with others

Organization & Management Skills
- Managing class schedules and assignments
- Teaching and mentoring learners
- Being detail oriented in the preparation of materials

Research & Planning Skills
- Creating original presentations and educational activities

Technical Skills
- Utilizing basic digital technology and personal computers

Human Environment

ESL teachers often have students from around the world and may therefore interact with individuals from different cultures and educational backgrounds. Face-to-face, email, and telephone communications are essential parts of the ESL field and prospective ESL teachers much be comfortable working with nearly constant interaction during working hours. In addition, ESL instructors should be comfortable and creative in communicating with others to better facilitate student participation and group interaction in the classroom.

Technological Environment

ESL teachers often use word processing software as part of their job and must also be familiar with digital communication methods such as using email and smart devices. Some ESL programs may ask teachers to use specialized software-based learning tools in the classroom or for delivering/grading tests for students.

EDUCATION, TRAINING, AND ADVANCEMENT

High School/Secondary

High school students interested in pursuing a career as ESL teachers should focus on meeting basic education requirements with a focus on English and composition. Training in foreign languages is also helpful and students who focus on becoming fluent in a specific foreign language may be eligible for jobs focusing on educating individuals from specific linguistic backgrounds. Classes in computer technology will also be helpful for those entering the field.

Suggested High School Subjects
- English
- Composition
- Literature
- World Languages
- Linguistics
- Social Studies
- Computer Technology

Famous First

In 1966, pioneering linguistic anthropologist Dell Hymes created the concept of "communicative competence," which is the ability to use language correctly and appropriately towards completing certain communicative goals. Communicative competence became one of the cornerstones of ESL education and is still considered one of the primary goals in teaching English to non-English speakers. Hymes' concept is now divided into a variety of more specific levels of competence, including discourse competence, strategic competence, and sociolinguistic competence.

College/Postsecondary

Individuals interested in pursuing a career as ESL instructors should begin by obtaining a Bachelor's Degree in English or English education. Further, individuals seeking to become ESL teachers might consider taking classes in adult education offered in some Bachelor's degree programs. In addition to English composition and analysis, prospective ESL teachers will benefit from classes in public speaking and from some exposure to intercultural studies and sociology. While a Bachelor's degree may be sufficient for some ESL teacher positions, those seeking to work in colleges, universities, or junior colleges will benefit from obtaining a Master's degree or higher degree and should therefore take classes towards the goal of applying for graduate studies programs.

Related College Majors
- English
- English Education
- Education
- Education Administration
- Composition
- Writing as a Profession

Adult Job Seekers

Individuals with degrees in English or Education can apply for open positions. In some cases, individuals with teaching degrees may be eligible for internships in ESL education offered through some institutions of higher learning and private ESL education companies. Job postings may be found by joining one of several professional ESL organizations around the nation.

Professional Certification and Licensure

Most ESL teachers are required to obtain and maintain state certification as a teacher, though teacher certification is not required in all states. Some states further require special certification in adult education for ESL teachers, whether working for an educational institution or private company. To obtain an adult education license, applicants must typically participate in a training program and pass a test.

Additional Requirements

ESL teachers need excellent communication skills as their job necessitates frequent interaction with individuals form different cultures and with different levels of fluency in English. As a result, ESL teachers benefit from having sensitivity to cultural, economic, and sociological differences, and from the ability to think creatively when communicating with others. In addition, patience, critical thinking, and leadership skills are important traits for success in the ESL field.

Fun Fact

The Census Bureau tells us that more than 350 languages are spoken in the U.S. After English, Spanish is most common, followed by Chinese, Tagalog (spoken in the Philippines), Vietnamese and French (including Patois and Cajun.)
Source: http://fusion.net/story

EARNINGS AND ADVANCEMENT

The median annual wage for ESL and adult literacy teachers was $50,280 in 2015. The lowest 10 percent of ESL teachers earned less than $28,000, while the highest paid 10 percent of ESL professionals earned salaries in excess of $80,000 annually. The highest paid jobs in the field tend to be offered in elementary, secondary, and higher education institutions, while salaries for ESL teachers in private or alternative ESL programs tend to be lower. The lowest paid positions in the ESL field are typically in the healthcare and social services industries.

Metropolitan Areas with the Highest Employment Level in this Occupation

Metropolitan area	Employment	Employment per thousand jobs	Hourly mean wage
New York-Jersey City-White Plains, NY-NJ	3,590	0.55	$32.22
Seattle-Bellevue-Everett, WA	2,960	1.93	$27.71
Houston-The Woodlands-Sugar Land, TX	2,530	0.86	$28.58
Los Angeles-Long Beach-Glendale, CA	1,170	0.42	$35.48
Anaheim-Santa Ana-Irvine, CA	1,520	1.00	$25.92
Chicago-Naperville-Arlington Heights, IL	1,470	0.41	$31.41
Boston-Cambridge-Newton, MA	930	0.53	$19.83
Washington-Arlington-Alexandria, DC-VA-MD-WV	930	0.38	$26.27
Minneapolis-St. Paul-Bloomington, MN-WI	890	0.47	$19.71
Tampa-St. Petersburg-Clearwater, FL	830	0.69	$24.25

Source: Bureau of Labor Statistics

EMPLOYMENT AND OUTLOOK

The Bureau of Labor Statistics estimates that the ESL field will grow by 7 percent between 2014 and 2024, which is considered average growth across all industries. The decline in immigration rates since the early 2000s has also slowed the growth of domestic ESL education. Individuals with Spanish language experience are in high demand in states with large Spanish-speaking immigrant populations, while individuals with Chinese or Korean language experience will have an advantage in other areas. Future job availability will depend on the progress of federal and state immigration reform and the job outlook for the ESL field may therefore shift after the 2016 Presidential Election season.

Employment Trend, Projected 2014–24

ESL teachers: 13%

Education, training, and library occupations: 8%

Total, all occupations: 7%

Note: "All Occupations" includes all occupations in the U.S. Economy. Source: U.S. Bureau of Labor Statistics, Employment Projections Program

Related Occupations
- Social Workers
- Special Education Teachers
- Kindergarten and Elementary School Teachers
- Middle School Teachers
- High School Teachers
- School and Career Counselors
- Technical Education Teachers
- Curriculum Specialist

Related Military Occupations
- Military Foreign Language Instructor
- Language Department Lead

Conversation With . . .
GABRIELLA TAGLIAFERRO

ESL & Bilingual Teacher
Brophy Elementary School, Framingham, MA
Teacher, 22 years

1. **What was your individual career path in terms of education/training, entry-level job, or other significant opportunity?**

I grew up in Argentina, so my native language is Spanish, but I went to an English school. So I started off in kindergarten being bilingual myself. Also, my father's family is Italian and we visited grandma every Sunday, so I speak Italian. After I became a teacher, I went to live in the south of Argentina to work specifically with the indigenous Mapuche. I was always curious about the social and the emotional part of integrating into a new culture. The Mapuche are as Argentinian as anybody else, yet they needed to integrate into the wider population. That was very enlightening. I liked it a lot.

After five years, I moved to Italy and taught kindergarten. Of course, they spoke Italian and I was teaching English, so it was English as a Second Language, but for Italians. When I came to the U.S. five years later, I had a lot of experience and got a job very quickly. I taught middle school science and math and language arts in Spanish to newcomers. And I really loved it. The idea is to keep feeding and teaching them grade-appropriate content in their native language and they of course receive an hour or two of English every day.

Right now, I teach all subjects in Spanish to second graders. I co-teach with the ESL teacher who comes into the class. I have a master's degree in applied linguistics and am certified as an ESL teacher and as a bilingual Spanish and bilingual Italian teacher.

2. **What are the most important skills and/or qualities for someone in your profession?**

Being sensitive to cross-cultural issues. As a teacher, you have to make a real connection with the person you're teaching and understand the difficulties of incorporating a second language. You need to have knowledge of how applied linguistics works, how language development works.

3. What do you wish you had known going into this profession?

I wish I could have traveled a little more to know more cultures. And I definitely would have liked to know how the American system of education worked because it took me a while to figure it out. For example, besides the many steps I took to translate and validate my certification from Argentina, I did not know that teachers needed to take several Massachusetts Tests for Educator Licensure (MTELs) to earn their license. And as the parent of kids who went to school here, I saw a general assumption that families coming to the country should know how to navigate the system and support their children.

4. Are there many job opportunities in your profession? In what specific areas?

Yes. The immigrant population is growing in size and as a percent of the total population.

5. How do you see your profession changing in the next five years? What role will technology play in those changes, and what skills will be required?

Massachusetts now requires new teachers to have instruction in teaching English Language Learners, which should make things better. Technology has helped with finding resources in the native language. Spanish is so common in the U.S. now, yet in academics it's hard to find, for example, school books that are appropriate. Having ebooks and online resources will make it easier. We also are using technology to create books online in different languages.

6. What do you enjoy most about your job? What do you enjoy least about your job?

I love the contact with cultures. Even though all my students speak Spanish, there's such a diversity of customs and ways of viewing the world, because they do come from different countries. That makes it a lot of fun and so rich. We spend a lot of time getting to know each other. For example, vocabulary—how do you say this in your country and your country and your country? Students get a sense of being valued for their diversity.

Also, the relationships I have with the families are very, very close. They are parents who are very lost sometimes because they don't understand this educational system that is very different from the system they knew before. It helps that I am an immigrant, because trust can be an issue. It's still happening that people pity them or condescend. The human connection is really important to me. And through that, these parents can push the kids to do what I want them to do at home!

What I like least is that the system still has a long way to make it easier for ESL students to achieve. People who don't speak the language are at a great disadvantage with all the mandatory testing. There has been a lot of progress, but there is a long way to go.

7. **Can you suggest a valuable "try this" for students considering a career in your profession?**

Learning a language is not just "this is the grammar and these are the words and put it together and off you go." If you are drawn to, or curious about, the human part of the student who is trying to learn English, this job could be for you. Try to volunteer at after-school programs or summer school for ESL students.

MORE INFORMATION

Teachers of English to Speakers of Other Languages, Inc. (TESOL)
1925 Ballenger Avenue, Suite 550
Alexandria, Virginia 22314
www.tesol.org

National Association for Bilingual Education (NABE)
11006 Viers Mills Road, L-1
Wheaton, MD 20902
www.nabe.org

National Council of Teachers of English (NCTE)
1111 W. Kenyon Road
Urbana, Illinois, 61801
www.ncte.org

American Association for Applied Linguistics (AAAL)
1827 Powers Ferry Road, Building 14
Suite 100
Atlanta, Georgia, 30339
www.aaal.org

American Council on the Teaching of Foreign Languages (ACTFL)
1001 N. Fairfax Street, Suite 200
Alexandria, Virginia, 22314
www.actfl.org

International Language Testing Assocation (ILTA)
3416 Primm Lane
Birmingham, Alabama 35216
www.iltaonline.com

Micah Issitt/Editor

Human Resources Manager

Snapshot

Career Cluster: Business Administration; Human Services

Interests: Organizations, human behavior, working life, solving problems, resolving conflict

Earnings (Yearly Average): $100,800

Employment & Outlook: Faster Than Average Growth Expected

OVERVIEW

Sphere of Work

Human resources managers, also referred to as human resources professionals or benefits specialists, provide job training and job placement support services to individuals and companies, recruit new workers, conduct job interviews, refer clients for jobs, or supervise the hiring process. Human resources managers may also provide training for employees and staff on benefits-related issues such as health benefits, paid time off, educational benefits, insurance and retirement benefits, and taxes.

Work Environment

Human resources managers spend their workdays seeing clients in a wide variety of settings, including corporate human resources or staffing departments, job counseling and placement agencies, and college and university career counseling offices. Human resources managers have a fixed office where they see clients but may also travel to see potential job candidates or attend job fairs. Given the diverse demands of human resources work, human resources managers may need to work days, evenings, and weekends to meet client, department, or company needs.

Profile

Working Conditions: Work Indoors
Physical Strength: Light Work
Education Needs: Bachelor's Degree, Master's Degree
Licensure/Certification: Recommended
Physical Abilities Not Required: No Heavy Labor
Opportunities For Experience: Internship, Apprenticeship, Military Service, Volunteer Work
Part-Time Work
Holland Interest Score*: ESR

* See Appendix A

Occupation Interest

Individuals drawn to the human resources profession tend to be intelligent and have the ability to quickly assess situations and people, find resources, resolve conflicts, and solve problems. Those most successful at the job of human resources manager display traits such as time management, knowledge of human behavior, computer skills, and business savvy. Human resources managers should enjoy spending time with a wide range of people, including those from diverse cultural, social, and educational backgrounds.

A Day in the Life—Duties and Responsibilities

The daily occupational duties and responsibilities of human resources managers will be determined by the individual's area of job specialization and work environment. Specialties of human resources managers include recruiting, vocational assessment, staffing, interviewing, job training, job placement, and benefits training.

Human resources managers may recruit job candidates, interview possible job candidates, visit job fairs at colleges and universities, and conduct job candidate evaluations to assess vocational aptitude, work history, and job readiness. They make hiring recommendations, conduct background checks, and may coordinate drug tests for new hires. Human resources managers also review job listings and forums to stay informed about available jobs within their business and industry, and they must develop connections and familiarity with local employment agencies. Supervising a staff of human resources specialists or assistants also falls under the purview of this job.

Human resources managers must keep up to date on current best practices in their field. They may be expected to write or update an employee handbook describing company policies such as dress, work relationships, email standards, and paid time off. They must take time to stay informed about current labor laws, trends, and regulations. They are responsible for conducting benefits workshops and training seminars for employees and staff on benefits-related issues such as health benefits, paid time off policies, educational benefits, life insurance and retirement benefits, and taxes. Human resources managers also direct human resources employees and the human resources department at large.

In addition, all human resources managers are responsible for completing employee records and required documentation, such as job referral forms, on a daily basis

Duties and Responsibilities

- Recruiting, testing and orientating new employees
- Investigating and resolving questions of equal employment
- Preparing job descriptions
- Reporting on the effects of industry trends on workers
- Promoting the use of public employment programs
- Devising ways of assuring fair compensation
- Designing and administering benefits programs
- Planning and implementing employee training programs
- Promoting occupational safety and health
- Negotiating agreements to disputes involving a company
- Supporting management in labor negotiations
- Advising both labor and management to resolve disputes
- Deciding disputes to bind both labor and management to contracts

OCCUPATION SPECIALTIES

Occupational Analysts

Occupational Analysts do research to classify jobs and describe the effects of trends on workers.

Labor Relations Specialists

Industrial Relations Directors formulate policy, oversee labor relations and negotiate agreements involving unions.

Benefits Managers

Benefits Managers specialize in handling a company's employee benefits, especially health insurance and pensions.

Education and Training Managers

Education and Training Managers supervise employees in skill development, learning and morale.

Recruiting Managers

Recruiting Managers oversee the recruiting and hiring responsibilities of the human resources department.

Payroll Specialists

Payroll Specialists handle the operations of an organization's payroll department, ensuring that all aspects of payroll are processed correctly and on time

WORK ENVIRONMENT

Physical Environment

The immediate physical environment of human resources managers varies according to their company size, geographical location, and job specialization. Human resources managers involved in job placement and benefits training spend their workdays seeing clients in corporate human resources and staffing departments while human resources managers involved in employee recruitment spend their workdays visiting job training and placement programs and college and university career counseling offices.

Relevant Skills and Abilities

Communication Skills
- Persuading others
- Speaking effectively

Interpersonal/Social Skills
- Being patient
- Cooperating with others
- Understanding conflict

Organization & Management Skills
- Coordinating tasks
- Managing people/groups
- Managing time
- Meeting goals and deadlines
- Performing duties that change frequently

Research & Planning Skills
- Developing evaluation strategies
- Solving problems

Technical Skills
- Working with both people and data

Human Environment

Human resources managers work with a wide variety of people. They should be comfortable meeting with potential job candidates, colleagues, staff, supervisors, college and university students, and unemployed people.

Technological Environment

Human resources managers use computers, cell phones, cars, and Internet communication tools to perform their job. They should be comfortable using computers to access employee records as well as post available positions online

EDUCATION, TRAINING, AND ADVANCEMENT

High School/Secondary

High school students interested in pursuing a career in human resources should prepare themselves by developing good study habits. High school courses in foreign languages, psychology, and writing will provide a strong foundation for work as a human resources specialist and manager or college-level work in the field. Due to the range of human resources job requirements, high school students interested in this career path will benefit from seeking internships or part-time work that expose the students to managerial roles and diverse professions.

Suggested High School Subjects
- Business
- College Preparatory
- English
- Humanities
- Mathematics
- Psychology
- Social Studies
- Statistics

Famous First

The first pension plan was offered by American Express Company to its employees in 1875. The plan included employees 60 years of age or older with at least 20 years of employment. Approved beneficiaries received 50 percent of the average salary they had earned over the preceding 10 years, with a cap of $500.

College/Postsecondary

Postsecondary students interested in becoming human resources specialists or managers should work towards the bachelor's degree in human resource management or a related field. Classes in psychology, business administration, and foreign languages may also prove useful in their future work. Advanced positions in this field often require a master's degree in human resources development. Postsecondary students can gain work experience and potential advantage in their future job searches by obtaining internships or part-time employment in career placement or job training programs.

Related College Majors
- Business Administration
- Human Resources Management
- Labor/Personnel Relations & Studies
- Management

Adult Job Seekers

Adults seeking employment as human resources managers should have earned, at a minimum, a bachelor's degree in human resource management or a related field, such as business administration, personnel administration, or labor relations. Employers may require human resources managers to have a master's degree and related national certification. Adult job seekers should educate themselves about the educational and professional license requirements of their home states and the organizations where they seek employment. They may also benefit from joining professional associations, such as the Society for Human Resource Management and the National Employment Counseling Association, which generally offer help with networking and job searching.

Professional Certification and Licensure

Certification for human resources managers is voluntary but often recommended or requested by employers. The main human resources specialist and manager certifications are the Professional in Human Resources (PHR) designation, the Senior Professional in Human Resources (SPHR) designation, and the Global Professional in Human Resources (GPHR) designation offered by the Human Resources Certification Institute. The PHR, SPHR, and the GPHR certifications are earned by passing a national examination testing knowledge of human resources practices and federal employment rules and regulations including affirmative action and the American with Disabilities Act. Continuing education coursework is a condition of ongoing certification.

Additional Requirements

Successful human resources managers engage in ongoing professional development to maintain their certifications. Because human resources managers have access to personal information and hiring or job placement influence, they must adhere to strict codes of professional ethics. Membership in professional human resources associations is encouraged among all human resources managers as a means of building professional community and networking

Fun Fact

The National Cash Register Company, known today as NCR, established the first personnel management department in the aftermath of a 1901 strike and lockout. Other factories followed in an effort to deal with grievances, safety, wages, and other issues that are handled by today's Human Resources departments.

Source: http://www.brighthubpm.com/resource-management/77387-a-history-of-human-resource-management/

EARNINGS AND ADVANCEMENT

According to a salary survey by the National Association of Colleges and Employers, individuals with a bachelor's degree in human resources were offered starting salaries of $49,359 in 2012.

Median annual earnings of human resources managers were $100,800 in 2013. The lowest ten percent earned less than $59,000, and the highest ten percent earned more than $177.000. The annual earnings of non-managerial human resources specialists averaged $61,560 in 2013.

Human resources managers may receive paid vacations, holidays, and sick days; life and health insurance; and retirement benefits. These are usually paid by the employer

Metropolitan Areas with the Highest Employment Level in This Occupation

Metropolitan area	Employment[1]	Employment per thousand jobs	Hourly mean wage
New York-White Plains-Wayne, NY-NJ	7,230	1.38	$65.61
Chicago-Joliet-Naperville, IL	4,000	1.08	$49.54
Los Angeles-Long Beach-Glendale, CA	3,750	0.94	$55.69
Washington-Arlington-Alexandria, DC-VA-MD-WV	3,340	1.41	$65.02
Minneapolis-St. Paul-Bloomington, MN-WI	2,860	1.60	$55.08
Atlanta-Sandy Springs-Marietta, GA	2,610	1.13	$55.36
Boston-Cambridge-Quincy, MA	2,460	1.40	$59.93
Houston-Sugar Land-Baytown, TX	2,130	0.77	$59.26
Seattle-Bellevue-Everett, WA	2,010	1.39	$56.80
Phoenix-Mesa-Glendale, AZ	1,860	1.05	$47.73

[1] Does not include self-employed. Source: Bureau of Labor Statistics.

EMPLOYMENT AND OUTLOOK

Human resources managers held about 102,000 jobs nationally in 2012; human resources specialists, on the other hand, held about 418,000 jobs in 2012. The private sector accounted for nearly 90 percent of jobs, primarily in the services industry in the areas of administrative and support services; professional, scientific and technical services; manufacturing; health care and social assistance; and finance and insurance.

Employment of human resources managers is expected to grow about as fast as the average for all occupations through the year 2022, which means employment is projected to increase 9 percent to 16 percent. Legislation and court rulings setting standards in various areas, such as occupational safety and health, equal employment opportunity, wages, health care, pensions, and family leave will increase demand for human resources managers. In addition, employers are expected to devote greater resources to job-specific training programs in response to the increasing complexity of many jobs, the aging of the workforce, and technological advances that can leave employees with obsolete skills.

Employment Trend, Projected 2012–22

Human Resources Managers: 13%

Total, All Occupations: 11%

Management Occupations: 7%

Note: "All Occupations" includes all occupations in the U.S. Economy. Source: U.S. Bureau of Labor Statistics, Employment Projections Program.

Related Occupations

- Court Administrator
- Employment Specialist
- General Manager & Top Executive
- Lawyer
- Management Analyst & Consultant
- Psychologist

Related Military Occupations

- Emergency Management Officer
- Personnel Manager
- Recruiting Manager
- Teacher & Instructor
- Training & Education Director

Conversation With . . .
KAREN STONE MICKOOL

Executive Director, Stone Associates
Human Resource Consulting Firm, 5 years
Santa Fe, NM

1. What was your individual career path in terms of education/training, entry-level job, or other significant opportunity?

Before moving into traditional human resources, I spent many years training and developing leaders — first college students, then corporate executives. My Master's Degree is in higher education administration and counseling; my undergraduate degree is in special education. I worked my way up the ranks in higher education working in student life departments, where I focused on student leadership. When I took a position as a management development specialist with the Bank of New York, Delaware, my focus shifted to leadership development for mid-level executives. Over time, I held several leadership training positions with major companies and have had interesting assignments such as helping to run a global management development program for an engineering firm with state-of-the-art training facilities.

After that employer started struggling financially and I was laid off, a headhunter called to see if I'd be interested in a human resources job. I told him that I wasn't qualified! He called back to say his client still wanted to talk to me because they felt I had the ability to sit with senior leadership and help guide an organization. I was hired because they felt they could train me to manage HR functions like payroll and benefits.

In 2009, I moved to Santa Fe, NM for personal reasons and was able to start my own consulting practice. My company specializes in partnering with small businesses. We manage the full employment cycle of an employee from hiring to orienting and training, to developing the employee, to, sometimes, exiting the employee if that's the appropriate thing to do.

Business needs change quickly and layoffs are common. But you can reinvent yourself, and ultimately benefit from that change. Be conscientious about maintaining your professional network because those contacts will help you through transitions and job changes. I have been laid off three times in my career and every time I landed back on my feet with a better job with more responsibility and a better compensation package.

2. What are the most important skills and/or qualities for someone in your profession?

Discretion. You must be ethical and trustworthy. You are in a position to know highly sensitive information and maintaining confidentiality is key. You won't succeed if you cant keep a lot of secrets.

To be effective you must keep up with what's going on in employment law. Unfortunately we live in a litigious society, and these issues come into play on a daily basis. There's a fine line here—we don't give legal advice, but we need to know when legal advice is needed.

Finally, it's critical that you go into an organization and learn about the business: how the organization works, how they make money, what the key business propositions are and how they affect the company's goals and outcomes. The only way to be a credible voice is to show that you understand the business.

3. What do you wish you had known going into this profession?

I wish I'd had more background with basics like payroll and benefits early on. But, I had invaluable opportunities at a very senior level that most HR people don't get until much later in their careers.

4. Are there many job opportunities in your profession? In what specific areas?

There are always going to be jobs, and they're always going to be competitive.

5. How do you see your profession changing in the next five years? What role will technology play in those changes, and what skills will be required?

Today's HR leaders are truly involved in setting a company's strategy and direction. To sit at the table with business leaders, it's not enough to understand human resources; you need a good business foundation.

6. What do you like most about your job? What do you like least about your job?

Every day is different. I coach senior level executives and small business owners, and I'm truly helping people better themselves and build their businesses. I also fill the role of HR manager for some clients, handling daily responsibilities like helping to fill job vacancies.

It's hard to make difficult decisions. Sometimes, what's in the best interest of the business is not in the best interest of the employee and you have to find a way to reconcile that.

7. Can you suggest a valuable "try this" for students considering a career in your profession?

Get an internship, and become involved with the professional organization, SHRM, the Society for Human Resource Management (www.shrm.org.) Many colleges have student chapters which give you the opportunity to get involved early in your career.

SELECTED SCHOOLS

Many colleges and universities, especially those with business schools, offer programs human resources development. The student can also gain initial training at a technical or community college. For advanced positions in large firms a master's degree (MBA) is often required. Below are listed some of the more prominent graduate institutions in this field.

Michigan State University
Eli Broad College of Business
632 Bogue Street
East Lansing, MI 48824
517.355.8377
broad.msu.edu

Northwestern University
Kellogg School of Management
2169 Campus Drive
Evanston, IL 60208
847.467.7000
www.kellogg.northwestern.edu

Purdue University
Krannert School of Management
403 W. State Street
West Lafayette, IN 47907
765.496.4343
www.krannert.purdue.edu

Stanford University
Stanford Graduate School of Business
655 Knight Way
Stanford, CA 94305
650.723.2146
www.gsb.stanford.edu

University of California, Berkeley
Haas School of Business
S450 Student Services Building #1900
Berkeley, CA 94720
510.642.1421
haas.berkeley.edu

University of Chicago
Booth School of Business
5807 S. Woodlawn Avenue
Chicago, IL 60637
773.702.7743
www.chicagobooth.edu

University of Michigan, Ann Arbor
Ross School of Business
701 Tappan Avenue
Ann Arbor, MI 48109
734.763.5796
michiganross.umich.edu

University of Southern California
Marshall School of Business
3670 Trousdale Parkway
Los Angeles, CA 90089
213.740.8674
www.marshall.usc.edu

University of Wisconsin, Madison
Wisconsin School of Business
Grainger Hall
975 University Avenue
Madison, WI 53706
608.262.1550
bus.wisc.edu

Vanderbilt University
Owen Graduate School of
Management
401 21st Avenue South
Nashville, TN 37203
615.322.2534
www.owen.vanderbilt.edu

MORE INFORMATION

**American Management
Association**
1601 Broadway
New York, NY 10019
212.568.8100
www.amanet.org

**American Society for Training
and Development**
Fulfillment Department
1640 King Street, Box 1443
Alexandria, VA 22313-2043
800.628.2783
www.astd.org

American Staffing Association
277 South Washington St., Suite 200
Alexandria, VA 22314
703.253.2020
www.staffingtoday.net

**Human Resources Certification
Institute**
1800 Duke Street
Alexandria, VA 22314
www.hrci.org

**International Association of
Workforce Professionals**
1801 Louisville Road
Frankfort, KY 40601
888.898.9960
www.iawponline.org

**International Foundation of
Employee Benefit Plans**
P.O. Box 69
Brookfield, WI 53008-0069
888.334.3327
www.ifebp.org

**International Public
Management Association for
Human Resources**
1617 Duke Street
Alexandria, VA 22314
703.549.7100
www.ipma-hr.org

**National Association of
Personnel Service**
131 Prominence Lane, Suite 130
Dawsonville, GA 30534
706.531.0060
www.naps360.org

**National Employment
Counseling Association**
6836 Bee Cave Road, Suite 260
Austin, TX 78746
www.employmentcounseling.org

**Society for Human Resource
Management**
1800 Duke Street
Alexandria, VA 22314
800.283.7476
www.shrm.org

World at Work
14040 N. Northsight Boulevard
Scottsdale, AZ 85260
877.951.9191
www.worldatwork.org

Simone Isadora Flynn/Editor

Librarian

OVERVIEW

Sphere of Work

A librarian is an information specialist who helps patrons locate various kinds of information quickly and effectively within a library setting. He or she is responsible for the selection, organization, and circulation of library materials, including print media, books, magazines and periodicals, and digital and electronic media. A librarian also manages non-print materials, including films, tapes, CDs, maps, and microfiche. He or she generally performs administrative, technical, and customer service tasks.

Work Environment

A librarian assists patrons in finding and reaching books and information sources. A librarian usually works in a public or academic library, as well as in a school library media center or special library. In all cases, a librarian works in a pleasant, comfortable environment, either independently or under the supervision of a library director. A librarian generally works a standard thirty-five to forty-hour workweek and may be required to work during the evenings or on weekends.

Profile

Working Conditions: Work Indoors
Physical Strength: Light Work
Education Needs: Bachelor's Degree, Master's Degree, Doctoral Degree
Licensure/Certification: Required
Opportunities For Experience: Internship, Volunteer Work, Part Time Work
Holland Interest Score*: SAI

* See Appendix A

Occupation Interest

People looking to become librarians should find satisfaction in learning about the ways in which ideas and information are communicated within modern society. They should be passionate about working with people and helping them locate and obtain various kinds of information effectively and accurately. Librarians often work alone or with a small staff and must be comfortable managing and overseeing all aspects of a public or private library. Aspiring librarians should be extremely organized, with a passion for cataloging and arranging information systematically.

A Day in the Life—Duties and Responsibilities

Librarians primarily manage the day-to-day operations of the libraries in which they work. Most librarians select and procure print, audiovisual, and electronic information sources for the various sections of the library. They organize, classify, and maintain library materials according to physical or electronic catalogs and databases. They assist library patrons and respond to any reference questions patrons may have. In smaller libraries, librarians are responsible for checking out and receiving materials.

Librarians often act as teachers, transferring library skills to customers or groups of customers. They sometimes hold regular tutoring sessions, which orient new patrons to the library. Some librarians schedule a daily or weekly storytelling or literacy meeting to read aloud to groups of small children visiting the library. In larger libraries, librarians specialize in a specific subject area and must coordinate with other librarians and library staff to make sure each section or department runs smoothly. Librarians also take on various administrative tasks, such as preparing budgets and other reports and maintaining employee and circulation records. In many cases, librarians hire, train, and supervise other library personnel.

In recent years, technology has begun to decrease the public's reliance on print and hardcopy materials. As a result, librarians are now responsible for remote and electronic databases, Internet research and cataloging, and web content management. They also instruct patrons on the use of various electronic library systems.

Duties and Responsibilities

- Maintaining the library's collection of print and non-print materials
- Selecting, ordering, cataloging and classifying materials
- Assisting patrons in obtaining library services and materials
- Utilizing the Internet and electronic databases

OCCUPATION SPECIALTIES

Technical Services Librarians

Technical Services Librarians obtain, prepare, and organize electronic and print library materials. They arrange resources to make it easier for patrons to find information.

Reference Librarians

Reference Librarians assist groups and individuals in locating and obtaining library materials.

Children's Librarians

Children's Librarians manage library programs for children and select books and other materials of interest to children for the library to acquire. They plan and conduct programs for children to encourage reading, viewing, listening and using of library materials and facilities.

Acquisitions Librarians

Acquisitions Librarians select and order books, periodicals, articles and audiovisual materials on particular subjects.

Special Collections Librarians

Special Collections Librarians collect and organize materials on select subjects used for research.

Bibliographers

Bibliographers work in research libraries and compile lists of books, periodicals, articles and audiovisual materials on particular subjects.

Classifiers & Catalogers

Classifiers and Catalogers organize materials by subject and catalogue and describe books and other library materials.

WORK ENVIRONMENT

Physical Environment

Most librarians work in clean, quiet, and well-ventilated library spaces. They maintain a library's level of calm and serenity by monitoring patrons' behavior to ensure their compliance with library rules and regulations.

Relevant Skills and Abilities

Communication Skills
- Expressing thoughts and ideas
- Speaking effectively
- Writing concisely

Interpersonal/Social Skills
- Cooperating with others
- Working as a member of a team

Organization & Management Skills
- Coordinating tasks
- Making decisions
- Managing people/groups
- Paying attention to and handling details
- Performing duties which change frequently

Research & Planning Skills
- Developing evaluation strategies

Human Environment

Librarians regularly interact with library patrons, including young children, adolescents, college students, teachers, and members of community organizations. They report to a library supervisor or director and often manage library assistants, technicians, administrative staff members, and janitorial personnel.

Technological Environment

Librarians use a wide variety of tools and equipment to help them organize information. They regularly work with paper and electronic card catalogs, microforms, the Internet and e-mail, and computer programs. They also use projection equipment, audiovisual devices, and fax machines.

EDUCATION, TRAINING, AND ADVANCEMENT

High School/Secondary

High school students who wish to become librarians should focus on college preparatory courses that deal with business, communications, language and literature, technology, and public speaking. Students may also benefit from studying at least one foreign language. Interested students should spend time in their high school and local libraries, familiarizing themselves with current information systems and cataloging procedures as well as the structure of a library.

Suggested High School Subjects

- Arts
- Audio-Visual
- Business
- Business Data Processing
- College Preparatory
- Composition
- Crafts
- English
- Foreign Languages
- Government
- History
- Humanities
- Keyboarding
- Literature
- Mathematics
- Photography
- Political Science
- Science
- Social Studies
- Speech

Famous First

The first children's section in a library is thought to be that of the Minneapolis Public Library, which in 1889 separated out children's books from the rest of the holdings and, shortly thereafter, set aside a room for children (and parents or guardians).

College/Postsecondary

After high school, prospective librarians must obtain a bachelor's degree, preferably in library science. Employers generally give preference to students who graduate from American Library Association (ALA)-accredited schools. At the college level, students should prepare for a career in library science by studying librarianship, children's and adult literature, archival methods, humanities, science and technology, and subject reference and bibliography, among other subjects.

In order for a librarian to work in a public, academic, or special library, he or she must obtain a master's degree in library science (MLS) after completing an undergraduate degree. Graduate programs in library science usually cover the foundations of information science, censorship, user services, and automated circulation systems, in addition to other supplemental and elective courses. Though not required, some librarians choose to obtain a doctorate in library and information science.

Related College Majors
- Library Assistant Training
- Pre-Law Studies

Adult Job Seekers

Many aspiring librarians begin by volunteering or working part-time in local libraries. Those enrolled in an undergraduate or graduate program may also be able to participate in a work-study program or internship with a participating library. Prospective librarians can apply for employment directly with a library, through library associations, or through school placement services.

Experienced librarians may advance to supervisory or teaching positions. These positions may require more budgetary, administrative, and managerial skills and duties. Advancement is often dependent on seniority, education, and library size.

Professional Certification and Licensure

Librarians who work in public schools or local libraries are usually required to be certified. Certification and licensure requirements vary by state. Many states also require librarians to acquire teacher certifications, and some states require librarians to pass a comprehensive examination. Interested individuals should research and fulfill the education and certification requirements of their home state.

Librarians who specialize in certain subject areas, such as law, medicine, or the sciences, may also need to earn an advanced degree in their desired subject. For example, twenty states require school librarians to have an advanced degree in library science or education.

Additional Requirements

Librarians are responsible for maintaining large databases of information and must therefore be extremely organized and detail-oriented. They must also be passionate about information systems and interested in the changing trends in and improvements to those systems. They should enjoy continually learning about new research methods and classification technology.

Fun Fact

The Top 10 Most Frequently Challenged Books list compiled each year by the American Library Association was topped in 2015 by the novel "Looking for Alaska" by John Green. Also on the list: three books about homosexual or transgender teens and the Bible.

Source: http://www.ala.org

EARNINGS AND ADVANCEMENT

Earnings of librarians depend on the individual's qualifications and the type, size and geographic location of the library. Median annual earnings of librarians were $56,880 in 2015. The lowest ten percent earned less than $33,810, and the highest ten percent earned more than $88,530.

Librarians may receive paid vacations, holidays, and sick days; life and health insurance; and retirement benefits. These are usually paid by the employer.

Metropolitan Areas with the Highest Employment Level in this Occupation

Metropolitan area	Employment	Employment per thousand jobs	Annual mean wage
New York-Jersey City-White Plains, NY-NJ	6,550	1.01	$70,440
Chicago-Naperville-Arlington Heights, IL	3,310	0.93	$60,740
Washington-Arlington-Alexandria, DC-VA-MD-WV	3,310	1.37	$78,030
Boston-Cambridge-Newton, MA	2,740	1.56	$73,970
Los Angeles-Long Beach-Glendale, CA	2,680	0.65	$75,050
Nassau County-Suffolk County, NY	2,420	1.89	$78,010
Houston-The Woodlands-Sugar Land, TX	2,190	0.75	$60,580
Dallas-Plano-Irving, TX	2,120	0.91	$59,360
Atlanta-Sandy Springs-Roswell, GA	1,970	0.79	$59,050
Newark, NJ-PA	1,680	1.46	$67,190

Source: Bureau of Labor Statistics

EMPLOYMENT AND OUTLOOK

There were approximately 143,000 librarians employed nationally in 2014. About one-fourth worked part-time. Employment is expected to grow slower than the average for all occupations through the year 2024, which means employment is projected to increase 1 percent to 3 percent. Offsetting the need for librarians are government budget cuts and the increasing use of computerized information storage and retrieval systems in libraries that allow users to bypass librarians and conduct research on their own.

Employment Trend, Projected 2014–24

Total, all occupations: 7%

Librarians, curators, and archivists: 4%

Librarians: 2%

Note: "All Occupations" includes all occupations in the U.S. Economy. Source: U.S. Bureau of Labor Statistics, Employment Projections Program

Related Occupations
- Archivist and Curator
- Computer & Information Systems Manager
- Library Technician
- Media Specialist
- Research Assistant

Conversation With . . .
AUDREY CHURCH

President, American Association of School Librarians
Chicago, Illinois
Library sciences, 36 years

1. What was your individual career path in terms of education/training, entry-level job, or other significant opportunity?

I was a public school librarian for 20 years—three years at the primary school level and 17 years at the high school level. I completed my student teaching in both high school English and library science and loved both, but my first job offer was for the primary school librarian position, and the rest is history. I absolutely loved my time working as a school librarian. In fact, the only job better than being a school librarian is teaching people to be school librarians—which is what I do now as a professor of school librarianship at Longwood University in Farmville, Virginia.

School librarianship crosses two fields of study, education and library science. Most states require that school librarians first earn a teaching license. My initial teaching license is in Secondary English, but people come to the school librarianship career with teaching licenses in varied fields, from elementary education to social studies to physical education. In order to become a certified school librarian, I completed a master's degree in education with a concentration in school librarianship. People who have a master's degree in library science, and who perhaps have a background as a public librarian or an academic librarian but do not hold a teaching license must complete required education coursework.

I also serve as president of the American Association of School Librarians.

2. What are the most important skills and/or qualities for someone in your profession?

The most important qualities for a school librarian are a desire to work with children, the ability to work well with others, and the willingness to be a lifelong learner. Strong communication and leadership skills are also necessary, as are good organizational skills and proficiency with technology.

3. What do you wish you had known going into this profession?

I wish I had known the variety of jobs and roles that school librarians play on a daily basis: teacher, instructional partner, information specialist, instructional leader, technology integrator, professional development provider, program administrator. No two days are alike, and it is never boring. It would be difficult to describe a "normal" day in a 21st century school library.

4. Are there many job opportunities in your profession? In what specific areas?

In some areas of the United States, due to budget crises, school librarian positions have been cut. In other areas, however, there is a shortage of qualified persons to fill open positions. In some areas where jobs were previously cut (for example, in California and in Washington, DC), we now see the restoration of positions as budget situations improve.

5. How do you see your profession changing in the next five years? What role will technology play in those changes, and what skills will be required?

While school librarians will continue to work with print resources, more and more resources will be available in digital format. The teaching role of the librarian will become even more critical as school librarians continue to teach students digital literacy skills. Technology plays a key role as librarians help students and staff become effective users of ideas and information. Critical thinking and problem solving skills will be required, as will flexibility and adaptability.

6. What do you enjoy most about your job? What do you enjoy least about your job?

The facets of my job that I enjoy the most are working with people, helping students and staff gain the skills that they need to be independent, information-literate lifelong learners. I enjoy helping students become critical thinkers, enthusiastic readers, skillful researchers, and ethical users of information. I love the fact my job continues to evolve as technology and education change. I enjoy the opportunity to work with all students in the school, all teachers, administrators, parents, and community members.

The facet of my job that I enjoy the least is that there are never enough hours in the day to complete all the tasks that need to be done.

7. Can you suggest a valuable "try this" for students considering a career in your profession?

I would encourage students considering a career as a school librarian to spend time observing an elementary school library, a middle school library, and a high school library. Many people have very traditional views of what a school librarian does, believing that the library is still a place of books and quiet. While we certainly still have books, the library is a hub of information, inquiry, and instruction. It is an active and interactive place of learning.

MORE INFORMATION

American Association of Law Libraries
105 W. Adams Street, Suite 3300
Chicago, IL 60603-6225
312.939.4764
www.aallnet.org

American Association of School Librarians
50 E. Huron Street
Chicago, IL 60611
800.545.2433
www.aasl.org

American Library Association
50 E. Huron Street
Chicago, IL 60611
800.545.2433
www.ala.org

American Society for Information Society & Technology
1320 Fenwick Lane, Suite 510
Silver Spring, MD 20910
301.495.0900
www.asis.org

Library of Congress
101 Independence Avenue SE
Washington, DC 20540
202.707.5000
www.loc.gov

Medical Library Association
65 E. Wacker Place, Suite 1900
Chicago, IL 60601-7298
312.419.9094
www.mlanet.org

Special Libraries Association
331 South Patrick Street
Alexandria, VA 22314-3501
703.647.4900
www.sla.org

Briana Nadeau/Editor

Library Technician

Snapshot

Career Cluster(s): Education & Training; Media & Communications

Interests: Reading, customer service, communicating with others, organizing information

Earnings (Yearly Average): $32,310

Employment & Outlook: Average Growth Expected

OVERVIEW

Sphere of Work

Library technicians are responsible for the daily maintenance of a library. Their responsibilities include assisting librarians in purchasing materials for the library, reshelving books, creating displays, and assisting patrons. Technicians are also responsible for library organization, both physically and in the computer database, as well as issuing library cards to new patrons. Sometimes library technicians plan community outreach programs or fundraising events, such as book sales.

The range of responsibilities assigned to a library technician depends on the type of library

in which the technician works. Technicians in smaller libraries fulfill a wide variety of duties, while those in larger libraries tend to specialize in one area of work.

Work Environment

In addition to public libraries, library technicians may work in school libraries (elementary, secondary, or university), specialty libraries (legal or medical), or even bookmobiles with service to nursing homes and schools. With the exception of the latter, most library technicians work in a quiet, indoor environment.

Profile

Working Conditions: Work Indoors
Physical Strength: Light Work
Education Needs: On-The-Job Training, High School Diploma with Technical Education, Junior/Technical/Community College
Licensure/Certification: Usually Not Required
Opportunities For Experience: Part Time Work
Holland Interest Score*: CSE

* See Appendix A

Occupation Interest

An ideal library technician is extremely organized and physically fit enough to spend a lot of time shelving books. Technicians must also have good communication skills for working with patrons. A love of reading enhances a library technician's ability to recommend books to patrons and select new books to purchase for the library's collection.

Though most library technicians work for state and local governments and thereby serve all members of the local community, school library technicians in particular must be adept at meeting the needs of young students. For example, a familiarity with research practices or, for younger students, an understanding of childhood development and learning would be helpful on the job. Library technicians today are also well versed in computer technology.

A Day in the Life—Duties and Responsibilities

Library technicians in a small library will spend a large part of their day on the computer maintaining the library database, helping patrons find books and information, shelving books, organizing library resources, and, perhaps, planning outreach programs. The Albert Wisner Public Library in Warwick, NY, which the Library Journal voted the best small library in America in 2016, plays a significant role in its community and offers a number of valuable programs for residents.

At larger libraries, library technicians are able to focus on a much smaller range of responsibilities. They might work in one particular area of the library, such as the archives, where they would be responsible for assisting librarians in organizing materials and answering questions about the library's archival resources. Larger libraries also have the resources to provide a variety of specialized services; for example, technicians might assist patrons with visual impairment to find audiobooks or books written in Braille. The New York Public Library, which is one of the largest libraries in the country, provides a range of services for immigrants, the homeless, and the incarcerated. Technicians work with volunteers to organize and implement New York's vast constellation of outreach programs.

Some library technicians work in specialty libraries for corporations, government agencies, law firms, or medical centers and hospitals. Library technicians at a law firm, for example, are expected to exhibit some level of expertise in that field.

Library technicians are often responsible for their library's bookmobile programs. Bookmobiles travel to bring reading materials to patrons with mobility issues, such as the elderly, the ill, the incarcerated, and others who cannot travel to the library themselves.

Duties and Responsibilities

- Helping patrons to locate and use resource catalogs, indexes, audiovisual equipment and materials
- Issuing identification cards to borrowers
- Receiving, inspecting, repairing, sorting, shelving and checking out books and other materials
- Recording identifying user data and due dates
- Compiling lists of overdue books and issuing overdue notices
- Keeping current files of newspaper clippings and pictures
- Arranging displays and exhibits
- Mailing materials to patrons
- Answering routine inquiries

WORK ENVIRONMENT

Physical Environment

Library technicians, who are often supervised by librarians, work at desks or in offices within a library. Their time is divided between working at a computer and the often physically demanding work of shelving and reshelving books.

Relevant Skills and Abilities

Communication Skills
- Editing written information
- Speaking effectively
- Writing concisely

Interpersonal/Social Skills
- Cooperating with others
- Working as a member of a team

Organization & Management Skills
- Making decisions
- Paying attention to and handling details
- Performing duties which change frequently

Research & Planning Skills
- Developing evaluation strategies

Human Environment

Library technicians interact with patrons and students. If library technicians are working with young children in a school library, they will be more active participants in their environment and might even devise and lead fun activities and programs. Library technicians at a university library, on the other hand, would likely spend their time assisting college-aged students in conducting research. Library technicians also work with other libraries and library technicians to oversee interlibrary loans.

Technological Environment

It is becoming increasingly important for library technicians to be trained in computer technologies. They are responsible for managing vast databases of information and, in some cases, helping patrons conduct research and perform other tasks on the computer.

EDUCATION, TRAINING, AND ADVANCEMENT

High School/Secondary

Some small libraries will hire library technicians with only a high school diploma, but many require some form of higher education. Still, aspiring library technicians can study to improve their computer skills in high school, which will make it easier for them to learn on the job.

Suggested High School Subjects
- Audio-Visual
- Business & Computer Technology
- English
- Foreign Languages
- Keyboarding
- Literature
- Psychology
- Science
- Sociology

Famous First

The first computerized library network was OCLC, the Ohio College Library Center, established at Ohio State University, Columbus, OH, in 1971. It served a consortium of 54 academic libraries and was headed by Frederick G. Kilgour. OCLC was later expanded both nationally and internationally, its name being changed to the Online College Library Center. Today, as a global network called WorldCat, it serves 72,000 institutions in 170 countries.

College/Postsecondary

Some library technicians hold an associate's degree or a certificate. Students in library technician programs take courses in media technology, information research methods, cataloging, and management. Many community colleges offer both certificate programs and associate's degrees in library sciences.

Related College Majors
- Administrative Assistant/Secretarial Science, General
- General Office/Clerical & Typing Services
- Library Assistant Training

Adult Job Seekers

A number of retirees have found jobs as library technicians, particularly in smaller libraries. Libraries seek adults with flexible schedules and some level of postsecondary education. Much of the training required to complete the tasks associated with the job, particularly maintaining library databases, can be learned on the job. It is comparatively much easier for adult job seekers to find work as a library technician than as a librarian, a career that requires more education and training.

Professional Certification and Licensure

There is no professional licensure required to become a library technician. After acquiring an associate's degree or a certificate, if they so desire, library technicians can pursue further education and training through groups like the American Library Association (ALA).

 ## Additional Requirements

Library technicians spend their days with books and people and must, in some respect, have an affinity for both. They must be polite and willing to offer help to patrons. With regard to books, they might be asked to make recommendations; thus, a love of reading would certainly be an advantage. Additionally, library technicians can expand their knowledge in the field by becoming a member of the ALA or their state library association.

In a library, career ladders are most often based on further education, not experience. A library technician with fifteen years of experience will not qualify for a job as a librarian until he or she obtains a master's degree in library sciences, or MLS. With experience, however, library technicians can take on more responsibilities and become more independent in their work.

Fun Fact

Libraries and grammar go together: Aristophanes, who invented the comma and the colon, was a librarian in ancient Alexandria, Greec.
Source: https://interestingliterature.com

EARNINGS AND ADVANCEMENT

Earnings of library technicians depend on the size and geographic location of the community, the type and size of the library and the employee's skill and education. Median annual earnings of library technicians were $32,310 in 2015. The lowest ten percent earned less than $19,420, and the highest ten percent earned more than $51,620.

Library technicians may receive paid vacations, holidays, and sick days; life and health insurance; and retirement benefits. These are usually paid by the employer. Additional benefits offered by private businesses often include educational assistance programs.

Metropolitan Areas with the Highest
Employment Level in this Occupation

Metropolitan area	Employment	Employment per thousand jobs	Anuual mean wage
New York-Jersey City-White Plains, NY-NJ	4,620	0.71	$36,100
Chicago-Naperville-Arlington Heights, IL	4,230	1.18	$35,560
Washington-Arlington-Alexandria, DC-VA-MD-WV	1,850	0.76	$43,330
Los Angeles-Long Beach-Glendale, CA	1,830	0.45	$42,320
Boston-Cambridge-Newton, MA	1,700	0.96	$46,240
Nassau County-Suffolk County, NY	1,520	1.19	$32,760
Seattle-Bellevue-Everett, WA	1,320	0.86	$45,090
Atlanta-Sandy Springs-Roswell, GA	1,230	0.50	$28,570
St. Louis, MO-IL	1,210	0.91	$40,370
Portland-Vancouver-Hillsboro, OR-WA	1,000	0.92	$39,010

Source: Bureau of Labor Statistics

EMPLOYMENT AND OUTLOOK

Nationally, library technicians held about 102,000 jobs in 2014. Employment is expected to grow slower than the average for all occupations through the year 2024, which means employment is projected to increase 3 percent to 7 percent. The increasing use of library automation is expected to continue to create job growth among library technicians. Computerized information systems have simplified certain tasks, such as descriptive cataloguing, which can now be handled by library technicians instead of librarians.

Although efforts to contain costs may slow employment growth of library technicians in school, public, and college and university libraries, this may also result in the hiring of more library technicians than librarians. The best job prospects will be in special libraries because of the increase in their use by professionals and managerial workers.

Employment Trend, Projected 2014–24

Total, all occupations: 7%

Library technicians and assistants: 5%

Library technicians: 5%

Librarians, curators, and archivists: 4%

Note: "All Occupations" includes all occupations in the U.S. Economy. Source: U.S. Bureau of Labor Statistics, Employment Projections Program

Related Occupations
- File Clerk
- Health Information Technician
- Librarian
- Media Specialist
- Receptionist & Information Clerk

Conversation With . . .
AMANDA BELLIS

Library Technician, Pleasant Hill Public Library
Pleasant Hill, Iowa
Librarian, Des Moines Public Library, Des Moines, IA
Library technician, 5 years; Librarian, 2 years

1. What was your individual career path in terms of education/training, entry-level job, or other significant opportunity?

In college, I changed majors several times. I ultimately decided to major in English.

Then I started thinking about what I'd do with a bachelor's degree in English. It was kind of a joke when I first thought: I should be a librarian. Then I started thinking about it seriously and started learning about the profession. I talked to the staff at the library in Pleasant Hill, where I grew up, and asked about options.

The timing was perfect because they had a part-time Library Technician I position open. The librarian said it would give me a sense of the work. It did and I found I really liked it.

The library tech job is available to anyone with a high school diploma. It's more of an entry-level job. In it, I do a little bit of shelving, a little weeding of our materials and I handle donations. I also work at the front desk or at the public computers. I help people as they check out materials or if they have questions and need help.

Librarians have more responsibility. They're in charge of programs and events, handle more in-depth questions and searches for information, and do overall planning. You have to have a master's degree in library science to be a librarian. I went back to school and got that degree. I have a part-time librarian job in Des Moines and am hoping a full-time job will open. In the meantime, I'm also working my part-time library tech job.

2. What are the most important skills and/or qualities for someone in your profession?

Customer service skills and attention to detail. I work with the public all the time so I have to be able to interact with people and answer their questions and remain professional even if a customer is irate over something – a fine, for example. I'm a bit introverted so I had to develop an outgoing persona for work.

Attention to detail is essential in everything from making a library card to shelving to dealing with people. There are a lot of fine details that can mess things up if they are not correct.

3. What do you wish you had known going into this profession?

I wish I had learned more about the types of library jobs that are out there and the kind of experience and knowledge required for them. I also wish I'd compared that information against the offerings at different graduate schools because they can have different focuses. I made my grad school decision based on not having to pay out-of-state tuition but the program I attended focuses more on people who want to work in academic libraries. My interest is in public libraries and their youth services. If I'd known more, I could have tailored my education to my interests.

4. Are there many job opportunities in your profession? In what specific areas?

There are lots of jobs but, in Iowa, there aren't that many that are full-time or that pay a lot. There are a lot of small libraries and not a lot of big library systems in this state.

5. How do you see your profession changing in the next five years, what role will technology play in those changes, and what skills will be required?

It's funny how you keep hearing how some new technology will be the end of libraries, but it doesn't happen. Libraries have become a place that offers access to new technology, as well as assistance in using it, and I think that will only increase. Librarians are expected to be able to work with technology. I help people with computers as often as I help them find books.

But people are also still reading and watching movies and listening to music—all the things that people can get at the library. I don't see that changing.

6. What do you enjoy most about your job? What do you enjoy least about your job?

One of my favorite things is just being able to help people. If I can make someone happy with a book recommendation or by helping a person figure out an online job application or something else, I'm happy too. That's why I'm in this profession. My least favorite thing is when someone has a problem or is upset. That's never fun.

7. Can you suggest a valuable "try this" for students considering a career in your profession?

Volunteering at a library is certainly an option. Often, there's a clerk or aide position that's available to high school students, usually checking things in or shelving or helping people. It's a chance to see how the library works and if it's something they might like as a career. They can also talk to library staff. We're always happy to talk to people about the profession.

MORE INFORMATION

American Association of Law Libraries
105 W. Adams Street, Suite 3300
Chicago, IL 60603-6225
312.939.4764
www.aallnet.org

American Association of School Librarians
50 East Huron Street
Chicago, IL 60611
800.545.2433
www.aasl.org

American Library Association
50 E. Huron Street
Chicago, IL 60611
800.545.2433
www.ala.org

Association of Library Collections and Technical Services
50 E. Huron Street
Chicago, IL 60611
800.545.2433
www.ala.org/alcts

Library of Congress
101 Independence Avenue, SE
Washington, DC 20540
202.707.5000
www.loc.gov

Medical Library Association
65 East Wacker Place, Suite 1900
Chicago, IL 60601-7298
312.419.9094
www.mlanet.org

Office of Personnel Management
1900 E Street, NW
Washington, DC 20415-0001
202.606.1800
www.opm.gov

Special Libraries Association
331 S. Patrick Street
Alexandria, VA 22314-3501
703.647.4900
www.sla.org

Molly Hagan/Editor

Media Specialist

Snapshot

Career Cluster(s): Education & Training; Media & Communications

Interests: Library information and technology, library media, education, media acquisition, library services, library science

Earnings (Yearly Average): $57,770

Employment & Outlook: Slower Than Average Growth Expected

OVERVIEW

Sphere of Work

Media specialists are library professionals who manage collections of many different forms of media, including electronic and print periodicals, video and film recordings, audio recordings, and databases and software. They are often experienced in the use of information technology and other multimedia systems and equipment as well. Many of them work in education, helping teachers and administrators integrate the various types of media into school libraries and curricula; others work in public or specialized libraries, assisting patrons in locating the information they need.

Work Environment

Media specialists work in settings that are clean, quiet, organized, and well lit. Educational media specialists usually work in school or university libraries. The job may be stressful at times, especially when large groups are in the library, as media specialists must frequently manage multiple tasks at once. They typically work standard forty-hour work weeks, although they may work on weekends and during evenings. Media specialists may occasionally be required to bend down to check and adjust various systems, or lift and move heavy stacks of books or equipment.

Profile

Working Conditions: Work Indoors
Physical Strength: Light Work
Education Needs: Master's Degree
Licensure/Certification: Required
Opportunities For Experience:
  Volunteer Work
Holland Interest Score*: ESA

* See Appendix A

Occupation Interest

Media specialists may have a background in education or library science. Whether they work primarily with teachers or librarians, they are responsible for educating people on the use of all different types of media. They should be flexible and creative, with an aptitude for information technology, and find satisfaction in assisting others in their pursuit of knowledge.

A Day in the Life—Duties and Responsibilities

Media specialists tend to the informational needs of teachers, students, and members of the general public. They assist library patrons in locating different types of media. School media specialists develop integrated programs that enhance students' reading and research skills by selecting videos, audio recordings, books, and Internet-based materials to share with them. They also assist teachers in merging traditional reading assignments with non-print information, suggesting books, websites, videos, and other media of value, in order to ensure that the curricula being taught are up to date. School media specialists train teachers and students on how to locate, access, and download new online information, and frequently host workshops for fellow educators and librarians on the use of multimedia. A large number of them are also administrators, in which capacity they provide insight to fellow district leaders on the best ways to integrate multimedia-based educational approaches into school curricula.

Many media specialists are librarians who manage the day-to-day operations of the facility. In this capacity, they may oversee other employees, establish budgets for the library's media resources, educate patrons in the use of computers and other forms of information technology, or perform minor routine maintenance. Additionally, media specialists recommend policies that ensure that online resources and other non-print media are being used for their intended purposes and not being accessed for illegal activities.

Duties and Responsibilities

- Assisting users with locating information
- Classifying and organizing materials
- Maintaining records of the library's collections
- Ordering materials to be used or distributed
- Training teachers, students and/or library patrons in the use of various multimedia
- Designing media programs for a school system
- Advising department heads and teachers about new materials and equipmen

OCCUPATION SPECIALTIES

Audiovisual Librarians

Audiovisual Librarians coordinate the availability of audiovisual materials, such as films, videos, and recordings, in a library, and assist patrons in selecting materials. They evaluate materials, considering their technical, informational, and aesthetic qualities, and select materials for library collections.

Institutional Librarians

Institutional Librarians plan and direct library programs in settings such as government offices, medical facilities, corporations, and non-profit organizations.

Music Librarians

Music Librarians classify and file musical recordings, sheet music, original arrangements and scores for individual instruments.

WORK ENVIRONMENT

Physical Environment

Media specialists work in universities, schools, and other library settings, frequently localized to a media center within those facilities, although many oversee the entire library. These settings are spacious enough to house rows of books, periodicals, personal computer terminals, office equipment, private study rooms, and work tables. Libraries are generally very quiet, though there is usually a great deal of individual and/or group activity occurring at once.

Relevant Skills and Abilities

Interpersonal/Social Skills
- Cooperating with others
- Providing support to others

Organization & Management Skills
- Coordinating tasks
- Organizing information or materials

Research & Planning Skills
- Gathering information
- Identifying resources

Human Environment

Media specialists frequently work with librarians and library assistants, teachers, students, parents, computer technicians, school administrators and officials, and members of the general public.

Technological Environment

Media specialists rely largely on computer hardware and software, telecommunications equipment, and audiovisual systems. Among the technologies with which they work are personal and notebook computers, DVD players, multipurpose phone systems, and digital audio and video recorders. They also use different forms of software, including presentation and office suites, electronic cataloguing programs, online research databases such as LexisNexis, and website creation software.

EDUCATION, TRAINING, AND ADVANCEMENT

High School/Secondary

High school students should take classes that instill an understanding of various forms of non-print media, including computer science, graphic design, and audiovisual courses and activities. Additionally, they must build their reading, writing, and public speaking skills through courses in literature and communication. Students can also gain experience by volunteering in a library media center or working part-time for an audiovisual equipment manager or retailer.

Suggested High School Subjects
- Audio-Visual
- College Preparatory
- Composition

- Computer Science
- English
- Literature

Famous First

The first digital media device designed solely for the purpose of playing audiobooks was the Audible Player, from Audible Co., in 1997. Promoted as being smaller and lighter than a Walkman, the popular Sony cassette player of the time, the Audible Player retailed for $200 and held up to two hours of downloadable audio.

College/Postsecondary

Media specialists must have a bachelor's degree in a field such as literature, education, or library science. They are generally required to have a master's degree as well, in library science, educational media, or a similar discipline. Those individuals who pursue a PhD in these fields will have an advantage in a competitive job market.

Related College Majors
- Educational/Instructional Media Design
- Educational/Instructional Media Technology
- Library Science/Librarianship

Adult Job Seekers

Qualified library media specialists can apply directly to school districts, school boards, or general and specialist libraries that advertise openings. They may also gain an advantage by joining professional organizations, such as the Special Libraries Association, which provide networking opportunities and information about available positions.

Professional Certification and Licensure

All states require that librarians and library media specialists be certified, although the criteria for this certification vary from state to state. Some organizations offer media specialist certification programs, which frequently entail a combination of postgraduate education, classroom training, and on-the-job mentoring.

Additional Requirements

Media specialists must be highly knowledgeable of developments in the non-print media environment, including Internet resources, computer software, and social media. They should be patient and skilled educators, able to help different audiences understand concepts that may be confusing. They should also be effective managers and leaders, able to develop budgets and implement operational systems for others to follow.

EARNINGS AND ADVANCEMENT

Media specialists may advance to administrative or supervisory positions with experience. They may also choose to specialize in a particular area, such as law or medicine. Specialization in one area also leads to opportunities in government or private business libraries. In 2014, median annual earnings of media specialists were $57,770. The lowest ten percent earned less than $35,605, and the highest ten percent earned more than $88,521.

Media specialists may receive paid vacations, holidays, and sick days; life and health insurance; and retirement benefits. These are usually paid by the employer.

Metropolitan Areas with the Highest
Employment Level in this Occupation

Metropolitan area	Employment	Employment per thousand jobs	Annual mean wage
Los Angeles-Long Beach-Glendale, CA	7,260	1.77	$54,120
Minneapolis-St. Paul-Bloomington, MN-WI	710	0.38	$57,320
New York-Jersey City-White Plains, NY-NJ	580	0.09	$48,840
Atlanta-Sandy Springs-Roswell, GA	480	0.19	$59,410
Las Vegas-Henderson-Paradise, NV	480	0.52	$52,760
Portland-Vancouver-Hillsboro, OR-WA	450	0.41	$43,590
Fort Worth-Arlington, TX	440	0.45	$51,940
Phoenix-Mesa-Scottsdale, AZ	420	0.23	$36,380
Washington-Arlington-Alexandria, DC-VA-MD-WV	330	0.14	$70,220
Tampa-St. Petersburg-Clearwater, FL	330	0.27	$44,000

Source: Bureau of Labor Statistics

EMPLOYMENT AND OUTLOOK

Librarians, of whom media specialists are a part, held about 145,000 jobs nationally in 2014. Most were in school and academic libraries; others were in public and special libraries. Employment is expected to grow slower than the average for all occupations through the year 2024, which means employment is projected to increase 3 percent to 5 percent. The most opportunities will be available for those who specialize in a particular area. Job openings will also occur from the need to replace workers who retire.

Employment Trend, Projected 2014–24

Total, all occupations: 7%

Media specialists: 4%

Librarians: 2%

Note: "All Occupations" includes all occupations in the U.S. Economy. Source: U.S. Bureau of Labor Statistics, Employment Projections Program

Related Occupations
- Archivist and Curator
- Librarian
- Library Technician
- Research Assistant

MORE INFORMATION

American Association of Law Libraries
105 W. Adams Street, Suite 3300
Chicago, IL 60603-6225
312.939.4764
www.aallnet.org

American Association of School Librarians
50 East Huron Street
Chicago, IL 60611
800.545.2433
www.aasl.org

American Library Association
50 East Huron Street
Chicago, IL 60611
800.545.2433
www.ala.org

Association for Educational Communications and Technology (AECT)
PO Box 2447
Bloomington, IN 47402-2447
877.677.2328
www.aect.org

Council on Library/Media Technicians
202-231-3836
colt.ucr.edu

Library and Information Technology Association (LITA)
American Library Association
50 East Huron Street
Chicago, IL 60611-2795
800.545.2433 x4270
www.ala.org/ala/mgrps/divs/lita

Library of Congress
101 Independence Avenue, SE
Washington, DC 20540
202.707.5000
www.loc.gov

Medical Library Association
65 East Wacker Place, Suite 1900
Chicago, IL 60601-7298
312.419.9094
www.mlanet.org

Special Libraries Association
331 South Patrick Street
Alexandria, VA 22314-3501
703.647.4900
www.sla.org

Michael Auerbach/Editor

Placement Specialist

Snapshot

Career Cluster: Business Administration; Human Services
Interests: Human resources, career research, working with people, helping others
Earnings (Yearly Average): $56,630
Employment & Outlook: Average Growth Expected

OVERVIEW

Sphere of Work

Placement specialists, also referred to as staffing specialists or job placement professionals, provide job placement support services to individuals and staffing support services to employers. Placement specialists may recruit workers for employers, conduct initial job interviews, and refer clients for jobs. Placement specialists may work with recent college graduates, people interested in changing careers, unemployed adults, or adults living in situations that impact or limit employment options. Placement specialists

also support clients in their efforts to develop career goals and apply for job training and employment.

Work Environment

Placement specialists spend their workdays seeing clients in a wide variety of settings, including employment agencies, human resources offices, and college and university career counseling offices. Placement specialists may have a fixed office where they see clients, or they may travel to meet potential job candidates or attend job fairs. Given the diverse demands of employment specialist work, placement specialists may need to work days, evenings, and weekends to meet client needs.

Profile

Working Conditions: Work Inside
Physical Strength: Light Work
Education Needs: Bachelor's Degree
Licensure/Certification:
Recommended
Physical Abilities Not Required: No
Heavy Labor
Opportunities For Experience:
Internship, Military Service, Part-Time
Work
Holland Interest Score*: SEC

* See Appendix A

Occupation Interest

Individuals drawn to the employment specialist profession tend to be intelligent and have the ability to quickly assess situations and people, find resources, and solve problems. Those most successful in this profession display traits such as good time management, initiative, and tact. Placement specialists should enjoy matching people with jobs and have a background in human resources.

A Day in the Life—Duties and Responsibilities

The daily occupational duties and responsibilities of placement specialists will be determined by the individual's area of specialization and work environment. Specialties in employment counseling include recruiting, vocational assessment, staffing, and first-round interviewing.

An employment specialist's daily duties and responsibilities may include meeting with employers to discuss their staffing needs; developing a candidate pool of executive, professional, technical, managerial, and clerical workers; recruiting job candidates for specific employers; and conducting initial candidate interviews. They may also meet with job seekers to assess their vocational aptitude, work history, and job readiness, help them develop professional goals and objectives, and match them with available jobs. At temporary staffing agencies, placement specialists may continue mediating the relationship between employer and employee after a position is filled. placement specialists are responsible for completing required documentation, such as job referral forms, on a daily basis, and they must stay informed about current labor laws, trends, and regulations.

Duties and Responsibilities

- Reviewing completed applications and evaluating applicants' work history, education, training, skills, desired salary and qualifications
- Recording skills, knowledge, abilities, interests and test results
- Searching files of employer job orders to match requirements to qualifications
- Informing applicant of job duties, pay, benefits, conditions and opportunities
- Referring applicants to interview with prospective employers
- Testing or arranging for tests of skills and abilities
- Keeping informed of labor market developments, educational and occupational requirements, labor laws, government training programs and various regulations
- Maintaining case files on job seekers and completing counseling activity reports

OCCUPATION SPECIALTIES

Recruiters

Recruiters identify and interview individuals in order to recruit them for organizations. They advise individuals on matters concerning career opportunities, incentives, rights and benefits, and advantages of a particular career or organization.

Placement Specialists

Placement Specialists match employers with qualified jobseekers. They search for candidates who have the skills, education, and work experience needed for jobs, and they try to place those candidates with employers. They also may help set up interviews.

WORK ENVIRONMENT

Physical Environment

The immediate physical environment of placement specialists varies based on their caseload and area of specialization. They spend their workdays seeing clients in a wide variety of settings, including employment agencies, human resources offices, job training and placement programs, and college and university career counseling offices.

Human Environment

Placement specialists work with a wide variety of people and should be comfortable meeting with employers, potential job candidates, colleagues, staff, supervisors, college and university students, and unemployed people.

Relevant Skills and Abilities

Communication Skills
- Expressing thoughts and ideas
- Speaking effectively
- Writing concisely

Interpersonal/Social Skills
- Cooperating with others
- Working as a member of a team

Organization & Management Skills
- Making decisions
- Performing duties that change frequently

Research & Planning Skills
- Developing evaluation strategies
- Using logical reasoning

Technological Environment

Placement specialists use computers, cell phones, cars, and Internet communication tools to perform their job. For instance, placement specialists must be comfortable using computers to access student and client records, as well as for posting job listings and navigating online forums.

EDUCATION, TRAINING, AND ADVANCEMENT

High School/Secondary

High school students interested in pursuing a career as an employment specialist should prepare themselves by developing good study habits. High school courses in foreign languages, psychology, and writing will provide a strong foundation for work as an employment specialist. High school students interested in this career path will benefit from seeking internships or part-time work that exposes the students to managerial roles and diverse professions.

Suggested High School Subjects
- Applied Communication
- College Preparatory
- Composition
- Computer Science
- English
- Foreign Languages
- Psychology

Famous First

The first employment office established by a city was the office established in Seattle in 1894. Initially set up in a simple wooden shanty consisting of a single small room, the office soon moved to larger quarters in City Hall.

College/Postsecondary

Postsecondary students interested in becoming placement specialists should work toward a bachelor's degree in human resource management or a related field. Coursework in psychology, business administration, and foreign languages may also prove useful in their future work. Postsecondary students can gain work experience and potential advantage in their future job searches by securing internships or part-time employment in career placement or job training programs.

Related College Majors
• Human Resources Management

Adult Job Seekers

Adults seeking work as placement specialists should have a bachelor's degree and preferably some experience in business or personnel administration. Adult job seekers should educate themselves about the educational and professional licensure requirements of their home states and the organizations where they seek employment. Professional employment associations, such as the American Staffing Association and the National Association of Professional Employer Organizations, generally offer job-finding workshops and maintain lists and forums posting available jobs.

Professional Certification and Licensure

Certification for placement specialists is voluntary but may be required as a condition of employment or promotion at professional employment agencies. The American Staffing Association and the National Association of Personnel Services offer the leading voluntary certification options for placement specialists. The American Staffing Association's Certified Staffing Professional designation and the Technical Services Certified designation are each earned by completing training requirements and passing a national examination. The Certified Staffing Professional credential demonstrates competency in general labor and employment law, while the Technical Services Certified credential demonstrates competency in labor and employment laws applicable to technical, IT, and scientific staffing. The National Association of Personnel Services' Certified Personnel Consultant designation, Certified Temporary-Staffing Specialists designation, Certified Employee Retention Specialist designation, and Physician Recruiting Consultant designation are also earned through completing training requirements and passing national examinations. State licensing is not generally required for placement specialists.

Additional Requirements

Successful placement specialists engage in ongoing professional development to maintain their certifications. A high degree of personal integrity and professionalism are required of placement specialists because they have access to the personal information of employment candidates and influence over the hiring or job placement process. Membership in professional human resources associations is encouraged among all placement specialists as a means of building professional community and networking.

EARNINGS AND ADVANCEMENT

Earnings depend on the type, size and geographic location of the employer and the employee's education and experience. Placement specialists in personnel consulting firms are usually paid on a commission basis, while those in temporary help service companies receive a salary. Commissions are usually based on the type, as well as on the number, of placements. Those who place more highly skilled or hard-to-find employees usually earn more

Median annual earnings of Placement specialists were $56,630 in 2013. The lowest ten percent earned less than $33,240, and the highest ten percent earned more than $96,470.

Placement specialists may receive paid vacations, holidays, and sick days; life and health insurance; and retirement benefits. These are usually paid by the employer.

Metropolitan Areas with the Highest
Employment Level in this Occupation

Metropolitan area	Employment[1]	Employment per thousand jobs	Hourly mean wage
New York-White Plains-Wayne, NY-NJ	9,830	1.88	$32.62
Washington-Arlington-Alexandria, DC-VA-MD-WV	7,040	2.97	$36.22
Atlanta-Sandy Springs-Marietta, GA	5,580	2.42	$30.34
Phoenix-Mesa-Glendale, AZ	5,510	3.10	$27.03
Los Angeles-Long Beach-Glendale, CA	5,460	1.37	$29.57
Dallas-Plano-Irving, TX	5,000	2.33	$30.64
Houston-Sugar Land-Baytown, TX	4,300	1.56	$30.71
Philadelphia, PA	4,190	2.28	$31.45
Chicago-Joliet-Naperville, IL	4,020	1.09	$29.48
Minneapolis-St. Paul-Bloomington, MN-WI	3,730	2.08	$28.93

[1]Does not include self-employed. Source: Bureau of Labor Statistics

EMPLOYMENT AND OUTLOOK

Placement specialists held about 200,000 jobs nationally in 2012. Most placement specialists worked in the private sector in the areas of administrative and support services; professional, scientific and technical services; manufacturing; health care and social assistance; and finance and insurance firms. Employment is expected to grow as fast as the average for all occupations through the year 2022, which means employment is projected to increase 9 percent to 15 percent. Increasing efforts throughout all industries to recruit and retain quality employees should create many jobs for placement specialists.

Employment Trend, Projected 2010–20

Business Operations Specialists: 15%

Placement Specialists: 13%

Total, All Occupations: 11%

Note: "All Occupations" includes all occupations in the U.S. Economy. Source: U.S. Bureau of Labor Statistics, Employment Projections Program

Related Occupations
- Human Resources Specialist/Manager
- Rehabilitation Counselor
- School Counselor
- Social Worker
- Vocational Rehabilitation Counselor

Related Military Occupations
- Personnel Manager
- Personnel Specialist
- Recruiting Specialist

Conversation With . . .
STACY KYLE

Program Specialist
AHEDD, Camp Hill, Pennsylvania
Employment Specialist field, 21 years

1. What was your individual career path in terms of education/training, entry-level job, or other significant opportunity?

I majored in psychology with a concentration in deafness, and after I graduated, worked at a group home for delinquent girls. After two years, I moved to a job as a vocational counselor at a private rehab facility. I was an agent of the insurance company and helped people who had been on Workers' Compensation for more than a year find suitable jobs. I worked there for about two years, but didn't like that type of vocational counseling. Many clients had lawyers, which required me to send any communication to the lawyer, not the individual. This seriously hampered success because it caused delays and many opportunities were time-sensitive. In my current job with Association for Habilitation and Employment of Developmentally Disabled (AHEDD), I hire and train staff, manage projects, write grants, do data management and reporting, and do public speaking.

2. What are the most important skills and/or qualities for someone in your profession?

It's not just about finding jobs. The best employment specialists learn to ask the right questions. They are adept at talking to customers and understanding their concerns. They gain knowledge about external factors like Social Security benefits that can impact an individual's willingness to work or to work full time. You must have attention to detail and a willingness to learn. You have to understand how services are funded, so that you can work effectively with limited resources. You must constantly learn about different industries and employer expectations. You have to be able to effectively manage your own schedule, and be flexible enough to change your focus when unexpected needs arise.

The skills of those who perform well in this role are often under-appreciated. Sometimes staff are really good on the people end of things, but may not be good at assertively working the marketing/outreach side of things to find or create job opportunities.

3. What do you wish you had known going into this profession?

I knew the money was not big in this industry. I knew the supports available for clients don't always meet their needs, that program guidelines aren't always easy to understand, and that you can't always get the best results.

I think some employment specialists are surprised by the level of performance and outcomes expected. Here at AHEDD, of course we care about the satisfaction of the individuals with disabilities who are our clients, but we also have to meet the performance expectations of taxpayers, businesses, sponsors, etc. It's not good enough to just get people jobs. We want them to be working toward the maximum independence possible.

4. Are there many job opportunities in your profession? In what specific areas?

In current workforce development budgets, employment services for people with disabilities get a very small piece of the pie.

5. How do you see your profession changing in the next five years? What role will technology play in those changes, and what skills will be required?

Technology is huge. We have moved to a cloud environment, allowing staff easier access to data and other resources necessary to do their jobs in the community. We're working on an improved data system with participant-specific information outcomes. More and more, data will drive who gets money.

AHEDD is piloting an app that could help better quantify success in training individuals, by tracking their job performance and appropriate behaviors. This will help us make better decisions about whether to continue supporting someone in a specific position, and to justify requests for additional hours. The creator of this app is interested in trying out the use of remote job coaching, via webcam and other technology. That could reduce overall costs for employment services and, when appropriate, allow job coaches or employment specialists to be less obtrusive when an individual is trying to be integrated and accepted into his or her work environment.

6. What do you enjoy most about your job? What do you enjoy least about your job?

Hearing success stories is really my favorite part. When you learn that someone has been able to move out on their own, buy a car, or even take a friend out for lunch, it really drives home the purpose of AHEDD. Work gives people choices and power. The actual task I love most is doing presentations and selling employers on the value of working with us.

Documentation, while necessary, is my least favorite.

7. **Can you suggest a valuable "try this" for students considering a career in your profession?**

Customer service jobs can be a great opportunity, especially in an environment that requires you to deal with a variety of people who don't always understand things or are sometimes angry.

Selling or marketing jobs would also be helpful, because you have to learn about your potential customers and identify concerns or questions they might have with your product or program.

SELECTED SCHOOLS

Many colleges and universities have bachelor's degree programs in human resources management, counseling, and related subjects. The student may also gain an initial grounding at a technical or community college. Consult with your school guidance counselor or research area post-secondary programs to find the right fit for you.

MORE INFORMATION

American Staffing Association
277 South Washington St., Suite 200
Alexandria, VA 22314
703.253.2020
www.staffingtoday.net

Association of Executive Search Consultants
12 East 41st Street, 17th Floor
New York, NY 10017
212.398.9556
www.aesc.org

Human Resources Certification Institute
1800 Duke Street
Alexandria, VA 22314
866.898.4724
www.hrci.org

International Association of Workforce Professionals
1801 Louisville Road
Frankfort, KY 40601
888.898.9960
www.iawponline.org

National Association of Personnel Service
131 Prominence Lane, Suite 130
Dawsonville, GA 30534
706.531.0060
www.recruitinglife.com

Simone Isadora Flynn/Editor

Preschool Aide

Snapshot

Career Cluster(s): Education & Training; Human Services
Interests: Education, early childhood development, teaching, psychology, language development, student care
Earnings (Yearly Average): $22,310
Employment & Outlook: Average Growth Expected

OVERVIEW

Sphere of Work

Preschool aides, sometimes called paraeducators, support early childhood professionals in their teaching and child-care efforts. Preschool aides are employed by public and private preschools, which focus on the educational needs of three to five year old children.

Preschool aides take direction from the lead or head classroom teachers and participate in the teaching of the preschool curriculum as specified by their job description or the preference of their lead teacher.

Preschool aides help with the daily care of young students as well as the students' socio-emotional development, pre-literacy skills, fine and gross motor skills, practical life skills, and language acquisition.

Work Environment

Preschool aides spend their workdays in early childhood classrooms arranged primarily to meet the social and educational needs of young children. In the preschool environment, furniture tends to be low to the ground, and preschool teachers must be sufficiently physically fit to carry children when needed, squat, bend, and sit on the floor. Preschool classroom resources such as art supplies, music lessons, fieldtrips, and support staff, differ depending on the school's financial resources and the educational philosophy directing the curriculum. Preschools may be private or public and may be part of an elementary school or may be an independent entity with no higher grades. Preschools are also found in businesses, high schools, colleges, social service agencies, and religious organizations.

Profile

Working Conditions: Work Indoors, Work Outdoors
Physical Strength: Light Work
Education Needs: On-The-Job Training, High School Diploma or GED, Apprenticeship
Licensure/Certification: Usually Not Required
Opportunities For Experience: Internship, Apprenticeship, Volunteer Work, Part Time Work
Holland Interest Score*: ESR

* See Appendix A

Occupation Interest

The occupation of preschool aide draws individuals who are responsible, responsive, patient, observant, playful, and caring. Preschool aides, who nurture children in the years between infancy and elementary school-age, should enjoy spending long hours with young children. Preschool aides may have experience in drama, natural sciences, child rearing, music, games, arts and crafts, reading and literacy, and educational theory.

A Day in the Life—Duties and Responsibilities

Preschool aides support the lead teacher's vision and curriculum. A preschool aide's daily duties and responsibilities include classroom preparation and clean up as well as student care. Classroom preparation and cleaning duties may include labeling materials, organizing work areas such as the art area or reading area, emptying student cubbies, preparing food for students, setting up daily projects, and cleaning and sanitizing at the end of the day. Preschool aides provide student care by greeting students in the morning, calming fears and separation anxiety, promoting a supportive and nurturing classroom environment, maintaining safety and health, providing consistent discipline, preventing conflict, and building students' relationship and cooperation skills.

Preschool aides with experience and seniority may plan student lessons, teach, participate in family outreach efforts, and take on other school duties. Planning learning activities includes lesson preparation, research, and buying or securing donations for project supplies. Teaching responsibilities include teaching lessons and leading activities that improve student vocabulary, mathematical thinking, early literacy, nature awareness, and motor skills. Family outreach includes greeting families at school drop-off and dismissal times as well as regularly communicating with families about their student's successes and challenges. Preschool aides must attend school functions such as staff meetings and open houses for prospective families.

Duties and Responsibilities

- Working with children according to parents' wishes
- Working with children individually and in small groups
- Feeding, changing, dressing and caring for infants
- Preparing meals and supervising eating periods
- Caring for children that don't feel well or are troubled

OCCUPATION SPECIALTIES

School Child Care Attendants

School Child Care Attendants take care of the personal needs of disabled children in school.

Children's Institution Attendants

Children's Institution Attendants care for groups of children housed in city, county, state or private institutions.

Playroom Attendants

Playroom Attendants organize games and entertainment for children of parents patronizing stores, theaters, hotels and similar organizations.

WORK ENVIRONMENT

Physical Environment

A preschool aide's physical environment is the preschool classroom. Preschool aides generally work 40-hour weeks or more, engaged in physically demanding activity. Many preschool aides follow an annual academic schedule with ample (usually unpaid) winter, spring, and summer vacations. Preschool aides enjoy vacation-teaching opportunities in preschools, child-care centers, and camps.

Human Environment

Preschool aides are in constant contact with young children, students' families, and lead teachers. Preschool aides may be responsible for students with physical and mental disabilities as well as students who are English language learners (ELL). Preschool aides must be comfortable working with people from a wide range of backgrounds.

Relevant Skills and Abilities

Communication Skills
- Speaking effectively
- Writing concisely

Interpersonal/Social Skills
- Being patient
- Being sensitive to others
- Cooperating with others
- Teaching others
- Working as a member of a team

Organization & Management Skills
- Making decisions
- Managing people/groups
- Organizing information or materials

Research & Planning Skills
- Using logical reasoning

Technological Environment

Preschool classrooms increasingly include computers for student use and learning. Preschool aides should be comfortable teaching children to use educational software and games.

EDUCATION, TRAINING, AND ADVANCEMENT

High School/Secondary

High school students interested in becoming preschool aides should develop good study habits and seek out child-care experience. Interested high school students should take courses in psychology, education, child development, physical education, and the arts. Internships or part-time child-care work with children at camps, after school programs, preschools, or child-care centers may also be helpful to those interested in the field of early childhood educationr.

Suggested High School Subjects
- Arts
- Child Care
- Child Growth & Development
- Crafts
- English

- Family & Consumer Sciences
- First Aid Training
- Foods & Nutrition
- Health Science Technology
- Psychology
- Theatre & Drama

Famous First

The first teacher's manual in the field of early childhood education was *The Paradise of Childhood*, written in 1869 by Edward Wiebe and published in Springfield, MA, by Milton Bradley & Co. (the toy manufacturer).

College/Postsecondary

College students interested in the field of early childhood education should consider majoring in education and earning initial teaching certification as part of their undergraduate education program. College students interested in early childhood education should complete coursework in psychology, education, child development, physical education, and the arts. The majority of preschool aide jobs do not require a college degree and, as a result, postsecondary students may be hired as preschool aides either during college or upon graduation.

Related College Majors
- Child Care & Guidance Workers & Managers, General

Adult Job Seekers

Adults seeking jobs as preschool aides should research the education and certification requirements of their home states as well as of the preschools where they seek employment. Adult job seekers in the early childhood education field may benefit from the employment workshops and job lists maintained by professional teaching associations such as the National Association for the Education of Young Children (NAEYC) and the American Federation of Teachers (AFT).

Professional Certification and Licensure

Professional certification and licensure requirements for preschool aides vary between states and schools. The range of child-care and early childhood teaching requirements is vast and includes high school education, child-care or teaching experience, the national Child Development Associate (CDA) credential, the Child Care Professional (CCP) designation, college-level education courses, associate's degree, bachelor's degree, master's degree, and state teaching certification. Some states also require first aid and CPR certification before beginning work in a preschool. Successful job seekers will find out the requirements that apply to them and satisfy the requirements prior to seeking employment.

Additional Requirements

Individuals who find satisfaction, success, and job security as preschool aides will be knowledgeable about the profession's requirements, responsibilities, and opportunities. Preschool aides must have high levels of integrity and ethics as they care for young children and have access to their families' personal information. Preschool aides need to find satisfaction in the work itself as the compensation offered preschool aides tends to be low and opportunities for professional advancement are few.

EARNINGS AND ADVANCEMENT

Earnings of preschool aides are generally low, but they increase based on experience and the type of institution in which they are employed. Most preschool aides advance by moving into supervisory positions, obtaining further education and entering the teaching profession, or by becoming administrators in institutional settings.

Mean annual earnings for preschool aides were $22,230 in 2015. The lowest ten percent earned less than $16,900, and the highest ten percent earned more than $30,750. Self-employed preschool aides had earnings that varied due to hours worked, number and ages of children and the location of the facility.

Preschool aides generally have few, if any, fringe benefits. This situation varies widely, however, with some employers offering advanced training to aides, and in some cases offering to pay for college coursework.

Metropolitan Areas with the Highest Employment Level in this Occupation

Metropolitan area	Employment	Employment per thousand jobs	Annual mean wage
New York-Jersey City-White Plains, NY-NJ	31,020	4.79	$26,970
Atlanta-Sandy Springs-Roswell, GA	15,010	6.05	$21,360
Los Angeles-Long Beach-Glendale, CA	14,230	3.47	$25,080
Houston-The Woodlands-Sugar Land, TX	13,510	4.61	$20,080
Dallas-Plano-Irving, TX	10,510	4.51	$21,220
Washington-Arlington-Alexandria, DC-VA-MD-WV	9,870	4.08	$25,170
Chicago-Naperville-Arlington Heights, IL	9,230	2.59	$24,100
Charlotte-Concord-Gastonia, NC-SC	6,990	6.27	$22,260
Minneapolis-St. Paul-Bloomington, MN-WI	6,960	3.70	$24,130
Riverside-San Bernardino-Ontario, CA	6,340	4.84	$26,570

Source: Bureau of Labor Statistics

EMPLOYMENT AND OUTLOOK

Childcare workers, of which preschool aides are a part, held about 1.2 million jobs nationally in 2014. Over one-third worked part-time. Employment is expected to grow as fast as the average for all occupations through the year 2024, which means employment is projected to increase 3 percent to 7 percent. The number of children enrolled in full or part-time preschool programs is likely to continue to increase, resulting in the need for more preschool aides.

Employment Trend, Projected 2014–24

Human services occupations: 13%

Total, all occupations: 7%

Preschool aides: 5%

Note: "All Occupations" includes all occupations in the U.S. Economy. Source: U.S. Bureau of Labor Statistics, Employment Projections Program

Related Occupations
- Childcare Worker
- Preschool Teacher
- Social and Human Services Assistant
- Teacher Assistant

Conversation With . . .
CAITLIN MULLENS

Full-time assistant preschool teacher
Fayetteville Tech. Community College Children's Center
Fayetteville, North Carolina
Preschool assistant teacher, 7 months

1. What was your individual career path in terms of education/training, entry-level job, or other significant opportunity?

I started my training in this field my freshman year of high school in Florida. That year, they started an early childhood program and just randomly put kids in it. That's how I landed in it and I ended up really liking it. By the end of my freshman year, I was certified in areas like child nutrition and child abuse and neglect.

I also got experience caring for children because the school opened a small center without about eight kids. I ended up getting asked back by the teacher who ran the program and I took the course every semester through my senior year. I just took to it really well. It's what kept me going to school.

After high school, I decided I might as well go to college to study early childhood education. My family moved up here and I enrolled at FTCC, and I learned so much more. The instructors were incredible. I got to work at the school's center part-time before I graduated. A full-time job opened up last March and I was hired.

2. What are the most important skills and/or qualities for someone in your profession?

Patience. And being able to think outside of your own self. Not everybody lives the same way you do. People have different points of view and different experiences and different life situations and that doesn't necessarily make their decisions and actions wrong. You have to learn to try to understand parents and help them because that helps the child.

3. What are the most important skills and/or qualities for someone in your profession?

I think loving children and loving working with them are probably the most important qualities.

4. **Are there many job opportunities in your profession? In what specific areas?**

    There are a lot of job opportunities, but not a lot of great ones. Not a lot of other childcare centers or preschools offer health insurance and retirement. This is the best place to work for around here if you're going to go into this field because it's a state agency. If I weren't here, I would probably still work in this field – but I'd probably need to have a second job to support myself. Even now I sometimes feel like I need a second job to keep up with my expenses.

5. **How do you see your profession changing in the next five years, what role will technology play in those changes, and what skills will be required?**

    I think the field is changing for the better and will continue to do so. We're becoming more diverse and we're becoming more open. We're not as judgmental as we used to be. We have all sorts of families – single parents, same-sex parents, mixed families – and we're accepting of all that. We just want to be there for your kids.

    I don't see technology playing a big role in those changes. I do see us looking for more ways to communicate with children and to help them express their feelings. For example, we teach older babies simple sign language now so they can tell us when they're hungry. We also look for ways to learn about the families, especially if they're from a different culture.

6. **What do you enjoy most about your job? What do you enjoy least about your job?**

    There isn't really a whole lot that I don't enjoy. I love watching the children learn and progress and develop. It's amazing.

7. **Can you suggest a valuable "try this" for students considering a career in your profession?**

    Some might think babysitting would be good preparation but I don't agree. There's a difference between working at a preschool or childcare center and babysitting. With babysitting, you're either at their house or your house and you don't have the rules that you will have if you're at a center. I think volunteering is the best way to start. Then you learn rules and best practices vs. just what's your opinion. Then, if you like it, you can work part-time until you figure out what you want to do for sure. Some people will find it's too much for them.

MORE INFORMATION

American Federation of Teachers
555 New Jersey Avenue NW
Washington, DC 20001
202.879.4400
www.aft.org

**Association for Childhood
Education International**
17904 Georgia Avenue, Suite 215
Olney, MD 20832
800.423.3563
www.acei.org

**Center for the Child Care
Workforce**
555 New Jersey Avenue, NW
Washington, DC 20001
202.662.8005
www.ccw.org

**Council for Professional
Recognition**
2460 16th Street NW
Washington, DC 20009-3547
800.424.4310
www.cdacouncil.org

**National Association for the
Education of Young Children**
1313 L Street, NW, Suite 500
Washington, DC 20005
800.424.2460
www.naeyc.org

National Child Care Association
1325 G Street NW, Suite 500
Washington, DC 20005
800.543.7161
www.nccanet.org

**National Child Care Information
and Technical Assistance Center**
9300 Lee Highway
Fairfax, VA 22031-6050
800.616.2242
nccic.acf.hhs.gov

**National Early Childhood
Technical Assistance Center**
517 S. Greensboro Street
Carrboro, NC 27510
919.962.2001
www.nectac.org

Simone Isadora Flynn/Editor

Preschool Teacher

Snapshot

Career Cluster(s): Education & Training; Human Services
Interests: Education, teaching, early childhood development, leading activities, language development, arts and crafts
Earnings (Yearly Average): $28,570
Employment & Outlook: Average Growth Expected

OVERVIEW

Sphere of Work

Preschool teachers are early childhood professionals who focus on the educational needs of three to five year old children. Preschool teachers plan their teaching curriculum with their students' socio-emotional development, pre-literacy skills, fine and gross motor skills, practical life skills, and language acquisition needs in mind. Preschool teachers tend to be generalists with knowledge and talents in a wide range of subjects including drama, natural sciences, child rearing, music, games, arts and crafts, reading and literacy, and educational theory.

Work Environment

Preschool teachers work in early childhood classrooms arranged primarily to meet to the social and educational needs of young children. In the preschool environment, furniture tends to be low to the ground, and preschool teachers must be sufficiently physically fit to carry children when needed, squat, bend, and sit on the floor. The amounts of preschool classroom resources, such as art supplies, music lessons, field trips, and assistant teachers, differ depending on the school's financial resources and the educational philosophy directing the curriculum. Preschools may be private or public and may be part of an elementary school or may be an independent entity with no higher grades. Preschools are also found in businesses, high schools, colleges, social service agencies, and religious organizations.

Profile

Working Conditions: Work Indoors
Physical Strength: Light Work
Education Needs: Bachelor's Degree
Licensure/Certification: Required
Opportunities For Experience:
Internship, Volunteer Work, Part Time Work
Holland Interest Score*: SAE

* See Appendix A

Occupation Interest

The profession of preschool teacher draws individuals who are responsible, responsive, patient, observant, playful, and caring. Preschool teachers, who nurture children in the years between infancy and elementary school-age, should enjoy spending long hours with young children. Preschool teachers excel at long-term scheduling, planning, problem solving, and social interaction.

A Day in the Life—Duties and Responsibilities

A preschool teacher's daily duties and responsibilities include planning, teaching, classroom preparation and clean up, student care, family outreach, school duties, and professional development. Preschool teachers plan and teach lessons, research, buy or secure donations for project supplies, and lead activities that improve student vocabulary, mathematical thinking, early literacy, nature awareness, and motor skills. Classroom preparation and cleaning duties may include labeling materials, organizing work areas such as the art area or reading area, emptying student cubbies, preparing food for students, setting up daily projects, and cleaning and sanitizing at the end of the day. Preschool teachers provide student care by greeting students in the morning, calming fears and separation anxiety, promoting a supportive and nurturing classroom environment, maintaining safety and health, providing consistent discipline, preventing conflict, and building students' relationship and cooperation skills. Family outreach includes greeting families at school drop-off and dismissal times as well as regularly communicating with families about their student's successes and challenges. Preschool teachers must attend school functions such as staff meetings and open houses for prospective families. Their professional development duties include attendance at professional meetings, continued training, and ongoing and up to date licensure and certification.

Preschool teachers must work on a daily basis meet the needs of students, families, fellow teachers, and school administrators.

Duties and Responsibilities

- Using activities and games to teach colors, numbers and the alphabet
- Helping the physical coordination of students by play and exercise
- Teaching health and safety to children

WORK ENVIRONMENT

Physical Environment

A preschool teacher's physical environment is the preschool classroom. Preschool teachers tend to have a significant amount of autonomy in deciding the classroom layout and curriculum, particularly in private school settings. Preschool teachers generally work 40-hour weeks and often follow an annual academic schedule with ample winter, spring, and summer vacations. Part-time schedules are also widely available. Summer teaching opportunities in preschools and summer camps are common.

Relevant Skills and Abilities

Communication Skills
- Expressing thoughts and ideas
- Speaking effectively
- Writing concisely

Interpersonal/Social Skills
- Being patient
- Cooperating with others

Organization & Management Skills
- Coordinating tasks
- Managing people/groups
- Performing duties which change frequently

Human Environment

Preschool teachers are in constant contact with young children, students' families, fellow teachers, administrators, and preschool workers. Preschool teachers may have students with physical and mental disabilities as well as students who are English language learners (ELL). Preschool teachers must be comfortable working with people from a wide range of backgrounds and able to incorporate lessons on diversity into their teaching. Given the demands of the job and laws governing student to teacher ratios, preschool teachers should anticipate working in a teaching team.

Technological Environment

Preschool classrooms increasingly include computers for student use. Preschool teachers should be comfortable using internet communication tools and teaching children to use educational software and games.

EDUCATION, TRAINING, AND ADVANCEMENT

High School/Secondary

High school students interested in becoming preschool teachers should develop good study habits and take courses in psychology, education, child development, physical education, and the arts. Internships or part-time work with children and teachers at camps, after school programs, preschools, or child-care centers are helpful to those interested in the field of early childhood education.

Suggested High School Subjects
- Arts
- Audio-Visual
- Child Care
- Child Growth & Development
- Crafts
- English
- Health Science Technology
- Instrumental & Vocal Music
- Literature
- Mathematics
- Physical Education
- Pottery
- Psychology
- Science
- Sociology

Famous First

The first preschool (or nursery school, as it was called) was established in New York City in 1827 by the Infant School Society. The school was set up "to relieve parents of the laboring classes from the care of their children while engaged in the vocations by which they live, and provide for the children a protection from weather and idleness and the contamination of evil example besides affording them the means of early and efficient education.".

College/Postsecondary

College students interested in the field of early childhood education should consider majoring in education and earning initial teaching certification as part of their undergraduate education program. They should complete coursework in psychology, education, child development, physical education, and the arts. Prior to graduation, students intent on becoming preschool teachers should gain experience, through internship or part-time work, teaching preschool-age children as well as exploring requirements for early childhood education master's degree programs and individual state teaching certification.

Related College Majors

- Bilingual/Bicultural Education
- Child Care & Guidance Workers & Managers, General
- Elementary/Pre-Elem/Early Childhood/Kindergarten Teacher Education
- English Teacher Education
- Mathematics Teacher Education
- Science Teacher Education, General
- Speech Teacher Education

Adult Job Seekers

Adults seeking jobs as preschool teachers should research the education and certification requirements in their home states, as well the requirements of the schools in states where they may seek employment. Adult job seekers in the early childhood education field can benefit from the employment workshops and job lists maintained by professional teaching associations such as the National Association for the Education of Young Children (NAEYC) and the American Federation of Teachers (AFT).

Professional Certification and Licensure

Professional certification and licensure requirements for preschool teachers vary between states and schools. The range of preschool teaching requirements is vast and includes high school education, teaching experience, the national Child Development Associate (CDA) credential, associate's degree, bachelor's degree, or master's degree, and state teaching certification. Some states also require first aid and CPR certification before beginning work in a preschool. Savvy and successful job seekers will find out which requirements apply to them and satisfy the requirements prior to seeking employment.

Additional Requirements

Individuals who find satisfaction, success, and job security as preschool teachers will be knowledgeable about the profession's requirements, responsibilities, and opportunities. Successful preschool teachers engage in ongoing professional development. Preschool teachers must have high levels of integrity and ethics as they work with young children and have access to their families' personal information. Membership in professional teaching associations is encouraged among beginning and tenured preschool teachers as a means of building status in a professional community and networking.

EARNINGS AND ADVANCEMENT

Earnings depend on the size and geographic location of the employer and the individual's education and experience. Median annual earnings of preschool teachers were $28,570 in 2015. The lowest ten percent earned less than $19,130, and the highest ten percent earned more than $51,590.

Preschool teachers may receive paid vacations, holidays, and sick days; life and health insurance; and retirement benefits. These are usually paid by the employer.

Metropolitan Areas with the Highest Employment Level in this Occupation

Metropolitan area	Employment	Employment per thousand jobs	Annual mean wage
New York-Jersey City-White Plains, NY-NJ	3,530	0.55	$65,850
Chicago-Naperville-Arlington Heights, IL	1,530	0.43	$81,110
Tampa-St. Petersburg-Clearwater, FL	1,320	1.08	$46,500
Nassau County-Suffolk County, NY	800	0.62	$70,630
Denver-Aurora-Lakewood, CO	600	0.44	$55,220
Silver Spring-Frederick-Rockville, MD	470	0.82	$70,970
Minneapolis-St. Paul-Bloomington, MN-WI	440	0.23	$60,780
Las Vegas-Henderson-Paradise, NV	390	0.43	$53,150
Atlanta-Sandy Springs-Roswell, GA	380	0.15	$50,260
Albany-Schenectady-Troy, NY	360	0.81	$57,120

Source: Bureau of Labor Statistics

EMPLOYMENT AND OUTLOOK

Preschool teachers held about 440,000 jobs nationally in 2014. Employment of preschool teachers is expected to grow faster than the average for all occupations through the year 2024, which means employment is projected to increase 5 percent to 9 percent. This is due to an expected increase in overall student enrollment in preschools in the coming years.

Employment Trend, Projected 2014–24

Preschool teachers: 7%

Total, all occupations: 7%

Preschool, primary, secondary, and special education school teachers: 6%

Note: "All Occupations" includes all occupations in the U.S. Economy. Source: U.S. Bureau of Labor Statistics, Employment Projections Program

Related Occupations
- Elementary School Teacher
- Preschool Worker

Conversation With . . .
MADONNA MADSEN

Preschool teacher & Owner, Old MacDonald Preschool
North Platte, Nebraska
Preschool teacher, 16 years

1. What was your individual career path in terms of education/training, entry-level job, or other significant opportunity?

Honestly, it just fell into my lap. I had never considered doing this. My calling was to be a nurse and I did do that for a while but later left. When my youngest child was in school, I had the opportunity to come help the owner of this preschool. I became a teacher and figured out I loved kids and loved teaching them. After about my seventh year here, she decided to retire and offered me the chance to buy the business. I took the plunge. That was almost ten years ago.

2. What are the most important skills and/or qualities for someone in your profession?

First and foremost, you have to be a kid at heart. If you come in and you don't know how to act goofy or let loose so you can get down on their level, you can't communicate with them. I try to make learning fun. Patience is also key. And you need to know that every child is different and they don't all learn at the same pace. You have to be cognizant of their learning styles and skills and be able to adjust your teaching methods and lessons.

3. What do you wish you had known going into this profession?

I wish I'd known that I would love this work and that I should go to school for it before starting out. In Nebraska, you don't need a degree in early childhood education to teach at a preschool if you have sufficient experience and other types of training. Looking back, I think I would have been better off when I started out if I'd earned a degree in the field. At this point, though, I don't think it would help.

4. Are there many job opportunities in your profession? In what specific areas?

There are opportunities at good preschools if you're a good teacher and able to connect with the kids. You have to be funny, you have to be goofy, you have to be creative and you have to love kids. I have had staff who were good teachers but didn't have the spark you need to work with preschoolers. They didn't last.

5. **How do you see your profession changing in the next five years, what role will technology play in those changes, and what skills will be required?**

I don't see technology playing a big role here. I'm old-fashioned. We don't use any computers with the kids. I allow TV only once a year, when we have a pretend slumber party. I think it's important that they learn to play without electronics. That said, the preschool curriculum has changed dramatically since I started. It used to be very simple. Now they're learning skills that a few years ago they would have learned in kindergarten. For example, three-year-olds learn how to color and trace – which helps to strengthen their hand and their coordination – while five-year-olds learn basic reading and writing. I don't see the curriculum getting harder because it would start to make the children dislike learning. Preschool teachers need to be able to teach these skills and make them fun for the children.

6. **What do you enjoy most about your job? What do you enjoy least?**

I love the kids. You can be having the worst day ever, then you go down there and they give you hugs and they bring you right out of that bad mood. I love it when I see the light bulb click on – when they suddenly get something. What I like least is when parents don't have the time or patience to appreciate what their kids have done or learned. That's not usual. Most kids' parents will, say, put their drawing on the refrigerator. But there's always a kid who says his mom or dad threw it away. I try to make up for that with my own praise. But it hurts.

7. **Can you suggest a valuable "try this" for students considering a career in your profession?**

You could work as an aide. Or drop by a preschool to see what goes on. You could also go to a library and volunteer to read to preschool kids. At this age, they are the most fun kids to read to. I love reading stories to them because they get into it so much.

MORE INFORMATION

American Federation of Teachers
555 New Jersey Avenue NW
Washington, DC 20001
202.879.4400
www.aft.org

**Association for Childhood
Education International**
17904 Georgia Avenue, Suite 215
Olney, MD 20832
800.423.3563
www.acei.org

**Center for the Child Care
Workforce**
555 New Jersey Avenue, NW
Washington, DC 20001
202.662.8005
www.ccw.org

**Council for Professional
Recognition**
2460 16th Street NW
Washington, DC 20009-3547
800.424.4310
www.cdacouncil.org

**National Association for the
Education of Young Children**
1313 L Street, NW, Suite 500
Washington, DC 20005
800.424.2460
www.naeyc.org

**National Child Care Information
and Technical Assistance Center**
9300 Lee Highway
Fairfax, VA 22031-6050
800.616.2242
nccic.acf.hhs.gov

**National Early Childhood
Technical Assistance Center**
517 S. Greensboro Street
Carrboro, NC 27510
919.962.2001
www.nectac.org

Simone Isadora Flynn/Editor

Principal

Snapshot

Career Cluster(s): Education & Training
Interests: Education, management, school administration, budgeting, child development, resource planning
Earnings (Yearly Average): $90,410
Employment & Outlook: Average Growth Expected

OVERVIEW

Sphere of Work

Principals are educational administrators who manage elementary, middle, and secondary schools. Principals establish student and teacher performance goals, set school policies in accordance with the wishes of parents and teachers, hire and supervise school personnel, and enforce rules and discipline students as necessary. They manage the school's finances, make annual budgets, establish teacher and class schedules, and perform other administrative duties as necessary. Principals function as the school's representative within the community; they

meet with vendors and suppliers, organize fundraising activities, attend
conferences, and issue statements to the press.

Work Environment

Principals work from offices located inside the schools they oversee.
Although the principal has his or her own office, he or she spends much
of the workday walking the halls of the school, meeting with teachers,
students, facilities staff, administrative assistants, and others. Schools
are crowded, energetic environments during school hours. Principals
frequently respond to stressful situations, such as student fights,
angry parents, disciplinary issues, or school-wide emergencies. They
attend regular meetings of local government agencies, such as school
committees and boards of selectmen or city councils. Principals typically
work a forty-hour workweek, although they may work at the night for
public meetings and student activities. There are significant differences
in the job responsibilities of a principal depending on the ages of the
students and the size and location of the school.

Profile

Working Conditions: Work Indoors
Physical Strength: Light Work
Education Needs: Master's Degree
Licensure/Certification: Required
Opportunities For Experience:
 Internship
Holland Interest Score*: SEI

* See Appendix A

Occupation Interest

Principals are highly educated
individuals interested in school
administration who find job
satisfaction acting as managers
and leaders within elementary,
middle, and secondary schools.
Principals perform a variety of
activities and enjoy considerable
authority within the school. They
make final decisions regarding academic and disciplinary policies
as well as staffing and scheduling needs. They should have strong
communication skills as they frequently function in a public relations
capacity during meetings with families and community leaders.
Principals are financially well compensated for their years of education
and the demands of the job.

A Day in the Life—Duties and Responsibilities

Students often view the principal mainly as an enforcer of the school's
disciplinary and attendance rules, but in fact, his or her job duties
comprise a wide range of tasks. The principal meets with families to
discuss students' progress as well as relevant developments and policies

at the school. The principal is responsible for hiring qualified faculty members and supervises teachers on new materials, educational goals, testing requirements, teaching methods, and classes. He or she sets performance standards for staff, evaluating their progress and meeting with them to discuss ways to improve. The principal ensures that the school and its staff act in compliance with government-imposed standards and monitors the effectiveness of those standards, reporting periodically to the school superintendent and local school committee. The principal works with school officials and teachers to develop and implement the school's curriculum, programs, and standards.

The principal acts as the chief administrator of the school. He or she must develop mission statements, strategic plans budgets, and other important documents. The principal sets daily schedules, establishes administrative systems and protocols, and approves orders for food, repair work, and supplies.

The principal also manages the school's public relations efforts. When an emergency occurs, the principal communicates with the media, school officials, families, and the public. He or she also assists in raising funds for the school from local businesses during times of economic difficulty.

All principals spend some time addressing students' emotional needs and family situations. To that end, they may implement daycare programs, gifted programs, school breakfast or lunch programs, parent-teacher conferences, learning disability programs, or anti-bullying policies. Principals at high schools must often address and develop strategies to cope with complex behavioral issues, such as substance abuse, teenage pregnancy, safety and security, and poor student attendance. Principals are obligated to take thoughtful teaching approaches and make every effort to improve the quality of education for their students.

Duties and Responsibilities

- Setting standards, policies and procedures
- Developing academic programs
- Training and motivating teachers and staff
- Advising and meeting with students and parents
- Preparing budgets and reports

WORK ENVIRONMENT

Physical Environment

Principals work in elementary, middle, and secondary schools. They work in offices, usually located within the school's main administrative area. Schools are very active and complex, with sometimes hundreds of students, teachers, and other school personnel in the building and grounds at once. Principals also visit other schools and school systems and, when called upon, attend school board and other meetings at town or city halls and other local government offices.

Relevant Skills and Abilities

Interpersonal/Social Skills
- Being able to remain calm
- Cooperating with others
- Working as a member of a team

Organization & Management Skills
- Coordinating tasks
- Handling challenging situations
- Managing people/groups
- Managing time
- Organizing information or materials

Work Environment Skills
- Working in a fast-paced environment

Human Environment

Principals work with a wide range of people within and outside of the school. Within the school, they work with teachers, administrators, assistants, custodial staff, cafeteria workers, librarians, coaches, and students. Outside of the school, principals work with school officials and elected officials, vendors and suppliers, consultants, accountants, and students' families.

Technological Environment

Principals must be familiar with public address systems and two-way radios. They must also have skills with computers and school administrative and office management software, such as school attendance databases, budgeting programs, and enterprise resource planning (ERP) software.

EDUCATION, TRAINING, AND ADVANCEMENT

High School/Secondary

High school students should take courses that will help them build a career as an educator. Coursework in mathematics, science, social studies, and English will prepare students for college-level studies. Interested students are also encouraged to take child growth and development classes as well as psychology courses.

Suggested High School Subjects
- Algebra
- Biology
- Business
- Business English
- Business Math
- Calculus
- Child Growth & Development
- College Preparatory
- English
- Foreign Languages
- Geometry
- Literature
- Physical Science
- Psychology
- Social Studies
- Sociology
- Statistics

Famous First

The first and oldest public school in existence today is Boston Latin School, founded in 1635 (as Boston Public Latin School). Its purpose was to prepare boys for the ministry by schooling them in "ancient tongues." The first schoolmaster there was Philemon Pormort.

UPPOSED FIRST OR SECOND SCHOOL HOUS WHICH EZEKIEL CHEEVER PROBABLY BEGAN TO TE

College/Postsecondary

Elementary, middle and secondary school principals need to earn a master's or doctorate degree in education, psychology, education administration, or a related field. Interested college students should consider applying to graduate programs in education or education administration as most principals begin their careers as teachers.

Related College Majors

• Education Administration & Supervision, General

Adult Job Seekers

Qualified individuals seeking a job as a principal may apply directly to the city or town in which an open position is located (or in the case of private schools, directly to the school itself). They may also seek jobs as assistant principals in order to gain more experience and exposure as a potential principal.

A principal at a small school or an elementary school principal is often viewed as being in the first years of school administration. Moving to a larger school or one with older students and issues that are more complex is usually considered an advancement opportunity.

Professional Certification and Licensure

Most states require that a principal receive a license as a professional school administrator. Licensure may require passing a training course and examination. A master's or doctorate degree in education or a related field may be sufficient for such certification. Private school principals do not fall under this requirement, although an advanced degree is a prerequisite for these positions as well.

Additional Requirements

Principals must be effective managers. They should be able to lead, inspire, communicate effectively, cope calmly with difficult or fast-paced situations, and set educational, staffing, and facilities-related goals. They should also be perceptive, able to understand the motives and perspectives of those with whom they interact. They must have exceptional judgment and decision-making abilities, as well as a solid understanding of government standards and performance expectations. Finally, principals must be skilled at working with children of different socioeconomic backgrounds and development levels.

Fun Fact

The first schools didn't have a principal until they grew beyond the one-room schoolhouse. Once schools got even bigger and required more management, principals stopped teaching and the word "teacher" was dropped from their job titles.

Source: www3.nd.edu

EARNINGS AND ADVANCEMENT

Principals advance by moving up the administrative ladder or transferring to another school that might be larger or in a different system. Median annual earnings of principals were $92,188 in 2012. The lowest ten percent earned less than $61,798, and the highest ten percent earned more than $137,249.

Principals may receive paid vacations, holidays, and sick days; life and health insurance; and retirement benefits. These are usually paid by the employer.

Metropolitan Areas with the Highest Employment Level in this Occupation

Metropolitan area	Employment	Employment per thousand jobs	Annual mean wage
New York-Jersey City-White Plains, NY-NJ	13,780	2.13	$119,220
Chicago-Naperville-Arlington Heights, IL	6,610	1.85	$107,660
Houston-The Woodlands-Sugar Land, TX	5,300	1.81	$83,120
Washington-Arlington-Alexandria, DC-VA-MD-WV	4,560	1.89	$103,930
Los Angeles-Long Beach-Glendale, CA	4,480	1.09	$107,330
Atlanta-Sandy Springs-Roswell, GA	4,460	1.80	$89,120
Dallas-Plano-Irving, TX	4,400	1.89	$83,630
Boston-Cambridge-Newton, MA	3,190	1.81	$104,860
Baltimore-Columbia-Towson, MD	2,820	2.14	$97,390
Phoenix-Mesa-Scottsdale, AZ	2,720	1.45	$78,570

Source: Bureau of Labor Statistics

EMPLOYMENT AND OUTLOOK

Elementary and secondary school administrators, of which principals are a part, held about 240,000 jobs nationally in 2014. Employment is expected to grow about as fast as the average for all occupations through the year 2024, which means employment is projected to increase 4 percent to 8 percent. As education and training take on greater importance in everyone's lives, the need for education administrators will grow. Job opportunities should also be excellent because a large number of education administrators are expected to retire over the next ten years. Enrollments of school-age children will also have an impact on the demand for education administrators. Enrollment of students in elementary and secondary schools is expected to grow slowly over the next decade; however, preschool and childcare center administrators are expected to experience substantial growth as enrollments in formal child care programs continue to expand as fewer private households care for young children.

Employment Trend, Projected 2014–24

Total, all occupations: 7%

School principals: 6%

Management occupations: 6%

Note: "All Occupations" includes all occupations in the U.S. Economy. Source: U.S. Bureau of Labor Statistics, Employment Projections Program

Related Occupations
- Education Administrator
- Elementary School Teacher
- Secondary School Teacher

Conversation With . . .
WINSTON SAKURAI

Principal, Hanalani Upper School
Honolulu, Hawaii
School administration, 23 years

1. **What was your individual career path in terms of education/training, entry-level job, or other significant opportunity?**

From the time I was in elementary school, I wanted to be a principal. The reason was because every year from kindergarten all the way up to fifth grade, I had a new principal—which is disconcerting for everybody. The principal that came when I was in fifth grade stayed for 22 years. It was a National Blue Ribbon School twice. So that was really foundational for me.

My path was kind of different. I had been involved in student government in high school. My principal had given me an opportunity to be on the school accreditation committee. I got to learn a bit about how schools function. I was also the state student council president, which made me the student representative to the Hawaii Board of Education. I testified before the state legislature and was part of the Goals 2000 subcommittee on educator competency. I majored in political science. But the biggest opportunity was when the governor appointed me at age 20 to the state Board of Education.

When I left the board, I taught for a few years, then was vice principal in the elementary school and later principal for a few years. I've been the high school principal here for eight years. I've been at the same school—a private K-12 school—for the last 15 years and would like to be here for another 15. I got my master's in education leadership right after I became vice principal and am now working on my doctorate. I like being part of the action with the students right at the local level. That's where I've realized a lot of change happens. You can change one school at a time.

The National Association of Secondary School Principals (NASSP) named me 2016 National Digital Principal of the Year and 2016 Hawaii State Principal of the Year.

2. **What are the most important skills and/or qualities for someone in your profession?**

No two days are the same, so you have to be flexible and adaptable. You have to always think there's room for improvement. You have to be a good communicator because it's the number one thing that allows a school to move forward or not—internal communication with the staff and external communication with the families and community. You have to be a problem solver. You have to be a collaborator. You really need a good team around you as principal.

3. **What do you wish you had known going into this profession?**

One of the things I wish I knew was how deeply what you do affects thousands of people—everyone from the students to the teachers to the families and even the community. There have been times I could have been more conscious of how people sometimes have difficulty with change and that their feelings about changes need to discussed.

4. **Are there many job opportunities in your profession? In what specific areas?**

The average time spent as a principal is only five years. It's a stressful job. Here in Hawaii, we have principal shortages. So there are a lot of opportunities out there. There's the principal; many schools have multiple vice principalships; there are other school leadership opportunities, and there are district and state level administrators.

5. **How do you see your profession changing in the next five years? What role will technology play in those changes, and what skills will be required?**

The principalship has gone from someone who manages a building, manages a school, to someone who's innovative in making sure that learning at all levels, including professional development, takes place. Technology plays a big role because being connected with other educators allows ideas and best practices from all over the nation to be shared. There's a curation of information that was never possible before—Twitter education chats, online professional development, virtual conferences, and online resources that can be used in the classroom. What happens five years from now is going to be a totally different ball game.

6. **What do you enjoy most about your job? What do you enjoy least about your job?**

The thing I like most about the job is seeing students succeed, whether that's an essay that's done well or an international winning robotics team or sending someone to college to pursue a career that they really enjoy. What I struggle with most is that there just isn't enough time. You want to do so much and yet you can't put everything on a student's plate or a teacher's plate without burning them out or overburdening them.

7. **Can you suggest a valuable "try this" for students considering a career in your profession?**

If you have the opportunity to be on a school improvement committee, that would be a very good way to see if this work would appeal to you. Maybe shadow the principal one day. The nice thing is this is a career where you can just walk down the hall and talk to someone about it.

MORE INFORMATION

Administrative Leadership and Policy Studies Program
University of Colorado Denver
School of Education and Human Development
1380 Lawrence Street
Denver, CO 80204
303.315.4985

American Association of School Administrators
801 N. Quincy Street, Suite 700
Arlington, VA 82203-1730
703.528.0700
www.aasa.org

American Federation of School Administrators
1101 17th Street, NW, Suite 408
Washington, DC 20036
202.986.4209
www.admin.org

Association for Supervision and Curriculum Development
1703 N. Beauregard Street
Alexandria, VA 22311-1714
800.933.2723
www.ascd.org

National Association of Elementary School Principals
Educational Products Department
1615 Duke Street
Alexandria, VA 22314
800.386.2377
www.naesp.org

National Association of Secondary School Principals
1904 Association Drive
Reston, VA 20191-1537
703.860.0200
www.nassp.org

National Association of Student Personnel Administrators
111 K Street, NE, 10th Floor
Washington, DC 20002
202.265.7500
www.naspa.org

National Education Association
1201 16th Street, NW
Washington, DC 20036-3290
202.833.4000
www.nea.org

Michael Auerbach/Editor

Reading Specialist

Snapshot

Career Cluster(s): Education, English
Interests: English reading, composition, teaching, social services
Earnings (Yearly Average): $50,280
Employment & Outlook: Average growth expected

OVERVIEW

Sphere of Work

Reading specialists, sometimes called "Adult Literacy" teachers or "Reading Coaches," are educators specializing in helping individuals with reading difficulties. Reading specialists can focus on helping students at any level, from elementary school to adult and 57 percent work for elementary or secondary schools, or junior colleges, with the remaining 43 percent divided between colleges, universities, private educational companies, and social assistance/outreach organizations. Some reading specialists are ESL (English as a Second Language)

instructors who specialize in teaching reading to individuals from non-English speaking backgrounds.

Work Environment

Reading specialists typically work in a classroom or office setting meeting either with individual students or leading classes. Some reading specialists may work in different classrooms within a single school, while others may work out of several schools or offices and may therefore need to commute between work sites. Some reading specialists work as private tutors out of their home or visiting the homes of students.

Profile

Working Conditions: Work Indoors
Physical Strength: Light Work
Education Needs: Bachelor's Degree, Master's Degree
Licensure/Certification: Required for some positions
Opportunities For Experience: Part-Time Work, Student Teaching
Holland Interest Score*: SAE

* See Appendix A

Occupation Interest

Individuals looking to become reading specialists should have a strong interest in teaching, interpersonal communication, and English language and literature. In addition, as the position straddles the lines between education and social service, reading specialists should have a strong interest in helping others and providing community/social outreach.

Reading specialists should also be creative and artistic, as these qualities are helpful when creating lesson, and should be comfortable socializing with individuals from different cultural backgrounds.

A Day in the Life—Duties and Responsibilities

The typical duties of a reading specialist differ depending on whether the specialist focuses on a specific type of reading education and on their chosen teaching environment. Some reading specialists work for an entire school district and may help to supervise the district's reading and English staff. In other cases, reading specialists may work at a single school, college, or with a private company offering reading support and tutoring services. Adult education instructors may work irregular hours, in the mornings, evenings, and at night, to provide reading instruction for individuals who work during business hours.

During a typical day, a reading specialist may spend time meeting with students, grading and evaluating assignments, meeting with or supervising teachers or tutors, and preparing classroom materials and/or lesson plans. Reading specialists working for schools or districts may also meet with parents or family of students enrolled in reading programs.

Duties and Responsibilities

- Instructing students individually or in groups
- Providing feedback on class performance or homework
- Preparing lectures or classroom presentations
- Meeting with teachers or educational administrators
- Grading or evaluating homework or classwork
- Meeting with parents or family of students

OCCUPATION SPECIALTIES

ESL Teacher

ESL teachers are English teachers specializing in teaching writing, reading, and English speaking to non-English speakers. ESL teachers typically need proficiency in reading and writing and familiarity or interest in working with individuals from different cultures and educational backgrounds.

Literacy Coach

A literacy coach typically works with teachers to create and implement reading instruction programs used in school curricula. Literacy coaches may work directly with students or may take a supervisory role, helping teachers to develop the skills needed to work with students who have reading/writing difficulties.

Remedial Reading Teacher

Remedial reading teachers are English teachers specializing on helping students whose reading level is below average for the student's age or level of educational attainment. Remedial reading teachers typically work with individual students or with student groups.

Private Reading Tutor

A private reading tutor is an individual who works independently or for a private tutoring company and provides reading assistance for students with literacy or reading difficulties. Private tutors may be hired by a student or a student's family directly or may work for a reading/writing assistance center in an educational institution.

WORK ENVIRONMENT

Physical Environment

Reading specialists typically work in office or classroom environments. Literacy coaches and some other reading specialists may work for an entire school district and so may spend time traveling between schools within the district. Private reading tutors may work out of their home or may visit student homes for teaching sessions. Adult reading instructors tend to work in the morning, evenings, or at night, to work around the schedules of working students.

Human Environment

Reading specialists spend much of their time interacting directly with students, teachers, parents/family, and administrators and so must be comfortable with frequent daily interaction. Effective reading specialists develop relationships with students or teachers under their supervision, thereby helping the specialist to tailor his or her instruction to the needs of individual learners.

Relevant Skills and Abilities

Communication Skills
- Speaking effectively
- Writing clearly and concisely

Interpersonal/Social Skills
- Being able to work independently
- Being able to work with groups
- Being able to lead group projects/discussions

Organization & Management Skills
- Managing people/groups
- Evaluating teacher and student performance
- Keeping detailed records of teacher/student progress

Research & Planning Skills
- Creating lesson plans
- Creating original educational material
- Researching teaching tools and technology

Technical Skills
- Working with digital technology
- Working with desktop publishing and word processing equipment

Technological Environment

In the 2010s, reading specialists often use personal computers, tablets, smartphones, and electronic communication in their jobs. Familiarity with basic computing, word processing, spreadsheet creation, and desktop publishing are also helpful skills for a reading specialist. In some cases, reading specialists may use specific software programs created to aid in teaching different types of students to read and may therefore need to familiarize themselves with available literacy software and digital aides. Modern reading teachnology, such as ebook readers, tablets, and e-book applications are also essential for the field and reading specialists need to become familiar and proficient at working with digital reading technology.

EDUCATION, TRAINING, AND ADVANCEMENT

High School/Secondary

Those interested in becoming reading specialists should begin by pursing a teaching degree at the Bachelor's level, with the expectation of continuing to the Master's degree level or higher. In high school, students should take classes focusing on English reading, analysis, and composition. Students will also benefit from classes in intercultural studies, social work or sociology, basic computer literacy and technology, and any classes specific to a future career in education, including psychology. Though English education is primary for future English and reading teachers, familiarity with other languages is a benefit and students should take classes in one or more world languages.

Suggested High School Subjects
- English
- English literature
- English Composition
- Technical Writing
- Public Speaking
- Social Studies
- Civics
- Introduction to Computers
- Psychology
- Child Psychology
- World Languages

Famous First

Marie Clay (1926-2007), born in New Zealand, was a pioneer in the study of how children acquire literacy. Clay developed a specialized curriculum designed to help children learn to read and to support remedial education for children having reading difficulty and Clay's methods soon spread to Europe and the United States and became standard in reading and writing educational programs. Clay's basic methods, immersing learners in language rich environments and encouraging learning by asking the student to read materials that match their interests, remain cornerstones of reading education.

College/Postsecondary

Reading specialists should pursue college degrees in education, educational theory, or English. In addition to core studies, future professionals will benefit from a varied education that includes classes in sociology, social studies, history, intercultural studies, and one or more world languages. More than half of reading specialists and adult education experts have Master's degrees and undergraduate students should therefore expect to apply for graduate studies in English education, Adult education, or teaching English as a second language depending on the students specific interests. Reading specialist degrees at the Master's level are typically Master's of Education (MEd) degrees.

Related College Majors

- Education
- Education Administration
- English Education
- English Composition
- English Literature
- Communications
- Social Work
- Linguistics
- English as a Second Language

Adult Job Seekers

Individuals with degrees in English or teaching can apply for open positions, though they may need supplementary training to apply for some positions. Applying for a position as a student teacher or assistant reading specialist may also help prepare individuals for a career in the field. Those with experience in management or education administration may quality for literary coach positions and other supervisory roles, while those with backgrounds in literature and English composition/analysis may qualify for starting positions as reading tutors or remedial reading teachers.

Professional Certification and Licensure

In some states, individuals working as reading coaches or specialists may be required to obtain and maintain a teaching license. The qualifications and process of obtaining a teaching license varies by state but typically involve participating in a class and passing a test administered by a state educational institution. Typically, a Bachelor's degree is needed before applying for admission to a teachers training program.

Additional Requirements

Reading specialists should have excellent communications skills, including the ability to compose and give public presentations, the ability to communicate with individuals from vastly different linguistic and cultural backgrounds, and comfort working with peers and subordinates in either training or collaborative working situations. Cultural sensitivity, and the ability to connect with and understand individuals with different linguistic backgrounds and from different socioeconomic groups is an essential skill for a reading specialist. In addition, reading specialists should be patient and exhibit creativity when crafting lessons or working with students.

Fun Fact

Move over, meditation. Reading can reduce stress by 68 in people with elevated heart rates and stress levels. Researchers believe that's because reading focuses the mind. As the saying goes: Get lost in a book!

Source: http://www.telegraph.co.uk

EARNINGS AND ADVANCEMENT

The average salary for a reading specialist can vary widely depending on the specifics of the position and the region. The website Payscale.com lists the average salary for a reading specialist at approximately $49,000 annually, with a range of $30-40,000 for those beginning in the field. The Bureau of Labor Statistics (BLS) estimates the average salary for Adult Literacy and High School Equivalency Diploma Teachers, a category that includes reading specialists, at approximately $50,280 in 2015, with the highest 10 percent earning in excess of $80,000 annually, while the lowest 10 percent earn less than $30,000 per year. According to the BLS, the highest payrates are provided by elementary and secondary schools, followed by colleges and universities. Junior colleges, private and alternative educational institutions and social outreach/assistance positions typically pay less on average. Because some reading specialists work only on off hours, such as mornings, evenings, nights, and weekends, part-time work is common in the field.

Metropolitan Areas with the Highest Employment Level in this Occupation

Metropolitan area	Employment	Employment per thousand jobs	Hourly mean wage
New York-Jersey City-White Plains, NY-NJ	3,590	0.55	$32.22
Seattle-Bellevue-Everett, WA	2,960	1.93	$27.21
Houston-The Woodlands-Sugar Land, TX	2,530	0.86	$28.58
Los Angeles-Long Beach-Glendale, CA	1,710	0.42	$35.48
Anaheim-Santa Ana-Irvine, CA	1,520	1.00	$25.92
Chicago-Naperville-Arlington Heights, IL	1,470	0.41	$31.14
Boston-Cambridge-Newton, MA	930	0.53	$19.83
Washington-Arlington-Alexandria, DC-VA-MD-WV	930	0.38	$26.27
Minneapolis-St. Paul-Bloomington, MN-WI	890	0.47	$19.71
Tampa-St. Petersburg-Clearwater, FL	830	0.69	$24.25

Source: Bureau of Labor Statistics

EMPLOYMENT AND OUTLOOK

The Bureau of Labor predicts 7 percent growth for the adult literacy industry, which includes reading specialists, and indicates average growth overall. Reductions in U.S. immigration, as a result of changes in immigration policy and shifting preferences among immigrants, have reduced the need for ESL reading specialists and teachers. Federal and state governments provide funding for reading education and the rise in charter schools in the United States has provided new opportunities for reading specialists. Some of the more promising metropolitan areas for reading specialists, especially in the adult education field, have seen job growth rates of as much as 14 percent, which is above average for all professions. To maximize job outlook and salary, prospective reading specialists may want to research the most active environments in the field and consider relocating for better opportunities.

Employment Trend, Projected 2014–24

Reading specialist: 12%

Education, training, and library occupations: 8%

Total, all occupations: 7%

Note: "All Occupations" includes all occupations in the U.S. Economy. Source: U.S. Bureau of Labor Statistics, Employment Projections Program

Related Occupations
- High School Teachers
- ESL Teachers
- Kindergarten and Elementary School Teachers
- Instructional Coordinators
- Librarians
- Middle School Teachers
- School and Career Counselors
- Social Workers
- Special Education Teachers
- Teacher Assistants

Related Military Occupations
- Military Language Specialist

Conversation With . . .
HEIDI CASEY

Certified Reading Specialist, K-12, Consultant
San Francisco, Califonia
Reading specialist, 20 years

1. What was your individual career path in terms of education/training, entry-level job, or other significant opportunity?

I wanted to be a teacher so, in college, I took basic elementary education. While there, I had the opportunity to study a new reading program called the Collaborative Literacy Intervention Project (CLIP). I was fortunate to be encouraged to become a CLIP specialist. I trained for a year through Arizona State University, and then was assigned a position as a CLIP teacher.

After working as a reading specialist for several years, I was confident in my ability and felt knowledgeable enough to train other staff members in the program. My husband used to be transferred a lot so I had to leave several jobs. But it was often easy to find a new one because my skills were in demand. One time, I was offered a job over the phone before we even moved.

2. What are the most important skills and/or qualities for someone in your profession?

Flexibility, patience, and the wisdom to recognize that each child is different. You also have to use bits of different methods sometimes. Since I've taught in so many school districts, I've been trained in various modes and that's given me the ability to use parts of each in creating reading intervention programs. I've always been open to the possibilities of new techniques but it takes time to see what works. Over the years, I've taken concepts that have been proven to work and added them to my reading program.

3. What do you wish you had known going into this profession?

I wish I'd known more about how each situation can be so unique. We must take into account the varied learning styles and adapt them for each student. A teacher needs to do some investigative work into what type of learning mode is best for a particular student. I believe learning differentiated education is a big bonus for any educator. It is not a one-size-fits-all situation.

4. Are there many job opportunities in your profession? In what specific areas?

Years ago, reading specialists were in high demand. I had no problems securing a position even though we moved around the country. But in 2009, I lost my job because of budget cuts in California. So did other specialized teachers. Classroom teachers were forced to try to meet the needs of at-risk readers while juggling everything else. That trend now seems to be reversing some.

5. How do you see your profession changing in the next five years, what role will technology play in those changes, and what skills will be required?

I see the profession taking a turn with the use of online programs in the classroom and with tutors and private companies servicing students in their homes. I know several online reading tutors who are adept at providing assistance online. Many of these professionals can tailor their home-based business to fit the needs of the student. Anyone contemplating this needs to be familiar with the standards and reading adoption program that the student is using at school. Consistency is very important. There also needs to be ongoing communication with the parent and the classroom teacher.

6. What do you enjoy most about your job? What do you enjoy least about your job?

I can think of no greater reward than to see non-readers become self-confident and acknowledge the fact that they can now read. It's a great gift. Many of my students continue to remember me with thank you cards and mention my name when they have successes.

On the down side, I'd have to say the struggle is with keeping the parent engaged throughout the tutoring process. The program works best when there is complete follow-through in the home.

7. Can you suggest a valuable "try this" for students considering a career in your profession?

I would suggest visiting several schools and observing their reading programs. Interested students could also shadow a reading specialist, take an in-depth look at test scores to see where weak areas lie within the reading component, and research online reading programs. Students could also look at standardized test scores in the language arts area. That can give great insight into what area needs the most work. That's always my most valuable tool.

MORE INFORMATION

American Federation of Teachers
555 New Jersey Ave., NW
Washington, DC 20001
www.aft.org

International Literacy Association
PO Box 8139
Newark DE 19714
www.literacyworldwide.org

National Council of Teachers of English (NCTE)
1111 W. Kenyon Road
Urbana, Illinois, 61801
www.ncte.org

American Association for Applied Linguistics (AAAL)
1827 Powers Ferry Road, Building 14
Suite 100
Atlanta, Georgia, 30339
www.aaal.org

National Education Association
1201 16th Street, NW
Washington, DC 20036
www.nea.org

Micah Issitt/Editor

Recreation Program Director

Snapshot

Career Cluster: Hospitality & Tourism; Human Services; Sports & Entertainment

Interests: Physical education, recreational activities, planning events and programs

Earnings (Yearly Average): $48,215

Employment & Outlook: Faster Than Average Growth Expected

OVERVIEW

Sphere of Work

Recreation program directors work for private institutions as well as municipalities, developing and coordinating recreation needs for residents and visitors, including children, seniors, and adults. Recreation program directors develop these recreation programs by assessing community or service audience recreation needs; hiring and evaluating recreation workers and additional staff; overseeing the safety and maintenance of grounds, equipment, and facilities; promoting the recreation program to the community; planning events; scheduling programs; keeping records on program

happenings and staff; and fundraising through direct solicitation and grant-writing. Recreation program directors manage both public and private recreation programs through a variety of host agencies or institutions such as schools, camps, resorts, public agencies, retirement facilities, and hospitals.

Work Environment

Recreation program directors spend their workdays overseeing recreation programs in a wide variety of indoor and outdoor settings, including schools, public recreation centers, private resorts, indoor childcare centers, playgrounds, sports fields, swimming pools, residential facilities, or day camps. A recreation program director's work environment may involve extremes of heat, cold, or noise. Given the diverse demands of the recreation profession, recreation program directors may need to work a combination of days, evenings, weekends, vacation, and summer hours to ensure program success.

Profile

Working Conditions: Work Both Indoors and Outdoors
Physical Strength: Light Work
Education Needs:
Technical/Community College, Bachelor's Degree
Licensure/Certification:
Recommended
Physical Abilities Not Required: No Heavy Labor
Opportunities For Experience:
Internship, Military Service Part-Time Work
Holland Interest Score*: ESA

* See Appendix A

Occupation Interest

Individuals drawn to the recreation field tend to be charismatic, intelligent, and organized people who have the ability to quickly assess situations, utilize resources, and solve problems. Successful recreation program directors are responsible leaders who display effective time management skills, a strong sense of initiative, and a concern for individuals and society. Recreation program directors should enjoy physical activity and spending time with a wide range of people, including those with special needs and those from diverse cultural, social, and educational backgrounds.

A Day in the Life—Duties and Responsibilities

The daily occupational duties and responsibilities of recreation program directors will be determined by the individual's area of job specialization and work environment. Recreation program directors must be able to assess the recreational needs and abilities of individuals, groups, or the local community. Before their busy season, they typically spend time interviewing, hiring, and evaluating recreation workers and staff, including food service workers and maintenance crews. They spend a portion of each day supervising seasonal and full-time recreation workers, such as lifeguards, coaches, and activity leaders, and overseeing the safety, upkeep, and maintenance of grounds, equipment, and facilities. Recreation program directors promote the recreation program to the local community through flyers, websites, e-mails, and press releases. They also plan and schedule program events such as tournaments, nature studies, leagues, dances, team sports, and classes, and periodically brainstorm new ways to recruit volunteers for all aspects of the recreation program. Conducting program assessment and evaluation through surveys and feedback requests is one way in which recreation program directors can gain an understanding of the success of their programming.

Recreation program directors have many legal, financial, and administrative responsibilities, such as ensuring that their recreation program meets national requirements for safety and the Americans with Disabilities Act, planning the short-term and long-term recreation program budget, and conducting background checks on staff, volunteers, and contractors. Recreation directors are sometimes responsible for raising money for programming through grant-writing, fundraising, and donation requests. Part of the job involves keeping the recreation program in the public eye so that it will continue to attract patrons and contributions. The recreation program director may represent the recreation program at conferences and meetings, including local and national recreation society meetings, or meet periodically with institutional supervisors, such as parks and recreation department commissioners, facility owners, or other stakeholders.

All recreation program directors are responsible for accurate record keeping on program safety, accidents, and staff performance.

Duties and Responsibilities

- Developing and overseeing recreational programs
- Setting up schedules and activities
- Soliciting financial resources
- Coordinating human resources
- Directing specialized activities and events
- Publicizing and promoting programs to the community
- Maintaining facilities in good working order
- Ensuring safety of all patrons and staff
- Dealing with emergencies as necessary

WORK ENVIRONMENT

Physical Environment

The immediate physical environment of recreation program directors varies based on the program's focus and location. Recreation program directors spend their workdays coordinating activities in a wide variety of settings including schools, public recreation centers, indoor childcare centers, ice skating rinks, hospitals, playgrounds, sports fields, pools and aquatic centers, residential facilities, or day camps. Most recreation directors spend part of their work day outdoors, but the majority of their time is spent inside an office.

Human Environment

Recreation program directors work with a wide variety of people and should be comfortable meeting with colleagues, supervisors, program benefactors, staff, children, the elderly, people with physical disabilities, and families. Because they represent the program to the public and function in a supervisory or administrative role, they should enjoy meeting new people and spending much of their job managing others. Excellent communication skills are an advantage.

Relevant Skills and Abilities

Communication Skills
- Promoting an idea
- Speaking effectively

Interpersonal/Social Skills
- Asserting oneself
- Being sensitive to others
- Motivating others

Organization & Management Skills
- Coordinating tasks
- Demonstrating leadership
- Managing people/groups

Other Skills
- Being physically active

Technological Environment

Recreation program directors must be comfortable using computers to access information and records, Internet communication tools for e-mail, social media, and program websites, and cell phones to ensure availability during on-call hours or in case of an emergency. Those recreation program directors coordinating a specialized recreation program, such as metalworking or a ropes course, may also need to be comfortable training others in the use of techniques they have just learned themselves. They should be certified in CPR and other lifesaving techniques, and be at ease using related equipment.

EDUCATION, TRAINING, AND ADVANCEMENT

High School/Secondary

High school students interested in pursuing a career as a recreation program director should prepare themselves by developing good study habits. High school study of physical education, foreign language, public safety, sociology, psychology, and education will provide a strong foundation for work as a recreation program director or college-level work in the field. High school students interested in this career path will benefit from seeking part-time or seasonal work that exposes the students to diverse groups of people and recreational activities. They can also obtain certification in lifesaving techniques through their school or town.

Suggested High School Subjects
- Accounting
- Algebra
- Applied Communication

- Arts
- Business
- Business Law
- Business Math
- Crafts
- English
- Physical Education
- Social Studies

Famous First

The first summer camp for boys was Camp Comfort in Milford, Conn, established in 1861. It was founded by Frederick William Gunn, founder of The Gunnery prep school. The camp took 50 boys on a two-week camping trip. Today there are about 7,000 overnight camps and 5,000 day camps in the United States; together they serve over 10 million children.

College/Postsecondary

Postsecondary students interested in becoming recreation program directors should earn an associate's or bachelor's degree in recreation or physical education. A small number of colleges (accredited by the National Recreation and Park Association) offer the bachelor's of parks and recreation degree. Courses in physical education, education, public safety, business management, accounting, and foreign languages may also prove useful in future recreation work. Postsecondary students can gain work experience and potential advantage in their future job searches by securing internships or part-time employment in parks and recreation departments or private recreation programs.

Related College Majors
- Adapted Physical Education/Therapeutic Recreation
- Parks, Recreation & Leisure Facilities Management
- Parks, Recreation & Leisure Studies
- Physical Education Teaching & Coaching
- Sport & Fitness Administration/Management

Adult Job Seekers

Adults seeking employment as recreation program directors should have, at a minimum, an associate's or bachelor's degree in recreation or a related field and extensive program directing experience. Some recreation programs require their directors to hold a master's degree and second language proficiency. Adult job seekers should educate themselves about the educational and professional license requirements of their home states and the organizations where they seek employment, and may benefit from joining professional associations that offer help with networking and job searches. Professional recreation associations, such as the American Camping Association and the Society of State Directors of Health, Physical Education & Recreation, generally offer job-finding workshops and maintain lists and forums of available jobs.

Professional Certification and Licensure

Professional certification and licensure is not required of general recreation program directors. Directors of specialized recreation programs, such as swimming or parks and recreation, may be required to earn specialized certification as a condition of employment. Lifeguard certification, pool operations certification, and CPR/First Aid certification is offered by the American Lifeguard Association and requires coursework and passing an examination. The National Recreation and Park Association (NRPA) certificate is offered in therapeutic recreation, park management, outdoor recreation, industrial or commercial recreation, and camp management. It also requires a bachelor's degree or its equivalent in education and work experience, as well as passing a national examination. Ongoing professional education is required for continued certification in both lifesaving techniques and NRPA disciplines.

Additional Requirements

Successful recreation program directors will be knowledgeable about the profession's requirements, responsibilities, and opportunities. High levels of integrity and personal and professional ethics are required of recreation program directors, as professionals in this role interact with staff in subordinate roles and have access to personal information. Membership in professional recreation associations is encouraged among all recreation program directors as a means of building status within a professional community and networking.

In most states, the names of those people working in the field of recreation are almost always required to be submitted for a criminal record check. This includes employees, volunteers, and those delivering special programs.

EARNINGS AND ADVANCEMENT

Recreation program directors advance based on their experience. Certification by the National Recreation and Park Association helps advancement. Recreation program directors had mean annual earnings of $48,215 in 2012.

Recreation program directors may receive paid vacations, holidays, and sick days; life and health insurance; and retirement benefits. These are usually paid by the employer.

Metropolitan Areas with the Highest Employment Level in this Occupation (Recreation Workers)

Metropolitan area	Employment	Employment per thousand jobs	Hourly mean wage[1]
New York-White Plains-Wayne, NY-NJ	15,200	2.95	$14.66
Chicago-Joliet-Naperville, IL	10,870	2.99	$12.02
Los Angeles-Long Beach-Glendale, CA	9,640	2.49	$12.21
Washington-Arlington-Alexandria, DC-VA-MD-WV	4,680	1.99	$14.80
Oakland-Fremont-Hayward, CA	4,080	4.20	$13.39
Phoenix-Mesa-Glendale, AZ	4,030	2.33	$12.63
Boston-Cambridge-Quincy, MA	3,980	2.32	$12.20
Philadelphia, PA	3,900	2.14	$13.15

[1]Figures are for all recreation workers, not specifically for directors. Source: Bureau of Labor Statistics

EMPLOYMENT AND OUTLOOK

Recreation workers, of which recreation program directors are a part, held about 310,000 jobs nationally in 2012. About one-third worked in the park and recreation departments of local governments. About another one-fourth worked in nursing and residential care facilities and civic and social organizations, such as the Boy Scouts or Girl Scouts or the YMCA/YWCA. Employment is expected to grow about as fast as the average for all occupations through the year 2022, which means employment is projected to increase 10 percent to 19 percent. This is primarily due to people spending more time and money on recreation. However, employment growth may be limited by budget constraints facing State and local governments over the next decade.

Employment Trend, Projected 2012–22

Personal Care and Service Occupations: 21%

Recreation Workers: 14%

Total, All Occupations: 11%

Note: "All Occupations" includes all occupations in the U.S. Economy. Source: U.S. Bureau of Labor Statistics, Employment Projections Program

Related Occupations
- Fitness Trainer and Aerobics Instructor
- Health Club Manager
- Park Ranger
- Recreation Worker

Related Occupations
- Caseworker & Counselor

Conversation With . . .
DAVID ANDERSON

Recreation Program Director
City of Gatlinburg, Tennessee
Recreation programs, 15 years

1. What was your individual career path in terms of education/training, entry-level job or other significant opportunity?

I went to Lincoln Memorial University in Tennessee where I played Division II baseball and double-majored in physical education/fitness and health. I planned to go into either teaching or recreation. My mom is a teacher and my dad was in recreation. After doing student teaching, I decided recreation was the field for me; I didn't like all the administrative issues the school system has to deal with. And I liked the fact that the people you work with in recreation are there because they want to be there. They're there to have fun, they're there to get healthy, they're there to meet people and make friends.

My first job in the field was as a recreation programmer in Pigeon Forge, Tennessee. I started that in August 2001. The following April, the recreation program director job in Gatlinburg became available and they hired me. I've been here ever since.

2. What are the most important skills and/or qualities for someone in your profession?

It's extremely important to be a people person since you're working with the public and with all age groups. You have to be able to get along with all ages and develop relationships with them. It's important to have knowledge of childhood development. You should also have knowledge about sports although recreation programs encompass more than sports. They also include special events, arts and crafts, summer camps. It's kind of like being a jack of all trades.

3. What do you wish you had known going into this profession?

I wish I'd known that not every program that you put out there is going to be successful. There's a very big difference between running a recreation program in a big city and running one in a small community. I grew up just outside of Toronto. It's a fairly large area and pretty much everything their recreation department offered would become full almost immediately. That's not the case in a smaller community. You really have to work hard to present the best programs available and if something is successful you need to stick with it.

4. Are there many job opportunities in your profession? In what specific areas?

There are definitely job opportunities. It kind of varies and a lot depends on how willing you are to relocate. I would say there are upwards of 50-100 job openings always posted on the National Recreation and Park Association's website. So there are definitely opportunities, especially for people coming out of college. There are lots of internships and lots of entry-level jobs. The higher-level jobs generally don't turn over as much as the others.

5. How do you see your profession changing in the next five years, what role will technology play in those changes and what skills will be required?

We are using social media and technology more to get the word out about our programs and to do registrations. The internet has simplified the registration process. But I don't see the job requirements changing much or technology becoming a bigger factor. We're kind of the alternative to technology because the programs and events we offer are usually outdoors and connected to physical activity. We don't need to be experts in technology.

6. What do you enjoy most about your job? What do you enjoy least about it?

I love that I get to work with different populations and different age groups and in different activities. I meet people from all walks of life. That's a lot of fun. But it can be challenging when a person has a problem with some aspect of a program – for example, if someone has a complaint about a referee. It can also be disheartening if you think a program is going to be tremendously successful and no one signs up. But I love my job and I'm excited to come to work every day. I don't know if a lot of people can say that.

7. Can you suggest a valuable "try this" for students considering a career in your profession?

Internships are a terrific means of getting experience in the field. Other excellent ways to gain experience include getting involved with intramural leagues and volunteering at summer camps, races and similar community activities.

SELECTED SCHOOLS

Many community colleges and four-year colleges and universities offer programs in physical education; a number of them also offer programs in parks and recreation management, arts and crafts management, and related fields. Interested student are advised to consult with a school guidance counselor.

MORE INFORMATION

American Academy for Park and Recreation Administration
P.O. Box 1040
Mahomet, IL 61853
217.586.3360
www.aapra.org

American Alliance for Health, Physical Education, Recreation & Dance
1900 Association Drive
Reston, VA 20192-1598
800.213.7193
www.aahperd.org

American Camping Association
5000 State Road 67 North
Martinsville, IN 46151
765.342.8456
www.acacamps.org

American Lifeguard Association
8300 Boone Boulevard, 5th Floor
Vienna, VA 22182
703.761.6750
www.americanlifeguard.com

Employee Services Management Association
P.O. Box 10517
Rockville, MD 20849
www.esmassn.org

National Council for Therapeutic Recreation Certification
7 Elmwood Drive
New City, NY 10956
845.639.1439
nctrc@NCTRC.org
www.nctrc.org

National Recreation and Park Association
22377 Belmont Ridge Road
Ashburn, VA 20148-4501
800.626.6772
www.nrpa.org

Society of State Directors of Health, Physical Educ. & Recreation
1900 Association Drive, Suite 100
Reston, VA 20191-1599
703.390.4599
www.thesociety.org

YMCA of the USA
101 N. Wacker Drive
Chicago, IL 60606
800.872.9622
www.ymca.net

Simone Isadora Flynn/Editor

Religious Activities & Education Director

Snapshot

Career Cluster: Human Services

Interests: Religious studies, social services, social work, psychology, education

Earnings (Yearly Average): $38,160

Employment & Outlook: Average Growth Expected

OVERVIEW

Sphere of Work

Religious activities and education directors work within spiritual communities. These communities are made up of people with a shared religion or spiritual belief system. They are often centered on a single church, mosque, temple, or other place of worship. Directors organize group functions such as community meals and fundraisers.

They also coordinate enrollment, staffing, and curriculums for faith-based education initiatives. While some religious activities and education directors are spiritual leaders or clergy members, it is not a requirement of the job. However, most directors share the faith or religious doctrine of the community they serve.

Work Environment

The work environment of a religious activities and education director varies. Directors can work at churches, temples, mosques, or other places of worship. Many work out of an office in or near a religious facility. Directors hold events in various locations, including cafeterias, meeting halls, libraries, and conference centers. The job's work environment can also include outdoor facilities such as parks and campgrounds.

Profile

Working Conditions: Work Indoors
Physical Strength: Light Work
Education Needs: Junior/ Technical/Community College, Bachelor's Degree
Licensure/Certification: Usually Not Required
Physical Abilities Not Required: No Heavy Labor
Opportunities For Experience: Volunteer Work, Part-Time Work
Holland Interest Score*: SEA

* See Appendix A

Occupation Interest

Any person interested in becoming a religious activities and education director should feel a strong allegiance to the spiritual denomination they wish to serve. A commitment to social services and education is equally important. Directors should possess administrative skills and enjoy working with others. Leadership skills are essential.

A Day in the Life—Duties and Responsibilities

The work of a religious activities and education director varies from day to day. A director's day often begins with a staff meeting to ensure that all projects and operations are running smoothly. These projects include religious-education classes, volunteer programs, and outreach missions. Some directors conduct various administrative duties related to their congregation, which can include updating community websites, sending e-mails, and making schedules for teachers, students, and clergy. Other directors manage charity initiatives such as fundraisers, meal programs for the homeless, and health clinics.

Some directors are responsible for oversight of family- or marriage-counseling services and substance-abuse programs. Activities and education directors also manage group programs such as summer camps and spiritual retreats for members of their community. They also recruit volunteers and conduct project-specific training seminars.

Duties and Responsibilities

- **Assisting in worship services**
- **Sharing in decision-making of the church or community**
- **Teaching and counseling**
- **Visiting in homes or institutions**
- **Planning and working at medical, educational, agricultural and social activities**
- **Fund-raising for charitable activities**

WORK ENVIRONMENT

Physical Environment

Religious activities and education directors work at religious facilities or in general social-service settings, such as schools, hospitals, and charitable institutions. Some work may be done outdoors at parks and summer camps. Outreach work can take place in cities and towns of varying size.

Relevant Skills and Abilities

Interpersonal/Social Skills
- Cooperating with others
- Working as a member of a team

Organization & Management Skills
- Coordinating tasks
- Demonstrating leadership
- Managing people/groups

Human Environment

Religious activities and education directors work in a community of people joined by a common religious faith. They work in groups of varying size and work one-on-one with clergy members, teachers, students, and volunteers.

Directors work regularly with fellow worshippers and the business community.

Technological Environment

Contemporary office and communications technology is part of the job of a religious activities and education director. Basic computer skills are required, and knowledge of social media is important.

EDUCATION, TRAINING, AND ADVANCEMENT

High School/Secondary

Many religious denominations do not require any formal education of their religious activities and education directors. In this case, personal charisma, religious commitment, basic literacy, and dedication to the work are the only requirements. In other religious settings, a formal education or religious education is preferred or required.

High school students interested in a career as a religious activities and education director should take classes in the humanities, especially English, philosophy, and history. Classes in political science and psychology are also beneficial. Foreign languages can be useful, as well as classes in instrumental and vocal music, as music is often a part of spiritual activities.

In addition to secular studies, a person should study the religion of their choice or calling. This is done through attending religious teachings offered at churches, synagogues, mosques, madrassas, temples, shrines, or other religious facilities.

Suggested High School Subjects
- College Preparatory
- English
- Foreign Languages
- History

- Humanities
- Instrumental & Vocal Music
- Mathematics
- Philosophy
- Political Science
- Psychology
- Social Studies

Famous First

The first religious activities specialists in the military emerged during World War II, when it was recognized that, in addition to the spiritual activities performed by chaplains, work was needed in the area of supplying services such as musical direction, audio-visual aids, and clerical support.

College/Postsecondary

Some churches and religious denominations require that activities and education directors have some form of postsecondary education. Individuals interested in the profession can consider advanced degree programs in education, religious studies, or social work. In the United States, a degree in religious studies provides a solid basis for work for in many Christian denominations. Similarly, a degree in Jewish studies or Islamic studies can prepare individuals for work in these religions. A bachelor's degree in sociology provides a secular foundation on which those interested in religious work can build. A master's degree in any of the above subjects can prepare a person for an advanced career as a religious activities and education director. Other postsecondary education options include doctoral programs in education, religious studies, sociology, or social work.

Related College Majors
- Bible/Biblical Studies
- Pastoral Counseling & Specialized Ministries
- Religion/Religious Studies

- Religious Education
- Theology/Theological Studies

Adult Job Seekers

Adult job seekers interested in a career as a religious activities and education director should have a background in teaching, social work, or administrative work. Doing volunteer work at a religious institution is a good way to become qualified for an official position. Experience in community service is also a plus. Many religious denominations welcome adult job seekers who experience a calling to become active in religious work. In some cases, being of strong spiritual conviction is considered as important as formal education, training, or job experience.

Professional Certification and Licensure

The job of a religious activities and education director does not require any professional certification or licensure. However, if a director engages in accounting, social work, counseling, or teaching, some professional credentials may be required depending on state and national regulations.

Additional Requirements

As their work is dedicated to serving and reaching out to people, religious activities and education directors need strong interpersonal skills. They must be compassionate and have an interest in social services.

EARNINGS AND ADVANCEMENT

Earnings depend on the type and geographic location of the employer, the type of work performed and the individual's amount of responsibility, academic preparation and experience. Median annual earnings of religious activities and education directors were $38,160 in 2013.

Religious activities and education directors may receive paid vacations, holidays, and sick days; life and health insurance; and retirement benefits. These are usually paid by the employer. Some employers may also provide free housing, use of an automobile, allowances for travel, and educational reimbursements.

Metropolitan Areas with the Highest Employment Level in this Occupation

Metropolitan area	Employment[1]	Employment per thousand jobs	Hourly mean wage
New York-White Plains-Wayne, NY-NJ	1,120	0.21	$21.98
Portland-Vancouver-Hillsboro, OR-WA	1,040	1.01	$19.97
Chicago-Joliet-Naperville, IL	610	0.17	$21.24
Philadelphia, PA	610	0.33	$24.95
Nassau-Suffolk, NY	540	0.43	$21.25
Washington-Arlington-Alexandria, DC-VA-MD-WV	480	0.20	$31.52
Los Angeles-Long Beach-Glendale, CA	450	0.11	$31.08
Warren-Troy-Farmington Hills, MI	440	0.40	$15.39
San Diego-Carlsbad-San Marcos, CA	380	0.29	$31.62
Atlanta-Sandy Springs-Marietta, GA	340	0.15	$19.14

[1] Does not include self-employed. Source: Bureau of Labor Statistics

EMPLOYMENT AND OUTLOOK

Nationally, there were about 10,000 religious activities and education directors employed in 2012. Employment is expected to grow about as fast as the average for all occupations through the year 2022, which means employment is projected to increase 8 percent to 114 percent.

Employment Trend, Projected 2010–20

Community and Social Service Occupations: 17%

Religious Activities and Education Directors: 12%

Total, All Occupations: 11%

Note: "All Occupations" includes all occupations in the U.S. Economy. Source: U.S. Bureau of Labor Statistics, Employment Projections Program

Related Occupations
- Clergy
- Marriage & Family Therapist
- School Counselor
- Social & Human Service Assistant
- Social Worker
- Substance Abuse Counselor

Conversation With . . .
ADINA NEWMAN

Religious Activities and Educational Director
Religious School Director, Maryland Synagogue, 6 months
In the Education field, 15 years

1. What was your individual career path in terms of education/training, entry-level job, or other significant opportunity?

I started teaching 3 and 4 year olds in religious school before my bat mitzvah, on Saturday mornings at my local synagogue. I made a little money and kept up my skill set going into college, when I continued to teach and became a professional Torah reader to prepare students for their bar and bat mitzvahs. I majored in education at Boston University, got a master's in education policy & management policy at Harvard University, and another master's in elementary education at Brandeis University. I'm currently working toward a doctorate in educational administration and policy studies at George Washington University.

After I got my master's degrees, I was a curriculum designer for a publishing company. But I felt I needed the "street cred" — to be in the classroom — so I left to teach fifth grade for a couple of years in public schools.

I'm a person who tries things out. I tried curriculum and liked that; I taught, and liked that. Now, I oversee K-10 in a synagogue's religious school that meets Sundays and Wednesdays. We instill a sense of Jewish identity and community in students, and prepare for b'nai mitzvah. This job is part-time and works for my family because my husband and I have a baby. I also like the challenge of this job. I hire teachers, oversee the budget, order books, work with the Hebrew curriculum, and ride the wave of what's going on in the school. We also prepare for the High Holy Days in September and the programming that involves. This position is very front-loaded — just like any school — from August through the end of September. Overall, this job has been my goal for awhile, and it's a good fit.

2. What are the most important skills and/or qualities for someone in your profession?

All educators need to have flexibility because something is going to happen: a teacher may call in sick, you may need to sub, a kid might have a behavior issue. You need to be prepared for not being prepared. You need to understand language acquisition, for example, if you want your kids to learn Hebrew. You also need a knowledge of what's happening in your field in traditional schools and in religious schools in general. For example, in a traditional classroom it's understood there are different kinds of learners. A lot of religious schools still rely only on books. Here, your book is a supplement. We create stations and rotate to allow for instruction through multiple modalities so that kids might be doing things that are more tactile, or more visual, because we recognize what's working for different types of learners.

3. What do you wish you had known going into this profession?

In this position, you play therapist to students, teachers and parents. You are a sounding board for them. It's great to be that person people confide in to get the job done, but it's definitely something I did not expect.

4. Are there many job opportunities in your profession? In what specific areas?

There's always going to be some sort of director job somewhere in Jewish education. You need to know where to look, such as New York, Boston, or Florida. There's also Hillel, for higher education.

5. How do you see your profession changing in the next five years, what role will technology play in those changes, and what skills will be required?

Technology is of utmost importance. Right now, we are working on finding a way to get iPads. That's how the kids are learning in their traditional schools, and that's how you're going to get them through the door. Kids don't have to come here. In some cases, kids have been at their traditional school all day and they come here for two hours on a Wednesday night and we need to keep them engaged. Technology is the best way.

6. What do you enjoy most about your job? What do you enjoy least about your job?

I definitely like going down the hall, checking the classrooms and seeing the kids having a good time. That's wonderful. Unfortunately, we just don't have enough time to do what we want to do. In winter, for instance, we have snow days, and they hurt consistency and continuity.

7. Can you suggest a valuable "try this" for students considering a career in your profession?

A lot of synagogues have opportunities for leading. In classes, we have madrichim, which literally means "leaders," who are teaching assistants. Some synagogues even pay them. If you're in college already, go for it and apply for a position as a teacher. See how you feel about it.

SELECTED SCHOOLS

Many colleges and universities have bachelor's degree programs in counseling and rehabilitation therapy, often with a specialization in occupational therapy. The student may also gain an initial grounding in the field at a technical or community college. Consult with your school guidance counselor or research area post-secondary programs to find the right fit for you. Below are listed some of the more prominent schools in this field.

MORE INFORMATION

Buddhist Churches of America
1710 Octavia Street
San Francisco, CA 94109
415.776.5600
www.buddhistchurchesofamerica.org

Catholic Campus Ministry Association
1118 Pendleton Street, Suite 300
Cincinnati, OH 45202-8805
888.714.6631
www.ccmanet.org

National Association of Temple Educators
633 Third Avenue, 7th Floor
New York, NY 10017-6778
212.452.6510
www.natenet.org

National Council of Churches of Christ in the USA
475 Riverside Drive, Suite 880
New York, NY 10115
212.870.2227
www.ncccusa.org

R. C. Lutz/Editor

School Counselor

Snapshot

Career Cluster: Education & Training; Human Services

Interests: Helping others, working with students, solving problems, human behavior

Earnings (Yearly Average): $53,600

Employment & Outlook: Average Growth Expected

OVERVIEW

Sphere of Work

School counselors, also called guidance counselors or educational counselors, provide educational and career counseling to students from elementary school through the postsecondary level. They may also assist students with their social and personal development, particularly those students with unique abilities and challenges. Most school counselors work from an office located within a school setting, specializing in counseling a particular age range of students; some school counselors specialize in career counseling and work in or maintain offices off campus.

School counselors support students in their efforts to succeed academically and

develop realistic career goals, learn to resolve conflict and develop relationships with peers, and cope with family abuse, addiction, or other health issues. The overall goal of a school counselor is to help students (or other clients) attain the highest possible developmental skill level based on each student's needs and challenges. In the course of their work, the school counselor must also take care to protect each student's right to privacy, and must adhere to strict ethical and legal standards articulated by the American School Counselor Association (ASCA) and the Family Education Rights and Privacy Act (FERPA).

Work Environment

School counselors spend their workdays seeing students in school settings, college and university career counseling offices, job training and placement programs, and private counseling practices. Most school counselors work from a private office within a school or college, although vocational counselors may work independently. Given the diverse demands of school counseling, school counselors may need to work days, evenings, and weekends to meet student, client, or program needs, but in general they should expect to be at work during school hours.

Profile

Working Conditions: Work Indoors
Physical Strength: Light Work
Education Needs: Master's Degree
Licensure/Certification: Required
Physical Abilities Not Required: No Heavy Labor
Opportunities For Experience: Military Service, Volunteer Work
Holland Interest Score*: SAE

* See Appendix A

Occupation Interest

Individuals drawn to the school counseling profession tend to be intelligent and have the ability to quickly assess situations, find resources, and solve problems. Further, they should demonstrate caring and find satisfaction in helping others. Those most successful at the job of school counselor display traits such as time management, knowledge of human behavior, initiative, and concern for individuals and society; they should also be capable of inspiring students' trust, confidence, and respect. School counselors should also be comfortable working with a wide range of people, including those considered at-risk and those from diverse cultural, social, and educational backgrounds.

A Day in the Life—Duties and Responsibilities

The daily occupational duties and responsibilities of school counselors will be determined by the individual's area of job specialization and work environment. Specialties of educational counseling include school counseling, vocational counseling, and college career planning and placement counseling.

A school counselor's primary role is to provide academic, social, and emotional support—both practical and empathetic—to students. Some ways in which a school counselor can accomplish this goal include using scientifically-researched intervention strategies with a student in crisis, helping a student evaluate his or her talents and interests to conceive realistic career goals, and serving as a mentor for students while maintaining the professional distance advised by ASCA ethical guidelines. School counselors, during the course of a day's work, may help a student cope with family issues or problems that are interfering with the student's educational or developmental goals, listen to and share coping strategies with a student who is being bullied by a peer, monitor a peer counseling group, and conduct routine interviews with high school students regarding future college and career goals. Although high school counselors do more career counseling than elementary-level school counselors, both types of students benefit from conversations about which particular careers best fit their emerging talents and abilities.

In addition to the range of responsibilities described above, all school counselors are responsible for completing student and client records and required documentation, such as referral forms, on a daily basis.

Duties and Responsibilities

- Appraising individual's interests, aptitudes, abilities and personality characteristics using records, tests, interviews and professional sources
- Assisting in understanding and overcoming individuals' social and emotional challenges
- Consulting with students, teachers, parents, social workers and other professionals
- Collecting educational, occupational and economic information
- Assisting in personal decisions and the planning and implementation of career decisions

OCCUPATION SPECIALTIES

School Counselors

School Counselors are primarily concerned with the personal and social development of students and with helping them plan and achieve their educational and vocational goals.

Employment Counselors

Employment Counselors are concerned with career planning, placement and adjustment to employment of youths and adults.

College Career Planning and Placement Counselors

College Career Planning and Placement Counselors assist college students in examining their own interests, values, abilities and goals in exploring career alternatives and in making career choices.

WORK ENVIRONMENT

Physical Environment

The immediate physical environment of school counselors varies based on their caseload and specialization. School counselors spend their workdays seeing students in elementary, junior high, and high schools, college and university career counseling offices, job training and placement programs, and private counseling practices.

Human Environment

School counselors work with a wide variety of people and should be comfortable working and talking with children of all ages, although most school counselors eventually focus on a specific age range of students. School counselors frequently interact with students, teachers, colleagues, supervisors, students' parents and other family members, unemployed people, and students living with mental, physical, developmental, or emotional disabilities. The ethical standards upheld by school counselors are strict and specific due to the nature of counseling students under the age of eighteen, and also the fact that some students may experience family abuse or face potential legal issues.

Relevant Skills and Abilities

Communication Skills
- Listening attentively
- Speaking effectively
- Writing concisely

Interpersonal/Social Skills
- Cooperating with others
- Providing support to others
- Working as a member of a team

Organization & Management Skills
- Coordinating tasks
- Demonstrating leadership
- Managing people/groups
- Performing duties that change frequently

Research & Planning Skills
- Analyzing information
- Developing evaluation strategies

Technological Environment

School counselors use a range of telecommunication tools to perform their job and should be comfortable using computers to access student and client records as well as job listings and forums. In addition, school counselors must learn how to maintain confidential records without compromising the privacy or future aspirations of juvenile clients. This may involve using a private recordkeeping system rather than storing information in a computer or database.

EDUCATION, TRAINING, AND ADVANCEMENT

High School/Secondary

High school students interested in pursuing a career as a school counselor should prepare themselves by developing good study habits. The study of foreign languages, public safety, sociology, psychology, and education will provide a strong foundation for work as a school counselor or college-level work in the field. Due to the range of school counseling job requirements, high school students interested in this career path will benefit from seeking internships, volunteer opportunities, or part-time work that expose the students to diverse educational programs and professions.

Suggested High School Subjects
- Child Growth & Development
- College Preparatory
- Composition
- English
- Literature
- Psychology
- Social Studies
- Sociology
- Speech

Famous First

The first person to develop a comprehensive school guidance program was Jesse B. Davis, principal of Grand Rapids Central High School, pictured, in Michigan in 1907. Davis instructed the school's English teachers to have students write weekly essays on topics related to career choice, their plans for the future, or what the model man or woman was like, in their view. In 1913 Davis was made director of vocational guidance for the Grand Rapids school district, and helped found the National Vocational Guidance Association (now the National Career Development Association).

College/Postsecondary

Postsecondary students interested in becoming school counselors should work towards a master's degree in counseling or a related field such as psychology or social work. Classes in education and foreign languages may also prove useful in their future work. Postsecondary students can gain work experience and potential advantage in their future job searches by securing internships or part-time employment in career placement or job training programs.

Related College Majors

- Counselor Education/Student Counseling & Guidance Services
- Psychology

Adult Job Seekers

Adults seeking employment as school counselors should have earned, at a minimum, a bachelor's degree in counseling or related field such as psychology or social work. Employers are increasingly requiring school counselors to have a master's of counseling, school guidance, rehabilitation counseling, or social work and related national certification. Adult job seekers should educate themselves about the educational and professional license requirements of their home states and the organizations where they seek employment. Professional counseling associations, such as the National Employment Counseling Association and the Commission on Rehabilitation Counselor Certification, generally offer career workshops and maintain lists and forums of available jobs.

Professional Certification and Licensure

School counselors should pursue the certification and licensure required of their job specialty. Certification options include school counseling certification, general counseling certification, school guidance certification, rehabilitation counseling certification, mental health counseling certification, or social work certification. School counselors working with students at the elementary, secondary, or college level, for example, may earn the National Certified School Counselor (NCSC) designation or certification awarded by the American School Counselor Association (ASCA). Those earning the NCSC certification will have successfully completed a master's degree in counseling or related field, two years of supervised counseling experience, supervisor references, and the National Counselor Examination for Licensure and Certification examination.

Specific requirements for counselor licensing, including additional coursework, continuing education, and supervised hours, vary by state.

Additional Requirements

Successful school counselors engage in ongoing professional development to maintain their certifications. High levels of integrity and personal and professional ethics are required of school counselors, as individuals in this role serve as a role model and mentor mainly to juveniles and have access to personal information. Membership in professional counseling associations is encouraged among all school counselors as a means of building status within the professional community and networking, and also of maintaining high ethical standards and knowledge of best practices in the field.

Fun Fact

The Teacher of the Year has been recognized in a ceremony at the White House every year since 1952, when President Harry S. Truman initiated the program. But it wasn't until 2015 that the School Counselor of the Year was recognized in a White House ceremony, after First Lady Michelle Obama made good on her promise while working with school counselors on her Reach Higher Initiative.

Sources: https://www.whitehouse.gov/the-press-office/2015/01/30/remarks-first-lady-presentation-school-counselor-year-award

http://www.mea-mft.org/Articles/paul_andersen_is_national_teacher_of_the_year_finalist.aspx

EARNINGS AND ADVANCEMENT

Earnings depend on the type, size, geographic location, and union affiliation of the employer, and the individual's education, experience and specialty. School counselors had median annual earnings of $53,600 in 2013. The lowest ten percent earned less than $31,850, and the highest ten percent earned more than $86,870.

Many school counselors are compensated on the same pay scale as teachers. School counselors can earn additional income working summers in the school system or in other jobs.

School counselors may receive paid vacations, holidays, and sick days; life and health insurance; and retirement benefits. These are usually paid by the employer.

Metropolitan Areas with the Highest Employment Level in this Occupation

Metropolitan area	Employment	Employment per thousand jobs	Hourly mean wage
New York-White Plains-Wayne, NY-NJ	10,650	2.03	$32.69
Los Angeles-Long Beach-Glendale, CA	9,700	2.44	$33.14
Chicago-Joliet-Naperville, IL	5,930	1.60	$31.51
Phoenix-Mesa-Glendale, AZ	4,650	2.61	$23.38
Washington-Arlington-Alexandria, DC-VA-MD-WV	4,630	1.95	$31.86
Houston-Sugar Land-Baytown, TX	4,460	1.62	$26.87
Philadelphia, PA	4,340	2.36	$26.78
Atlanta-Sandy Springs-Marietta, GA	3,530	1.53	$27.86
Dallas-Plano-Irving, TX	3,350	1.56	$27.95
Boston-Cambridge-Quincy, MA	3,270	1.87	$30.42

Source: Bureau of Labor Statistics

EMPLOYMENT AND OUTLOOK

School counselors held about 262,000 jobs nationally in 2013. Employment is expected to grow about as fast as the average for all occupations through the year 2022, which means employment is projected to increase 9 percent to 15 percent. Increasing elementary, middle school and secondary school enrollments and an expansion in the responsibilities of school counselors will all contribute to job growth in this field.

Employment Trend, Projected 2010–20

Community and Social Service Occupations: 17%

School Counselors: 12%

Total, All Occupations: 11%

Note: "All Occupations" includes all occupations in the U.S. Economy. Source: U.S. Bureau of Labor Statistics, Employment Projections Program

Related Occupations
- Clergy
- Employment Specialist
- Healthcare Social Worker
- Marriage & Family Therapist
- Parole & Probation Officer
- Psychologist
- Rehabilitation Counselor
- Religious Activities & Education Director
- Social & Human Service Assistant
- Social Worker
- Substance Abuse Counselor
- Vocational Rehabilitation Counselor

Related Military Occupations
- Personnel Specialist

Conversation With . . .
TAWNYA W. PRINGLE

School Counselor
Hoover High School, San Diego
School Counselor, 27 years

1. What was your individual career path in terms of education/training, entry-level job, or other significant opportunity?

My career path consisted of working with teenagers in a residential treatment facility right after I graduated with my bachelor's degree in psychology. I had also done some volunteer work at a crisis line near San Diego State University, where I went to school. While I was in graduate school, I had a part-time job as a guidance assistant in an elementary school, which also served as my internship for the field of school counseling. Now I work as a school counselor in The Academy of Literature, Media and Arts (ALMA) at Hoover High in San Diego. One hundred percent of students in the school qualify for free or reduced lunch.

2. What are the most important skills and/or qualities for someone in your profession?

To be an excellent school counselor, you must have a passion for helping youth; the ability to be an agent of change within a school; the ability to work with parents as well as school staff and administration; good presentation skills; and cultural sensitivity. It's a plus if you are bilingual.

3. What do you wish you had known going into this profession?

I wish I had more training in the areas of working with special needs students and how to collect data effectively. I took statistics, but when I went to graduate school, school data collection wasn't taught; it is now. The reason it's important is that it gives staff and parents a way to quantify and measure results.

4. Are there many job opportunities in your profession? In what specific areas?

There are school counseling positions in some states and, hopefully, with the new emphasis on school counseling, there will be more. In July 2014, First Lady Michelle

Obama spoke at the American School Counselor Association's annual conference and said, "School counseling is a necessity to ensure that all our young people get the education they need to succeed in today's economy."

Usually, there are more jobs at the middle and high school levels than at the elementary level. Elementary school counselors tend to play a preventive role.

5. **How do you see your profession changing in the next five years? What role will technology play in those changes, and what skills will be required?**

    In the next five years, school counseling will continue to move forward in the area of gathering data for the purposes of improving student success and closing the achievement gap. In addition, there is now a strong emphasis on preparing students to be college- and career-ready with the skills necessary to compete in a global society. School counselors will need to have additional training in preparing students for the post-secondary school world and in career exploration for all fields. Technology will be used to gather and analyze data that is relevant to student achievement. It also will continue to change and improve the efficiency of how we communicate with parents, students and other staff.

6. **What do you enjoy most about your job? What do you enjoy least about your job?**

    I love my job as a school counselor. Every day I feel lucky that I get to be a student advocate for high school youth from all cultures. I love the fact that I can be a part of making their dreams come true. I love helping at-risk students refuse to give up and helping them to realize that education in empowering!

    The one part of my job that I most dislike has to do with hand-counting credits when I am doing transcript reviews. Still today, there is no technology out there that will do this for you. It's exhausting and although you do it only a couple of times a school year, when your caseload is 450 students, it's hard not to make mistakes.

7. **Can you suggest a valuable "try this" for students considering a career in your profession?**

    I would advise working in a school setting, shadowing a school counselor at every level (elementary, middle and high school) for a few days in a row, and also working in a culturally diverse area. Any type of customer service job is good because you get exposure to all kinds of people. Almost any type of experience you have working around students between the ages of 5 and 18 would be valuable.

SELECTED SCHOOLS

Many colleges and universities have bachelor's degree programs in education; some offer a specialization in school counseling. The student may also gain an initial grounding in the field at a technical or community college. Consult with your school guidance counselor or research post-secondary programs in your area. Below are listed some of the more prominent schools in this field.

Ohio State University
Columbus, OH 43210
614.292.6446
www.osu.edu

Penn State University
University Park
State College, PA 16801
814.865.4700
www.psu.edu

University of Central Florida
4000 Central Florida Boulevard
Orlando, FL 32816
407.823.2000
www.ucf.edu

University of Florida
Gainesville, FL 32611
352.392.3261
www.ufl.edu

University of Georgia
Athens, GA 30602
706.542.3000
www.uga.edu

University of Maryland
College Park, MD 20742
301.405.1000
www.umd.edu

University of Minnesota
Minneapolis, MN 55455
612.625.5000
www.umn.edu

University of Missouri
Columbia, MO 65211
573.882.2121
missouri.edu

University of North Carolina, Greensboro
1400 Spring Garden Street
Greensboro, NC 27412
336.334.5000
www.uncg.edu

University of Wisconsin
Madison, WI 53706
608.263.2400
www.wisc.edu

MORE INFORMATION

American Counseling Association
5999 Stevenson Avenue
Alexandria, VA 22304
800.347.6647
www.counseling.org

American School Counselor Association
1101 King Street, Suite 625
Alexandria, VA 22314
800.306.4722
www.schoolcounselor.org

International Vocational Education and Training Association
186 Wedgewood Drive
Mahtomedi, MN 55115
www.iveta.org

National Career Development Association
305 N. Beech Circle
Broken Arrow, OK 74012
918.663.7060
www.ncda.org

National Organization for Human Services
1600 Sarno Road, Suite 16
Melbourne, FL 32935
www.nationalhumanservices.org

Simone Isadora Flynn/Editor

Secondary & Middle School Teacher

Snapshot

Career Cluster(s): Education & Training

Interests: Teaching, lesson planning, leading instructional activities, adolescent development, student safety, peer mentoring

Earnings (Yearly Average): $57,200 (high school); $55,860 (middle school)

Employment & Outlook: Average Growth Expected

OVERVIEW

Sphere of Work

Secondary and Middle school teachers, also called middle and high school teachers, are teaching professionals that focus on the educational needs of adolescents. Secondary and Middle school teachers may be generalists with knowledge and talents in a wide range of subjects, or they may have an academic specialization, such as history, language arts, mathematics,

physical science, art, or music. Secondary and Middle school teachers work in both public and private school settings. They may be assigned student and peer mentoring and administrative tasks in addition to their teaching responsibilities.

Work Environment

Secondary and Middle school teachers work in high schools and middle schools designed to meet the social and educational needs of adolescents. The amounts and types of resources in middle and high schools and middle and high school classrooms such as art supplies, music lessons, physical education facilities, fieldtrips, and assistant teachers, differ depending on the school's financial resources and the educational philosophy directing the curriculum. Middle and high schools may be private or public. They may be an independent entity or part of a larger school that encompasses more grade levels.

Profile

Working Conditions: Work Indoors
Physical Strength: Light Work
Education Needs: Bachelor's Degree, Master's Degree
Licensure/Certification: Required
Opportunities For Experience: Internship, Volunteer Work, Part Time Work
Holland Interest Score*: SAE

* See Appendix A

Occupation Interest

Individuals drawn to the profession of Secondary and Middle school teacher tend to be intelligent, creative, patient, and caring. Secondary and Middle school teachers, who instruct and nurture secondary and middle school students, should find satisfaction in spending long hours instructing and mentoring adolescents. Successful Secondary and Middle school teachers excel at long-term scheduling, lesson planning, communication, and problem solving.

A Day in the Life—Duties and Responsibilities

A Secondary and Middle school teacher's daily duties and responsibilities include planning, teaching, classroom preparation, student care, family outreach, school duties, and professional development.

Secondary and Middle school teachers plan and execute specific teaching plans and lessons. They may also be responsible for buying or securing donations for classroom or project supplies. They assign homework and projects, teach good study habits, grade student work, maintain accurate academic records for all students, and lead and administer activities such as lab sessions, reviews, exams, student clubs, and small group learning.

Classroom preparation and cleaning duties may include labeling materials, organizing desk and work areas, displaying student work on bulletin boards and display boards, and, depending on janitorial support, cleaning up and sanitizing spaces at the end of the school day.

Secondary and Middle school teachers greet students as they arrive in the classroom, promote a supportive learning environment, maintain student safety and health, provide appropriate levels of discipline in the classroom and school environment, build student cooperation and listening skills, and work to present lessons in multiple ways to accommodate diverse learning styles.

Some teachers may provide family outreach by greeting student families at school drop off and dismissal times and using a student school-family communication notebook when required. All teachers must communicate regularly with families regarding student academic performance.

Secondary and Middle school teachers must attend staff meetings, participate in peer mentoring, enforce school policies, and lead open houses for prospective families. Teachers may also be responsible for overseeing students in the school hallways and for supervising school fieldtrips. Their professional development duties include attendance at professional meetings, continued training, and recertification as needed.

Secondary and Middle school teachers must work on a daily basis to meet the needs of all students, families, fellow teachers, and school administrators.

Duties and Responsibilities

- Preparing lesson plans
- Guiding the learning activities of students
- Instructing students through demonstrations or lectures
- Evaluating students through daily work, tests and reports, or through a portfolio of the students' artwork or writing
- Computing and recording grades
- Maintaining discipline
- Counseling and referring students when academic or other problems arise
- Conferring with parents and staff
- Assisting with student clubs, teams, plays and other student activities
- Supplementing lecturing with audio-visual teaching aides

OCCUPATION SPECIALTIES

Resource Teachers

Resource Teachers teach basic academic subjects to students requiring remedial work using special help programs to improve scholastic levels.

WORK ENVIRONMENT

Physical Environment

A Secondary and Middle school teacher's physical environment is the middle and high school classroom. Secondary and Middle school teachers tend to have a fair bit of autonomy in deciding classroom layout and curriculum. Secondary and Middle school teachers generally work forty-hour weeks and follow an annual academic schedule with ample winter, spring, and summer vacations. Summer teaching opportunities in summer school and summer camps are common.

Relevant Skills and Abilities

Communication Skills
- Expressing thoughts and ideas
- Persuading others
- Speaking effectively
- Writing concisely

Interpersonal/Social Skills
- Being patient
- Cooperating with others
- Working as a member of a team

Organization & Management Skills
- Coordinating tasks
- Making decisions
- Managing people/groups

Research & Planning Skills
- Creating ideas
- Using logical reasoning

Human Environment

Secondary and Middle school teachers are in constant contact with adolescents, student families, school administrators, and fellow teachers. Secondary and Middle school teachers may have students with physical and mental disabilities as well as students who are English language learners (ELL). Secondary and Middle school teachers must be comfortable working with people from a wide range of backgrounds and able to incorporate lessons on diversity into their teaching.

Technological Environment

Secondary and Middle school classrooms increasingly include computers for student use. Teachers should be comfortable using Internet communication tools and teaching adolescent students to use educational software. Teachers may also use computers to perform administrative tasks and record student progress. Secondary and Middle school teachers should be comfortable with standard office and audiovisual equipment.

EDUCATION, TRAINING, AND ADVANCEMENT

Middle and high school/Secondary and Middle

Middle and high school students interested in becoming Secondary and Middle school teachers should develop good study habits. Interested middle and high school students should take a broad range of courses in education, child development, science, mathematics, history, language arts, physical education, and the arts. Those interested in the field of education may benefit from seeking internships or volunteer/part-time work with children and teachers at camps and afterschool programs.

Suggested High School Subjects
- Algebra
- Arts
- Audio-Visual
- Biology
- Child Growth & Development
- College Preparatory
- Composition
- Computer Science
- English
- Foreign Languages
- Government
- Graphic Communications
- History
- Humanities
- Literature
- Mathematics
- Political Science
- Psychology
- Science

- Social Studies
- Sociology
- Speech
- Theatre & Drama

Famous First

The first junior high school, or middle school, was the Indianola Junior High School in Columbus, OH, which opened in September 1909. The school served 7th, 8th, and 9th grade students along with "such of the first six grades as might be necessary to relieve neighboring districts."

College/Postsecondary

College students interested in working towards a degree or career in Secondary and Middle school education should consider majoring in education and earning initial teaching certification as part of their undergraduate education program. Aspiring teachers should complete coursework in education, child development, and psychology. Those interested in pursuing a career in secondary education often major in the subject area they wish to teach. Prior to graduation, college students intent on becoming Secondary and Middle school teachers should gain teaching experience through an internship or volunteer/part-time work; prospective teachers should also research master's of education programs and state teaching certification requirements.

Related College Majors
- Agricultural Teacher Education
- Art Teacher Education
- Bilingual/Bicultural Education
- Business Teacher Education (Vocational)
- Computer Teacher Education
- Education Admin & Supervision, General
- Education of the Blind & Visually Handicapped

- Education of the Deaf & Hearing Impaired
- Education of the Specific Learning Disabled
- Education of the Speech Impaired
- Elementary/Pre-Elem/Early Childhood/Kindergarten Teacher Education
- English Teacher Education
- Family & Consumer Science Education
- Foreign Languages Teacher Education
- Health & Physical Education, General
- Health Teacher Education
- Marketing Operations Teacher Education (Vocational)
- Mathematics Teacher Education
- Music Teacher Education
- Physical Education Teaching & Coaching
- Science Teacher Education, General
- Secondary and Middle/Jr. High/Middle School Teacher Education
- Special Education, General
- Speech Teacher Education
- Technology Teacher Education/Industrial Arts Teacher Education
- Trade & Industrial Teacher Education (Vocational)
- Vocational Teacher Education

Adult Job Seekers

Adults seeking jobs as Secondary and Middle school teachers should research the education and certification requirements of their home states as well of the schools where they might seek employment. Adult job seekers in the education field may benefit from the employment workshops and job lists maintained by professional teaching associations, such as the American Federation of Teachers (AFT).

Professional Certification and Licensure

Professional certification and licensure requirements for Secondary and Middle school teachers vary between states and between schools. Secondary and Middle school teachers generally earn a master's in education, with a single-subject teaching concentration in language arts, history, science, political science, music, physical education, or art, and obtain a state teaching license for grades eight through twelve. Single-subject teaching licenses for Secondary and Middle school teachers require academic coursework, supervised student teaching, and successful completion of a general teaching exam.

Background checks are also typically required. State departments of education offer state teaching licenses and require continuing education and recertification on a regular basis. Savvy and successful job seekers will find out the requirements that apply to them and satisfy the requirements prior to seeking employment.

Additional Requirements

Individuals who find satisfaction, success, and job security as Secondary and Middle school teachers will be knowledgeable about the profession's requirements, responsibilities, and opportunities. Successful Secondary and Middle school teachers engage in ongoing professional development. Secondary and Middle school teachers must have high levels of integrity and ethics as they work with adolescents and have access to the personal information of student families. Membership in professional teaching associations is encouraged among beginning and tenured Secondary and Middle school teachers as a means of building status in a professional community and networking.

Fun Fact

Teachers earn 14 percent less than people in other professions that require similar levels of education. They work 52 hours per week.

Sources: http://www.theteachersalaryproject.org

EARNINGS AND ADVANCEMENT

Earnings of Secondary and Middle school teachers depend on their education and experience, and the size and location of the school district. Pay is usually higher in large, metropolitan areas. Secondary and Middle school teachers in private schools generally earn less than public Secondary and Middle school teachers.

Median annual earnings of secondary school teachers was $57,200 in 2014; the comparable figure for middle school teachers was $55,860. Secondary and Middle school teachers receive extra pay for coaching sports and working with students in extracurricular activities. Some Secondary and Middle school teachers earn extra income during the summer working in the school system or in other jobs.

Secondary and Middle school teachers have vacation days when their school is closed, as in during the summer and over holidays. They may also receive life and health insurance and retirement benefits. These are usually paid by the employer.

Metropolitan Areas with the Highest Employment Level in this Occupation

Metropolitan area	Employment	Employment per thousand jobs	Annual mean wage
New York-Jersey City-White Plains, NY-NJ	40,590	6.26	$82,260
Los Angeles-Long Beach-Glendale, CA	29,170	7.11	$76,710
Chicago-Naperville-Arlington Heights, IL	24,010	6.72	$74,960
Houston-The Woodlands-Sugar Land, TX	22,930	7.83	$57,520
Dallas-Plano-Irving, TX	17,080	7.33	$55,330
Washington-Arlington-Alexandria, DC-VA-MD-WV	13,910	5.75	$73,330
Atlanta-Sandy Springs-Roswell, GA	13,300	5.36	$56,620
Minneapolis-St. Paul-Bloomington, MN-WI	12,650	6.73	$67,200
Nassau County-Suffolk County, NY	12,020	9.42	$101,950
Baltimore-Columbia-Towson, MD	11,570	8.80	$64,400

Does not include self-employed.

EMPLOYMENT AND OUTLOOK

There were approximately 1.6 million Secondary and Middle school teachers employed nationally in 2014. Employment is expected to grow about as fast as the average for all occupations through the year 2024, which means employment is projected to increase 4 percent to 8 percent. Most job openings will occur as a result of the expected retirement of a large number of teachers.

The supply of Secondary and Middle school teachers is likely to increase in response to growing student enrollment, improved job opportunities, more teacher involvement in school policy, greater public interest in education and higher salaries. Job prospects are greater in central cities and rural areas. However, job growth could be limited by state and local government budget deficits.

Employment Trend, Projected 2014–24

Total, all occupations: 7%

Preschool, primary, secondary, and special education school teachers: 6%

Secondary and Middle school teachers: 6%

Note: "All Occupations" includes all occupations in the U.S. Economy. Source: U.S. Bureau of Labor Statistics, Employment Projections Program

Related Occupations
- Career/Technology Education Teacher
- College Faculty Member
- Education Administrator
- Elementary School Teacher
- Principal
- Special Education Teacher
- Teacher Assistant

Conversation With . . .
JOHN VERSLUIS

Band Teacher and Director, Geneseo Middle School
Geneseo, Illinois
Teacher, 12 years

1. What was your individual career path in terms of education/training, entry-level job, or other significant opportunity?

Both of my parents were elementary school teachers and as I grew up I saw the impact they had on their students. My dad passed when I was a senior in high school and many of his former students came to the visitation, from kids he'd taught the previous year to adults who'd had him in school years before. I was already planning to be a teacher. That steered me even more to education.

I briefly studied elementary education but music had always been my passion and that's what I ultimately did my concentration in.

2. What are the most important skills and/or qualities for someone in your profession?

For teachers in general, I think patience is key, especially at the middle school level. I think it takes a special person to teach middle school, given the developmental pressures of the age. You have to learn about 'tween brain' and how it works.

For band directors specifically, I think it's important to know some background on all of the instruments that students will use. That way, you can help the students more.

It's also useful to be aware of technology that can help you connect with students. Technology has offered so many advantages in the form of apps and tools that students can use to get direct feedback from the band director. For example, if a student is having trouble with a piece while they're at home, say on the weekend or at night, they can record themselves and send it to me to watch and listen. They can even do video chats or Skype.

3. What do you wish you had known going into this profession?

I think the only thing I wasn't prepared for was how email could impact the job and how it can sometimes be misconstrued. I'll usually call the person instead. The thing with email is you can't hear tone or see nonverbal cues.

4. Are there many job opportunities in your profession? In what specific areas?

Over the past couple of years, I've had four student teachers and they all found jobs pretty quickly. There are plenty of band director positions opening in Illinois and Iowa as people now in those positions retire or move on to other things.

5. How do you see your profession changing in the next five years, what role will technology play in those changes, and what skills will be required?

Technology has changed so much since I first started and I hope improvements continue, whether it's through better instruments or school districts providing students with iPads or tablets to use. I think that's the next step – to give them tablets. For my students, the tablets could be used to write and record music. It could have a metronome and a tuner installed so they wouldn't have to go out and get any apps. And they could keep their music scores on the tablets. That way they'd always have it with them.

6. What do you enjoy most about your job? What do you enjoy least about your job?

I most enjoy the students. They really make this job for me. They're hard-working; they do everything they're asked to do to the best of their ability. They're just really good kids. Even when they have issues, if you sit down and talk to them on a one-to-one level they just need someone to listen.

What I probably like least is occasional conflict with colleagues who still don't get what it is that we do and why a student needs to come out of their class for an assessment with me. Yes, your class is important but this class is also important to the well-being of this child. That can be a little frustrating.

7. Can you suggest a valuable "try this" for students considering a career in your profession?

If they have a passion for music and want to become a music educator, they could try helping other students who may be struggling. I think the biggest trait is just to love music. Once you have a strong passion for something, it's hard not to go with that.

MORE INFORMATION

American Association for Employment in Education
3040 Riverside Drive, Suite 125
Columbus, OH 43221
614.485.1111
www.aaee.org

American Association for Health Education
1900 Association Drive
Reston, VA 20191-1598
800.213.7193
www.aahperd.org/aahe

American Association of Colleges for Teacher Education
1307 New York Avenue, NW
Suite 300
Washington, DC 20005-4701
202.293.2450
www.aacte.org

American Federation of Teachers
Public Affairs Department
555 New Jersey Avenue, NW
Washington, DC 20001
202.879.4400
www.aft.org

National Association for Sport and Physical Education
1900 Association Drive
Reston, VA 20191
800.213.7193
www.aahperd.org/naspe

National Board for Professional Teaching Standards
1525 Wilson Boulevard, Suite 500
Arlington, VA 22209
800.228.3224
www.nbpts.org

National Council for Accreditation of Teacher Education
2010 Massachusetts Avenue, NW
Suite 500
Washington, DC 20036-1023
202.466.7496
www.ncate.org

National Council of Teachers of English
1111 W. Kenyon Road
Urbana, Illinois 61801-1096
877.369.6283
www.ncte.org/second

National Council of Teachers of Mathematics
1906 Association Drive
Reston, VA 20191-1502
703.620.9840
www.nctm.org

National Education Association
1201 16th Street, NW
Washington, DC 20036-3290
202.833.4000
www.nea.org

National Science Teachers Association
1840 Wilson Boulevard
Arlington, VA 22201
703.243.7100
www.nsta.org

Simone Isadora Flynn/Editor

Special Education Teacher

Snapshot

Career Cluster: Education & Training; Human Services

Interests: Teaching, education, preparing lessons, child development, student care, psychology

Earnings (Yearly Average): $56,920

Employment & Outlook: Slower Than Average Growth Expected

OVERVIEW

Sphere of Work

Special education teachers are teaching professionals that focus on the educational needs of students with physical, emotional, cognitive, or behavioral special needs. Special education teachers may be generalists with knowledge and talents in a wide range of subjects and special needs. Alternatively, they may have an academic specialization and training with speech impairment, hearing problems, language delays, mental retardation, seizures, orthopedic impairment, visual impairments, autism, traumatic brain

injuries, or learning disabilities. Special education teachers help to develop and provide the services of the individualized education plans (IEP) for every child in the public school system with documented special needs.

Work Environment

Special education teachers work in schools designed to meet to the social and educational needs of mainstream and special needs children. They work at all grade levels in both public and private school settings. Some special education teachers work in discrete special needs classrooms focusing on one age level or type of special need such as autism or physical disabilities. Others work in integrated special needs classrooms with students of many ages and special needs. Still others work in classrooms that have integrated mainstream and special needs students working alongside one another. Classrooms have different types and amounts of resources, such as art supplies, music lessons, and physical education facilities. The resources available depend on the financial resources of the school and district as well as the educational philosophy directing the curriculum.

Profile

Working Conditions: Work Indoors
Physical Strength: Light Work
Education Needs: Bachelor's Degree, Master's Degree
Licensure/Certification: Required
Physical Abilities Not Required: No Heavy Labor
Opportunities For Experience: Internship, Volunteer Work, Part-Time Work
Holland Interest Score*: SEC

* See Appendix A

Occupation Interest

Individuals drawn to special education tend to be intelligent, resourceful, creative, patient, and caring. Special education teachers, who instruct and nurture students with special needs, should find satisfaction in spending long hours interacting with and instructing children. They should be physically fit and able to move, lift, and carry students with physical disabilities as well as physically redirect students with behavioral or emotional problems. Successful special education teachers excel at communication and problem solving.

A Day in the Life—Duties and Responsibilities

A special education teacher's daily duties and responsibilities include planning, teaching, classroom preparation, student care, family outreach, school duties, and professional development.

Special education teachers prepare and teach lessons, modify the mainstream curriculum for students with special needs, and buy or secure donations for classroom or project supplies. They assign homework and projects, teach good study habits and life skills, grade student work, provide students with special needs accommodations (such as extra test time and homework modification), and maintain accurate academic and behavioral records for all students.

Classroom preparation and cleaning may include labeling materials, organizing desk and work areas, displaying student work on bulletin boards and display boards, and, depending on janitorial support, cleaning up and sanitizing at the end of the school day.

Special education teachers greet students as they arrive in the classroom, engage in student behavior modification and redirection, and promote a supportive learning environment. They also maintain student safety and health, provide appropriate levels of discipline in the classroom and school environment, build student cooperation and listening skills, and work to present lessons in multiple ways to accommodate diverse learning styles.

Some special education teachers may greet student families at school drop off and dismissal times and use a student school-family communication notebook. All teachers must communicate regularly with families about student health, experience, and performance.

Special education teachers attend staff meetings and meetings with family and social workers. They lead IEP development and review meetings and coordinate special education and mainstream classrooms. They also enforce school policies and participate in peer mentoring. Their professional development duties include attendance at professional meetings, continued training, and recertification as needed.

Special education teachers work daily to meet the needs of all students, families, fellow teachers, and school administrators. All special education teachers must adhere to the educational standards and rights described in the Individuals with Disabilities Education Act (IDEA).

Duties and Responsibilities

- Planning curricula and preparing lessons
- Arranging and adjusting tools, work aids and equipment used by students in classrooms
- Conferring with other staff members and professionals to develop programs to make the most of the students' potential
- Instructing students in subject areas
- Observing, evaluating and preparing reports on the progress of students
- Conferring with and reporting to parents pertaining to students' programs and adjustments

OCCUPATION SPECIALTIES

Teachers of Physically Impaired Students

Teachers of Physically Impaired Students instruct students in the elementary and secondary levels who are physically impaired. They evaluate students' abilities to determine the best training program for each individual.

Teachers of the Mentally Impaired

Teachers of the Mentally Impaired teach social skills and/or basic academic subjects in schools, hospitals and other institutions to mentally impaired students.

Teachers of the Hearing Impaired

Teachers of the Hearing Impaired teach elementary and secondary school subjects and special skills to deaf or hard-of-hearing students using lip reading, manual communication or total communication.

Teachers of the Visually Impaired

Teachers of the Visually Impaired teach elementary and secondary school subjects to visually-impaired and blind students using large-print materials and/or the Braille system.

Teachers of the Emotionally Impaired

Teachers of the Emotionally Impaired teach elementary and secondary school subjects including education on socially acceptable behavior to students with emotional impairments.

WORK ENVIRONMENT

Physical Environment

A special education teacher works primarily in the classroom. Special education teachers may have the autonomy and responsibility to modify the classroom layout and curriculum to meet the academic and social needs of students with special needs. They generally work forty-hour weeks and follow an annual academic schedule with ample winter, spring, and summer vacations. Summer teaching opportunities in summer school and camps are common.

Human Environment

Special education teachers are in constant contact with students with physical, cognitive, or emotional challenges as well as with families, social workers, therapists, school administrators, and fellow teachers. They must be comfortable working with people from a wide range of backgrounds and able to incorporate lessons on diversity and differences into their teaching.

Relevant Skills and Abilities

Communication Skills
- Expressing thoughts and ideas
- Speaking effectively
- Writing concisely

Interpersonal/Social Skills
- Being flexible
- Being sensitive to others
- Providing support to others

Organization & Management Skills
- Coordinating tasks
- Making decisions
- Managing people/groups

Research & Planning Skills
- Using logical reasoning

Technological Environment

Special education teachers use a wide variety of adaptive and instructional technologies, such as touch screens and communication devices. Special education teachers should be comfortable using Internet communication tools and teaching students to use educational software. They also often help students to use and care for adaptive technologies such as wheelchairs, orthotics, hearing and feeding aids, and dressing aids.

EDUCATION, TRAINING, AND ADVANCEMENT

High School/Secondary

High school students interested in becoming special education teachers should develop good study habits. Interested high school students should take a broad range of courses in education, anatomy, psychology, child development, science, math, history, language arts, physical education, and the arts. Those interested in the field of education may benefit from seeking internships or part-time work with special needs children at camps and afterschool programs.

Suggested High School Subjects
- Arts
- Audio-Visual
- Biology
- Child Growth & Development
- College Preparatory
- Composition

- Crafts
- English
- History
- Humanities
- Literature
- Mathematics
- Psychology
- Science
- Sociology
- Speech

Famous First

The first nationally mandated program to integrate students with special needs into regular school systems (rather than teach them in separate facilities) came with amendments to the Individuals with Disabilities Act of 1997. The act formally recognized the concept of "inclusion," or "inclusive education," reflecting an interest among educators and the public in "mainstreaming" students with disabilities.

College/Postsecondary

College students interested in special education should consider majoring in education and earning initial teaching certification as part of their undergraduate education program. Aspiring teachers should complete coursework in education, child development, and psychology. Prior to graduation, interested college students should gain teaching experience with special needs children, through internships or work. They should also research master's of education programs and state teaching certification requirements.

Related College Majors
- Education Administration & Supervision, General
- Education of the Blind & Visually Handicapped

- Education of the Deaf & Hearing Impaired
- Education of the Specific Learning Disabled
- Education of the Speech Impaired
- Elementary/Pre-Elementary/Kindergarten Teacher Education
- Secondary/Jr. High/Middle School Teacher Education
- Special Education, General

Adult Job Seekers

Adults seeking jobs as special education teachers should research the education and certification requirements of their home states as well of the schools where they might seek employment. Adult job seekers may benefit from employment workshops and job lists maintained by professional teaching associations, such as the American Federation of Teachers and the National Clearinghouse for Professions in Special Education.

Professional Certification and Licensure

All special education teachers must be licensed. Professional certification and licensure requirements for special education teachers vary between states and between schools. Special education teachers generally earn a master's in general education, with additional training in a special education area, such as learning or physical disabilities, and obtain a special education teaching license for kindergarten through high school. A small number of states require special education teachers to complete a master's of special education. State departments of education offer state teaching licenses and require continuing education and recertification on a regular basis. Successful job seekers will find out the requirements that apply to them and satisfy the requirements prior to seeking employment.

 ## Additional Requirements

Individuals who find satisfaction, success, and job security as special education teachers will be knowledgeable about the profession's requirements, responsibilities, and opportunities. Successful special education teachers engage in ongoing professional development. Special education teachers must have high levels of integrity and ethics as they work with vulnerable minors and have access to the personal information of student families. Membership in professional teaching associations is encouraged among beginning and tenured special education teachers as a means of building status in a professional community and networking.

Fun Fact

The phrase "special education" entered our collective vocabulary in 1975, when the federal Individuals with Disabilities Education Act (IDEA) was enacted, requiring schools to provide "special education for children with qualifying disabilities." Eventually, the acronym "SPED" took on a derogatory quality.

Source: http://www.specialednews.com/the-history-of-special-education-in-the-united-states.htm

EARNINGS AND ADVANCEMENT

Earnings of special education teachers depend on the individual's education and experience and the type, size and geographic location of the employer. Median annual earnings of special education teachers were $56,920 in 2013. The lowest ten percent earned less than $38,550, and the highest ten percent earned more than $90,460.

The school calendar allows special education teachers to have national and state holidays off and receive winter and summer vacations. They may also receive life and health insurance and retirement benefits. These are usually paid by the employer.

Metropolitan Areas with the Highest
Employment Level in this Occupation

Metropolitan area	Employment[1]	Employment per thousand jobs	Hourly mean wage
New York-White Plains-Wayne, NY-NJ	10,720	2.05	$75,690
Chicago-Joliet-Naperville, IL	3,910	1.06	$71,710
Los Angeles-Long Beach-Glendale, CA	3,630	0.91	$66,050
Philadelphia, PA	3,580	1.94	$68,320
Nassau-Suffolk, NY	2,900	2.35	$96,650
Minneapolis-St. Paul-Bloomington, MN-WI	2,450	1.37	$68,560
Washington-Arlington-Alexandria, DC-VA-MD-WV	1,730	0.73	$76,220
Atlanta-Sandy Springs-Marietta, GA	1,720	0.75	$54,180
Houston-Sugar Land-Baytown, TX	1,680	0.61	$52,120
Boston-Cambridge-Quincy, MA	1,650	0.94	$69,040

[1] Does not include self-employed. Source: Bureau of Labor Statistics

EMPLOYMENT AND OUTLOOK

There were about 443,000 special education teachers employed nationally in 2012. Nearly all were employed in public and private elementary, middle, and secondary schools. Employment is expected to grow slower than the average for all occupations through the year 2022, which means employment is projected to increase 3 percent to 10 percent. Job openings will mostly be created by continued growth in the number of special education students needing services. The need to replace special education teachers who switch to general education, change careers or retire will lead to additional job openings. At the same time, many school districts report shortages of qualified special education teachers. The most job opportunities will be available in inner city and rural schools. However, job growth could be limited by state and local government budget deficits.

Employment Trend, Projected 2010–20

Total, All Occupations: 11%

Education, Training, and Library Occupations: 11%

Special Education Teachers: 6%

Note: "All Occupations" includes all occupations in the U.S. Economy. Source: U.S. Bureau of Labor Statistics, Employment Projections Program

Related Occupations
- Audiologist
- Career/Technology Education Teacher
- Elementary School Teacher
- Secondary School Teacher
- Speech-Language Pathologist
- Vocational Rehabilitation Counselor

Conversation With . . .
SUSAN CAMPBELL

Special Education Teacher
Lexington Public Schools, Lexington, MA
Special Education teacher, 35 years

1. What was your individual career path in terms of education/training, entry-level job, or other significant opportunity?

I received a BA in psychology from Smith College, but I wasn't sure what I wanted to do with my degree. I ended up working as a childcare worker at a residential school for children with special needs. I connected with the students and was quickly promoted, first to lead a group of teachers, then into administrative positions. While working there, I was fortunate that the school made a master's degree in special education available at a very reasonable price. I became certified in Intensive Special Education, which I did for eight years. My next job, of 12 years, was as an administrator at a private day school for young children with special needs. After having a child of my own, I realized that working long hours twelve months of the year didn't leave me much time with my son. I also realized that I truly missed working directly with students. I left the private sector and was delighted to find a job in Lexington, MA, at a public elementary school. For the past 15 years, I have worked to include students with special needs in general education classes. I also teach a graduate course on inclusion at Simmons College in Boston.

2. What are the most important skills and/or qualities for someone in your profession?

I believe there are many important qualities a special education teacher must possess to be truly effective. First, you must have a willingness to be a lifelong learner. The field is always changing and it is vital to change with it. Secondly, you must be a good communicator. As a special education teacher, I interface with a wide variety of people: general educators, parents, specialists, paraprofessionals and administrators. In order to do my job effectively, I have to be able to listen carefully, express myself clearly and be willing to compromise when necessary.

3. What do you wish you had known going into this profession?

I wish I had known that many of the skills you need as a special educator aren't necessarily tied directly to teaching. As mentioned above, communication skills and continuing your own learning are keys to this profession. Had I known this, perhaps I would have taken different electives in order to prepare myself better. My advice is to look for courses, perhaps in the business department, on leadership, effective communication, and building strong teams.

4. Are there many job opportunities in your profession? In what specific areas?

School districts across the country have a mandate to provide services in the least restrictive environment possible; therefore, more and more districts are adding special educators. In addition, the number of students with special needs is increasing significantly in some areas. When I started teaching, the rate of autism was 1 in 10,000; currently it is 1 in 68. Teachers who can work effectively with these students, as well as with those with behavioral and emotional challenges, are in high demand at elementary, middle and high school levels.

5. How do you see your profession changing in the next five years? What role will technology play in those changes, and what skills will be required?

I believe the field of special education will continue to evolve as it seeks to provide the best possible services to the widest range of learners. Technology is key in capturing the attention of many learners and in providing other learners with access to the curriculum. Teachers need to keep abreast of the newest technology in regards to smart boards, apps, data collection software, and other e-resources.

6. What do you enjoy most about your job? What do you enjoy least about your job?

The things I enjoy most are the progress I see my students make and working with colleagues. There's no better feeling than seeing a student succeed where they didn't before, or watching them take a risk in their learning. It's also a wonderful feeling to collaborate with a fellow teacher on the design of a lesson that successfully reaches a wide range of learners. It feels terrific to see students excited about their learning. Paperwork and meetings, while a necessary part of the job, are my least favorite!

7. Can you suggest a valuable "try this" for students considering a career in your profession?

I suggest setting up an observation at a local school with the age group you see yourself working with. Take notes on what you see. Do you get excited? Can you think of ways you could make the lesson better? Or improve the classroom layout? Are there students you feel drawn to because they might be struggling? In the graduate course that I teach, one of the assignments is a site visit. Students often tell me how eye opening this task is!

SELECTED SCHOOLS

Many colleges and universities have bachelor's degree programs in education; some offer a specialization in special education. The student may also gain an initial grounding in the field at a technical or community college. Consult with your school guidance counselor or research post-secondary programs in your area. Below are listed some of the more prominent schools in this field.

University of Florida
Gainesville, FL 32611
352.392.3261
www.ufl.edu

University of Illinois at Urbana, Champaign
Champaign, IL
217.333.1000
illinois.edu

University of Kansas
1450 Jayhawk Boulevard
Lawrence, KS 66045
785.864.2700
www.ku.edu

University of Minnesota
Minneapolis, MN 55455
612.625.5000
www.umn.edu

University of Oregon
1585 East 13th Avenue
Eugene, OR 97403
541.346.1000
uoregon.edu

University of Texas, Austin
Austin, TX 78712
512.471.3434
www.utexas.edu

University of Virginia
Charlottesville, VA
934.924.0311
www.virginia.edu

University of Washington
Seattle, Washington
206.543.2100
www.washington.edu

University of Wisconsin
Madison, WI 53706
608.263.2400
www.wisc.edu

Vanderbilt University
2201 West End Avenue
Nashville, TN 37235
615.322.7311
www.vanderbilt.edu

MORE INFORMATION

**Alexander Graham Bell
Association for the Deaf & Hard
of Hearing**
3417 Volta Place, NW
Washington, DC 20007
202.337.5220
www.agbell.org

**American Association for
Employment in Education**
3040 Riverside Drive, Suite 125
Columbus, OH 43221
614.485.1111
www.aaee.org

**American Association of Colleges
for Teacher Education**
1307 New York Avenue, NW
Suite 300
Washington, DC 20005-4701
202.293.2450
www.aacte.org

American Federation of Teachers
Public Affairs Department
555 New Jersey Avenue, NW
Washington, DC 20001
202.879.4400
www.aft.org

**Association for Education and
Rehabilitation**
of the Blind and Visually Impaired
1703 N. Beauregard St., Suite 440
Alexandria, VA 22311
703.671.4500
www.aerbvi.org

Council for Exceptional Children
2900 Crystal Drive, Suite 1000
Arlington, VA 22202-3557
888.232.7733
www.cec.sped.org

**Learning Disabilities Association
of America**
4156 Library Road
Pittsburgh, PA 15234-1349
412.341.1515
www.ldanatl.org

**National Association of State
Directors of Special Education**
1800 Diagonal Road, Suite 320
Alexandria, VA 22314
703.519.3800
www.nasdse.org

National Education Association
1201 16th Street, NW
Washington, DC 20036-3290
202.833.4000
www.nea.org

Simone Isadora Flynn/Editor

Speech-Language Pathologist

Snapshot

Career Cluster: Education & Training; Health Care; Human Services

Interests: Anatomy, physiology, speech pathology, patient assessment, creating treatment plans, speech and audiology research

Earnings (Yearly Average): $70,810

Employment & Outlook: Faster Than Average Growth Expected

OVERVIEW

Sphere of Work

Speech-language pathologists, more commonly referred to as speech therapists, are trained to assess and treat disorders of expressive and receptive speech, voice, swallowing, and language. Speech-language pathologists treat clients with a wide range of speech-related problems, including swallowing issues, inability to make speech sounds, stutters, receptive language disorders (i.e.,

language processing and comprehension), and voice disorders. Speech-language pathology skills tend to be well compensated and in demand in a variety of work settings.

Work Environment

Speech-language pathologists work in therapeutic settings, such as medical clinics or hospitals, and in schools. In medical environments, speech-language pathologists generally partner with medical and social service professionals, such as doctors and social workers, to treat communication and swallowing problems caused by medical events, such as strokes or premature birth. In school settings, speech-language pathologists partner with educational professionals, such as teachers and special education coordinators, to address a student's speech-related deficiency or issue. Speech therapy, provided by a speech-language pathologist, is a common component of a special-needs child's individualized education plan (IEP).

Profile

Working Conditions: Work Indoors
Physical Strength: Light Work
Education Needs: Bachelor's Degree, Master's Degree
Licensure/Certification: Required
Physical Abilities Not Required: No Heavy Labor
Opportunities For Experience: Internship, Military Service, Volunteer Work, Part-Time Work
Holland Interest Score*: SAI

* See Appendix A

Occupation Interest

Individuals attracted to the speech-language pathology profession tend to be active people who enjoy hands-on work and close interaction with others. Individuals who excel as speech therapists exhibit traits such as intellectual curiosity, problem solving, a desire to help, and a social conscience. Speech-language pathologists must understand and respect science and scientific inquiry and be able to work as part of a team to meet patient needs.

A Day in the Life—Duties and Responsibilities

A speech-language pathologist's daily duties and responsibilities include full days of hands-on patient interaction and treatment, as well as administrative duties. Patients seen by speech-language pathologists include those experiencing developmental delays, structural deformities, learning disabilities, cleft palate, cerebral palsy, stroke complications, trauma complications, mental retardation, or hearing loss.

As a medical or therapeutic professional, speech-language pathologists interact with patients or clients on a daily basis. Daily work includes quantitative and qualitative assessment of patient speech problems using standardized tests and interviewing techniques; creating patient treatment plans; advising patients on the use of hearing communication devices. Speech-language pathologists also teach sign language to hearing impaired individuals and their families; meet with patient treatment teams or patient families; and provide eating and swallowing therapy to patients.

A speech-language pathologist's daily administrative responsibilities include the record keeping involved with patient evaluation and treatment. Speech-language pathologists must draft treatment plans, record notes following patient treatment sessions, provide written updates to patient treatment teams, and provide insurance companies with patient records and progress notes as required. Independent speech-language pathologists, who work outside of a school or medical clinic, may also be responsible for patient appointment scheduling and billing.

Academic speech-language pathologists may work in a research capacity rather than patient or clinical capacity. Academic speech-language pathologists have daily teaching, research, and publication responsibilities.

Duties and Responsibilities

- Planning or conducting therapy for impairments such as aphasia, stuttering and articulation problems
- Guiding and counseling patients and their families
- Consulting others concerned with the patient's welfare, such as doctors, physical therapists, social workers and teachers
- Conducting research related to speech and audiology
- Determining the range, nature and degree of impairment
- Coordinating test results with other information such as educational, medical and behavioral data
- Differentiating between organic and nonorganic causative factors

WORK ENVIRONMENT

Physical Environment

Speech-language pathologists work in classroom settings, hospitals, and medical or therapeutic offices. Classroom settings are arranged for students with desks, chairs, and floor seating. Medical settings are usually sparse and sterile. Therapeutic office settings used by speech-language pathologists may be shared with other therapeutic professionals, such as occupational, physical, or recreational therapists.'

Relevant Skills and Abilities

Analytical Skills
- Analyzing data

Communication Skills
- Expressing thoughts and ideas clearly

Interpersonal/Social Skills
- Being patient
- Cooperating with others
- Working as a member of a team

Organization & Management Skills
- Managing conflict

Research & Planning Skills
- Developing evaluation strategies

Technical Skills
- Performing scientific, mathematical and technical work

Human Environment

Speech-language pathologists usually work as part of a patient treatment team, including patient families, teachers, doctors, and additional therapists. As a member of a treatment team, speech-language pathologists participate in frequent team meetings and are responsible for communicating patient progress to fellow team members.

Technological Environment

Speech-language pathologists use a wide variety of technology in their work. Computers and Internet communication tools are a ubiquitous part of speech-language pathology work. In addition, speech-language pathologists generally learn how to use and teach sign language and assistive technological devices, such as hearing aids and computer touch screens.

EDUCATION, TRAINING, AND ADVANCEMENT

High School/Secondary

High school students interested in pursuing the profession of speech-language pathology in the future should develop good study habits. High school level coursework in biology, psychology, anatomy, sociology, and mathematics will prepare students for college- and masters-level studies. Students interested in the speech-language pathology field will benefit from seeking internships or part-time work with speech pathologists or people who have speech-related problems.

Suggested High School Subjects
- Biology
- Chemistry
- Child Growth & Development
- College Preparatory
- English
- Literature
- Physiology
- Science
- Speech

Famous First

The first television series to depict someone stuttering was the 1976 series I, Claudius, about the Roman Emperor Claudius. To avoid the stigma surrounding stuttering, Claudius's family kept him out of the public eye until his coronation, at the age of 49, in 41 AD. The first major motion picture to deal with the same subject was *The King's Speech* in 2010, which focused on the British regent George VI. In both cases the main subjects learn how to stop stuttering and communicate normally.

CLAUDIUS DISCOVERED BY THE PRÆTORIAN GUARD AND HAILED AS EMPEROR.

College/Postsecondary

Postsecondary students interested in pursuing training in speech-language pathology should complete coursework in speech studies, if offered by their school, as well as courses on biology, psychology, anatomy, sociology, and mathematics. Postsecondary students interested in attending graduate school in speech-language pathology will benefit from seeking internships or work with speech pathologists or people who have speech-related problems. Membership in the National Student Speech Language Hearing Association (NSSLHA) may provide networking opportunities and connections. Prior to graduating, college students interested in joining the speech-language pathology profession should apply to graduate school in speech-pathology or secure related work, such as speech-therapy assistant or speech-research assistant.

Related College Majors
- Audiology/Hearing Sciences
- Communication Disorders, General
- Education of the Speech Impaired
- Speech & Rhetorical Studies
- Speech Pathology & Audiology
- Speech-Language Pathology

Adult Job Seekers

Adult job seekers in the field of speech-language pathology have generally completed master's- or doctoral-level training in speech pathology from an accredited university, as well as earned necessary professional certification and licensure. Speech-language pathologists seeking employment will benefit from the networking opportunities, job workshops, and job lists offered by professional speech pathology associations such as American Speech-Language-Hearing Association (ASHA).

Professional Certification and Licensure

Speech-language pathologists are required to have earned a professional certification prior to beginning professional practice. The leading speech-language pathology certification is the Certificate of Clinical Competence (CCC) awarded by the American Speech-Language-Hearing Association. The CCC is awarded in speech-language pathology (CCC-SLP) and audiology (CCC-A). The CCC application process involves the passing of an examination as well as the submission of official transcript and clinical fellowship evaluation. Consult credible professional associations within your field and follow professional debate as to the relevancy and value of any certification program.

Additional Requirements

Individuals who find satisfaction, success, and job-security as speech-language pathologists will be knowledgeable about the profession's requirements, responsibilities, and opportunities. Successful speech-language pathologists engage in ongoing professional development. Speech-language pathologists must have high levels of integrity and ethics, as they work with confidential and personal patient information. Membership in professional speech-language pathology associations is encouraged among junior and senior speech-language pathologists as a means of building status within a professional community and networking.

Fun Fact

The Centers for Disease Control estimate the lifetime costs for all people with hearing loss born in the year 2000 will total $2.1 billion, resulting mostly from lost wages due to inability or limited ability to work.

Source: CDC and The American Speech-Language-Hearing Association

EARNINGS AND ADVANCEMENT

Earnings depend on the type and geographic location of the employer and the individual's ability, experience and education. Median annual earnings of speech-language pathologists were $70,810 in 2013. The lowest ten percent earned less than $44,860, and the highest ten percent earned more than $109,800.

Speech-language pathologists usually receive paid vacations, holidays, and sick days; life and health insurance; and retirement benefits. These are usually paid by the employer.

Metropolitan Areas with the Highest Employment Level in this Occupation

Metropolitan area	Employment[1]	Employment per thousand jobs	Hourly mean wage
Chicago-Joliet-Naperville, IL	4,900	1.32	$37.93
New York-White Plains-Wayne, NY-NJ	4,780	0.91	$42.71
Houston-Sugar Land-Baytown, TX	2,670	0.97	$34.98
Dallas-Plano-Irving, TX	2,490	1.16	$34.40
Los Angeles-Long Beach-Glendale, CA	2,140	0.54	$39.95
Nassau-Suffolk, NY	2,100	1.70	$42.52
Boston-Cambridge-Quincy, MA	1,780	1.02	$37.81
Minneapolis-St. Paul-Bloomington, MN-WI	1,710	0.95	$35.61
St. Louis, MO-IL	1,660	1.28	$34.50
Edison-New Brunswick, NJ	1,500	1.53	$42.13

[1] Does not include self-employed. Source: Bureau of Labor Statistics

EMPLOYMENT AND OUTLOOK

There were approximately 134,000 speech-language pathologists employed nationally in 2012. About one-half were employed in preschools, elementary and secondary schools or colleges and universities. Others were in hospitals; physicians' offices; speech, language and hearing centers; home health agencies; child day care services and other facilities.

Employment of speech-language pathologists is expected to grow faster than the average for all occupations through the year 2022, which means employment is projected to increase 15 percent to 24 percent. This is due in part to growth in the population of middle age and older persons, when the possibility of speech, language, swallowing and hearing problems increases. Medical advances are also improving the survival rate of premature infants and trauma and stroke victims, who then need treatment. In addition, many states now require that all newborns be screened for hearing loss and receive appropriate early treatment.

Employment Trend, Projected 2010–20

Health Diagnosing and Treating Practitioners: 20%

Speech-Language Pathologists: 19%

Total, All Occupations: 11%

Note: "All Occupations" includes all occupations in the U.S. Economy. Source: U.S. Bureau of Labor Statistics, Employment Projections Program

Related Occupations
- Audiologist
- Special Education Teacher

Related Military Occupations
- Speech Therapist

Conversation With . . .
ANDREA RODRIGUEZ

Speech Language Pathology Researcher, Tallahassee, FL
Speech Pathologist, 8 years

1. **What was your individual career path in terms of education/training, entry-level job, or other significant opportunity?**

I first learned about speech-language pathology in a sociology course in my sophomore year of college. The professor was out sick, so her daughter, a speech-language pathologist (SLP), filled in for her. She told us that she helps kids improve their speech, language and social skills and that SLPs were in high demand. I was interested in finding a profession where I could make a difference and help kids with disabilities succeed, so I asked to shadow her for a day. After observing her work with children at an outpatient clinic, I was sure this was the field for me. She was helping kids learn skills such as using speech to communicate their wants and needs, and understand language in order to follow directions at home and school.

I got a bachelor's degree in communication disorders, which allowed me to work as a speech-language pathology assistant, but to be a licensed speech-language pathologist you need a master's degree. When I was getting my master's, I received specialized training in working with children from high poverty communities. I did internships in an elementary school, a private speech therapy clinic, a memory disorders clinic, and working with young children in an early intervention program. Then I worked for an early intervention agency serving infants and toddlers with communication delays and disorders. In early intervention, therapy is provided in a child's natural environment, so I spent most of my day conducting assessments and providing services either in people's homes or at preschools, working with the children, parents and teachers.

I decided to enroll in a doctoral program to learn more about research. I now have a doctorate in speech language pathology and work as a researcher at a university. My research focuses on how to use technology to improve speech and language outcomes for young children with communication disorders. I hope to eventually work as a college professor in speech-language pathology.

2. **What are the most important skills and/or qualities for someone in your profession?**

It's essential to have an authentic desire to help others. Excellent written and verbal communication skills are a big part of the job because SLPs frequently share information with clients, family members, doctors, teachers, reading specialists, and physical and occupational therapists. You have to have a love of learning – to do this job, you have to keep up with research on evidence-based practices as well as complete required continuing education. Efficient time management is another critical skill.

3. What do you wish you had known going into this profession?

I wish I had known how many ways there are to specialize. Most of us wear many hats and serve clients with a variety of disorders: expressive and receptive language, speech articulation, stuttering, autism, dyslexia, word finding difficulties, or motor-speech disorders. Some SLPS specialize in one of these areas, which can make them more marketable. I also wish I had known how important it is for SLPs to work as a team with other professionals, especially for clients with complex medical needs or significant impairments.

4. Are there many job opportunities in your profession? In what specific areas?

Speech-language pathologists are in high demand! The American Speech-Language Hearing Association cites several reasons for this, including an increase in older populations, increased rates of survival for premature babies and trauma/stroke victims, and an increase in students eligible for special education services (http://www.asha.org/Careers/Market-Trends/). Many school districts report a shortage of SLPs.

5. How do you see your profession changing in the next five years, what role will technology play in those changes, and what skills will be required?

Technology can play a huge role in speech and language assessment and intervention. Video/audio recording, in particular, has made documentation and feedback easier and more accessible. Many settings have moved to a 'paperless' system of record keeping. We're using mobile devices and apps to track clients' progress toward their communication goals. Telepractice, which uses technology to provide therapeutic services remotely—for instance, video conferencing in rural areas where the SLP isn't able to travel between schools—is on the rise. Using mobile device apps to support intervention service delivery is becoming more popular as well. For example, an individual with limited verbal ability can use an iPad to make requests via a picture board or to participate in conversations via text-to-speech applications.

6. What do you enjoy most about your job? What do you enjoy least about your job?

Every day, I feel like I'm making a difference by helping young children with communication disorders participate more fully in their typical activities. I also love that each day is different!

As with many professions, paperwork is a necessary part of the job, but it's a lot less fun than the rest of my workday!

7. **Can you suggest a valuable "try this" for students considering a career in your profession?**

See if you can shadow an SLP for a day. The American Speech-Language-Hearing Association website (http://www.asha.org/) is a great resource. The Careers section has good information about planning your education, salary data, etc. Look for speech-language pathology blogs. Many are geared toward parents and professionals.

SELECTED SCHOOLS

Many colleges and universities have bachelor's degree programs related to, or focusing on, speech-language pathology. The student may also gain an initial grounding at a technical or community college. Consult with your school guidance counselor or research post-secondary programs in your area. Below are listed some of the more prominent schools in this field.

Northwestern University
633 Clark Street
Evanston, IL 60208
847.491.3741
www.northwestern.edu

Purdue University
610 Purdue Mall
West Lafayette, IN 47907
765.494.4600
www.purdue.edu

University of Arizona
Tucson, AZ 85721
520.621.2211
www.arizona.edu

University of Kansas
1450 Jayhawk Boulevard
Lawrence, KS 66045
785.864.2700
www.ku.edu

University of Iowa
Iowa City, IA 52242
319.335.3500
www.uiowa.edu

University of Pittsburgh
4200 Fifth Avenue
Pittsburgh, PA 15260
412.624.4141
www.pitt.**edu**

University of Texas, Austin
Austin, TX 78712
512.471.3434
www.utexas.edu

University of Washington
Seattle, Washington
206.543.2100
www.washington.edu

University of Wisconsin
Madison, WI 53706
608.263.2400
www.wisc.edu

Vanderbilt University
2201 West End Avenue
Nashville, TN 37235
615.322.7311
www.vanderbilt.edu

MORE INFORMATION

**American Cleft Palate-
Craniofacial Association**
1504 E. Franklin Street, Suite 102
Chapel Hill, NC 27514
919.933.9044
www.cleftline.org

**American Speech-Language-
Hearing Association**
2200 Research Boulevard
Rockville, MD 20850-3289
800.638.8255
www.asha.org

**National Student Speech
Language Hearing Association**
2200 Research Boulevard, #322
Rockville, MD 20850
www.nsslha.org

Simone Isadora Flynn/Editor

Sports Instructor/ Coach

Snapshot

Career Cluster(s): Education & Training; Health Science; Sports & Entertainment

Interests: Physical education, kinesiology, physiology, game preparation, psychology, anatomy

Earnings (Yearly Average): $31,000

Employment & Outlook: Average Growth Expected

OVERVIEW

Sphere of Work

Sports instructors and coaches work to develop the athletic skills of young people and teach them to function in a team setting. They instruct individuals or teams in the rules, techniques, and strategies of a particular sport, and help them train in order to achieve success.

Work Environment

Sports instructors and coaches work with young athletes in a wide range of environments, including athletic fields, gymnasiums, and classrooms. Those who work outdoors will have to factor in the risks or limitations posed by different types of weather. Depending on their level of active participation, instructors and coaches may be at risk for sports-related injuries.

Profile

Working Conditions: Work both Indoors and Outdoors
Physical Strength: Light Work, Medium Work
Education Needs: Bachelor's Degree
Licensure/Certification: Usually Not Required
Opportunities For Experience: Internship, Volunteer Work, Part Time Work
Holland Interest Score*: ESR

* See Appendix A

Occupation Interest

A sports instructor or coach should possess a strong background in, and knowledge of, the various sports for which he or she will be responsible. This includes not only an understanding of the basic physical skills needed to participate in these sports, but also how to teach people to work in a group and develop team goals.

A Day in the Life—Duties and Responsibilities

Sports instructors and coaching professionals work in a setting that requires tremendous social communication skills, as well as knowledge of motivational and educational techniques. They impart the knowledge and understanding required to effectively participate in an individual or team sport, while teaching young athletes the benefits of working in a group setting toward a common goal. The instructor or coach implements a learning progression, using a variety of repetitive physical drills that allows the athlete to build confidence by properly executing the skills required to compete in the sport being practiced. This is done in team practice sessions, which work progressively from an individual skill development period to a group development period, ending with an exercise in which both individual and group development learning and repetitive drill work are incorporated into the complete team setting. This is essential preparation for athletic contests.

Duties and Responsibilities

- **Organizing and running practice sessions**
- **Developing an individual's athletic talent**
- **Directing and orchestrating workouts**
- **Creating and executing game strategy**

OCCUPATION SPECIALTIES

Head Coaches

Head Coaches work with groups of athletes through subordinate assistant coaches.

Coaches of Professional Athletes

Coaches of Professional Athletes work with groups of paid professional athletes and paid assistant coaches. Their duties often include not only game preparation and game coaching, but recruiting, assessing and selecting new professional talent.

Physical Instructors

Physical Instructors work with individuals and small groups in beginning or advanced exercises for reducing weight or improving health.

WORK ENVIRONMENT

Physical Environment

Sports instructors and coaches work in athletic fields, gymnasiums, weight rooms, pools, classrooms, and offices. In certain sports, athletes are introduced to the individual and comprehensive team concepts via classroom instruction.

Relevant Skills and Abilities

Communication Skills
- Speaking effectively
- Writing concisely

Interpersonal/Social Skills
- Being patient
- Cooperating with others
- Motivating others
- Providing support to others
- Teaching others
- Working as a member of a team

Organization & Management Skills
- Coordinating tasks
- Managing people/groups
- Managing time
- Organizing information or materials

Human Environment

Sports instructors and coaches work with athletes of varying ages and skill levels. They may also work with other coaching professionals, office and teaching personnel, the media, and the community at large.

Technological Environment

Sports instructors and coaches use a variety of tools, including sports-related physical equipment and audiovisual devices. The physical equipment is designed to improve individual kinetic skills and techniques, which in turn improves the athlete's ability to compete. Audiovisual equipment allows athletes to observe their drill work and exercises, so that they can properly gauge what they need to improve to be competitive.

EDUCATION, TRAINING, AND ADVANCEMENT

High School/Secondary

High school students should study biology, physical education, and computers. English, psychology, and speech communication courses are also helpful, as is participation in whichever sport(s) the student wants to teach. During the summer, students should consider attending athletic camps for further development of individual skills.

Suggested High School Subjects
- English
- First Aid Training
- Health Science Technology
- Physical Education
- Psychology
- Social Studies

Famous First

The first coach of a professional basketball team who as African American was Bill Russell, who began coaching the Boston Celtics in 1966 and, in the following year, led the team to the NBA championship.

College/Postsecondary

Over the years, the job of sports instruction has come to place more of an emphasis on the development of professional standards for those who enter the field. Sports instructors and coaches in schools usually have at least a bachelor's degree, and are often also teachers or other education professionals. Colleges and universities in the United States offer a variety of coaching degree programs, which include courses in subjects such as human kinesiology, biology, physiology, nutrition, sports science and medicine, and professional standards. University programs may also offer internships for interested students, which allow them to observe professionals at work in their chosen sports and develop professional contacts for the future.

Related College Majors

• Physical Education Teaching & Coaching

Adult Job Seekers

Sports instructors and coaching professionals are generally also educators seeking employment in local school districts. Depending on the economic conditions and availability of qualified teachers, college graduates may be required to work as substitute teachers until a full-time opportunity presents itself. Substitute teacher work does not preclude an individual from working as a sports coach in a school district at the same time, and doing so can afford a recent college graduate the opportunity to further develop his or her individual skills and knowledge, while also becoming familiar with the school district personnel and administration. This can be beneficial in the highly competitive job market, as can being certified to teach multiple disciplines.

Participation in professional associations can also provide good opportunities for employment and personal development of one's professional skills. Each state has an official organization for high school sports, coordinated through the National Federation of State High School Associations (NFHS). Other national organizations, such as the Amateur Athletic Union, may also be helpful.

Professional Certification and Licensure

At the high school level, various states have different requirements for professional certification or endorsements in coaching. Some states may require teaching certification. Students interested in pursuing this profession should investigate the requirements of the state and school district in which they wish to work.

Additional Requirements

As in education, a sports instructor or coaching professional's strong commitment to continued learning and training is important for his or her own professional development, as well as for the safety and instruction of the athletes being coached.

Fun Fact

With 621 wins, John McKissick, former head football coach of Summerville High School in Summerville, South Carolina, holds the record for most wins by a football coach at any level. He coached for 63 years before retiring in 2015.

Source: http://www.postandcourier.com

EARNINGS AND ADVANCEMENT

Earnings in this field span the range from zero to many hundreds of thousands of dollars. Most sports instructors and coaches earn very modest amounts of money and usually must supplement their incomes from other sources. Advancement is based on ability and experience. Median annual earnings of sports instructors and coaches were $31,000 in 2015. The lowest ten percent earned less than $17,930, and the highest ten percent earned more than $70,050.

Only successful professional coaches in established professional organizations or schools can usually expect any fringe benefits. These usually include paid vacations, holidays, and sick days; life and health insurance; and retirement benefits.

Metropolitan Areas with the Highest
Employment Level in this Occupation

Metropolitan area	Employment	Employment per thousand jobs	Anuual mean wage
Los Angeles-Long Beach-Glendale, CA	5,490	1.42	$47,000
New York-White Plains-Wayne, NY-NJ	4,320	0.84	$42,880
St. Louis, MO-IL	3,670	2.88	$25,040
Santa Ana-Anaheim-Irvine, CA	3,340	2.37	$41,390
Chicago-Joliet-Naperville, IL	3,320	0.91	$32,290
Seattle-Bellevue-Everett, WA	3,310	2.35	$43,150
Boston-Cambridge-Quincy, MA	3,160	1.85	$47,770
Washington-Arlington-Alexandria, DC-VA-MD-WV	2,840	1.21	$51,510
Denver-Aurora-Broomfield, CO	2,700	2.19	$37,610
Philadelphia, PA	2,600	1.43	$37,780

Source: Bureau of Labor Statistics

EMPLOYMENT AND OUTLOOK

There were about 250,000 sports instructors and coaches employed nationally in 2014. About half of all sports instructors and coaches worked part-time, and about one-fourth were self-employed, earning fees for lessons. Employment is expected to grow as fast as the average for all occupations through the year 2024, which means employment is projected to increase 4 percent to 8 percent. Job opportunities are expected for sports instructors and coaches as more people in our society are becoming interested in physical fitness. Employment will also increase with the growth of school and college athletic programs and demand for private sports instruction. Persons who are certified to teach academic subjects in addition to physical education will have the best chances of finding sports instructor and coach jobs.

Employment Trend, Projected 2014–24

Total, all occupations: 7%

Sports instructors and coaches: 6%

Sports and entertainment occupations: 6%

Note: "All Occupations" includes all occupations in the U.S. Economy. Source: U.S. Bureau of Labor Statistics, Employment Projections Program

Conversation With . . .
CHUCK KYLE

Head Football & Head Track Coach
Saint Ignatius High School, Cleveland, Ohio
Coaching and teaching, 44 years

1. What was your individual career path in terms of education/training, entry-level job, or other significant opportunity?

I majored in English and wanted to either go to law school or become a teacher. During sophomore year, I took the introductory education course and realized that was the path I wanted to take. I was playing football at John Carroll University here in Ohio and hurt my shoulder early my junior year. After that season, I had a conversation with the St. Ignatius head coach about helping him coach. It sounded like a great idea. I didn't think my shoulder was ever going to come back. So when I was a college senior, I scheduled my classes early in the day and drove down to St. Ignatius to work as an assistant coach. Fortunately, there was an opening the following April and I was hired to teach English. I've been here ever since.

The National Federation of State High School Associations inducted me into its 2016 Hall of Fame, which is humbling because it's not just the football hall of fame. It encompasses all of athletics as well as teachers of art and music. Since last year, I've been a youth football advisor for the Cleveland Browns. The Haslams (the team owners) firmly believe if a kid is involved in athletics, he or she will also do well in school. They want to be the model NFL team that works with youth. So far it's been wonderful.

2. What are the most important skills and/or qualities for someone in your profession?

If someone thinks he wants to get into this vocation—and I call it a vocation—it shouldn't be because he or she is an expert in strategy. It's really not that. It's the enjoyment of working with people. If you show you care about kids, they'll care about you, they'll care about the program. I find sports an excellent teaching tool. Teaching English is very interesting, but where does a young person learn how to work with other people? Where do they learn the idea of commitment? You learn it vividly on a practice field or in a gym. It's difficult to find a poem or a novel that clearly teaches that.

3. What do you wish you had known going into this profession?

As a young person, I don't think you realize the time commitment that it takes to do coaching right. That's an issue; it does take time. There's no shortcut.

4. Are there many job opportunities in your profession? In what specific areas?

Overall, there are. I'm an anomaly because I've been a head coach here for so many years. Usually, a person's coaching for 6, 7, 8 years at a place. Most coaches are also teachers. It really helps to be a teacher and a coach. It's important that you have as many coaches as you can in the school building, because things come up during the day, from other teachers or from the kids themselves.

5. How do you see your profession changing in the next five years? What role will technology play in those changes, and what skills will be required?

High school sports are struggling financially, because schools are struggling. It's a shame because they're a very important part of education. In Europe, all the sports are club sports. School ends and they shut the doors and the kids go to club sports. There's no connection to school spirit.

There are definitely good things about technology. Years ago, I would mail DVDs all over America, and an assistant coach at some college would have 500 of them stacked up. Nowadays, I push a button and highlight films are on the college coach's computer. He's at the airport and can analyze 10 kids as he waits for his plane. Also, you can film the game on an iPad so that when the defense comes off the field, you can say, "Hey fellas, this happened the last couple of plays, look at this."

6. What do you enjoy most about your job? What do you enjoy least about your job?

Working with young people keeps me young. When the day comes that I don't have that kind of energy, it'll be time to stop.

One thing I don't enjoy is the idea of the win. You build up that pressure and most of the time it's self-inflicted. You have to say, "Come on, the world's a big place, I'm not going to really worry about this football game we're having."

7. Can you suggest a valuable "try this" for students considering a career in your profession?

Help out with youth leagues or rec leagues. Starting with a younger, simpler age is a good idea. Just because a person is a great player doesn't mean he'll make a good coach. A lot of times, a second team player goes on to be a great coach because he or she had to know the technique well because he or she didn't have the speed or the size.

MORE INFORMATION

Amateur Athletic Union
P.O. Box 22409
Lake Buena Vista, FL 32830
407.934.7200
www.aausports.org

American Federation of Teachers
555 New Jersey Avenue NW
Washington, DC 20001
202.879.4400
www.aft.org

National Collegiate Athletic Association
700 West Washington Street
P.O. Box 6222
Indianapolis, IN 46206
317.917.6222
www.ncaa.org

National Federation of State High School Associations
P.O. Box 690
Indianapolis, IN 46206
317.972.6900
www.nfhs.org

National High School Athletic Coaches Association
P.O. Box 3181
Clearwater, FL 33767
407.592.9212
www.nhsaca.org

National Junior College Athletic Association
1631 Mesa Avenue, Suite B
Colorado Springs, CO 80906
719.590.9788
www.njcaa.org

Positive Coaching Alliance
1001 North Rengstorff Avenue
Suite 100
Mountain View, CA 94043
866.725.0024
www.positivecoach.org

Chuck Goodwin/Editor

Teacher Assistant

Snapshot

Career Cluster(s): Education & Training; Human Services
Interests: Teaching, Pedagogy, Curriculum Development
Earnings (Yearly Average): $24,900
Employment & Outlook: Average Growth Expected

OVERVIEW

Sphere of Work

Teacher assistants support lead teachers as needed. Teacher assistants are sometimes called paraprofessionals, paraeducators, teacher aides, or instructional aides. In most instances, teacher assistants offer instructional support, student support, and clerical help. As public school budgets decrease and class sizes grow, many public school districts in the United States are addressing growing class size issues by increasing the number of teacher assistants on staff.

Teacher assistants follow the teaching, lesson, and behavioral plans developed by the lead teacher and school administrators. The lead teacher may assign the teacher assistant tasks such as grading,

photocopying, project set up and clean up, tutoring, small group instruction, homework review, and student supervision during lunch, recess, and field trips. At the elementary level, teacher assistants tend to be generalists comfortable supporting instruction in a wide range of subjects. At the secondary school level, teacher assistants tend to be single-subject assistants trained to offer instructional support in math, science, language arts, or the social sciences.

Work Environment

Teacher assistants work in both public and private school settings and in all grade levels from preschool through high school. Teaching assistants work in schools built to meet to the social and educational needs of children and adolescents. Classrooms and schools have different types of and access to resources, such as art supplies, music lessons, physical education facilities, field trips, and assistant teachers. The resources available depend on the financial resources of the school and district, as well as the educational philosophy driving the curriculum.

Profile

Working Conditions: Work Indoors
Physical Strength: Light Work
Education Needs: Junior/ Technical/Community College
Licensure/Certification: Usually Not Required
Opportunities For Experience: Internship, Apprenticeship, Volunteer Work, Part Time Work
Holland Interest Score*: ESC, SCE

* See Appendix A

Occupation Interest

Individuals drawn to patient, and caring. Often, parents of school age children seeking part-time employment pursue teaching assistant positions, in order to align their children's schedule with their own. Those who work in special education settings may need to be able to move, lift, and carry students needing assistance. Teacher assistants, who instruct and nurture students, should enjoy spending long hours with children and adolescents. Successful teacher assistants excel at teamwork, communication, and problem solving.

A Day in the Life—Duties and Responsibilities

A teacher assistant's daily duties and responsibilities vary based on his or her area of specialization and job specifications. Areas of teacher assistant specialization include preschool, elementary, secondary, or special education support.

Teacher assistants working in a preschool setting support the lead teacher's vision and curriculum. A preschool teacher assistant's daily duties and responsibilities include classroom preparation and clean up, as well as student care. Classroom preparation and cleaning duties may include labeling materials; organizing work areas such as the art area or reading area; preparing student snacks and, in some cases, lunch; setting up daily projects; and cleaning up and sanitizing at the end of the day. Student care duties include greeting students in the morning; calming fears and addressing separation anxiety; promoting a supportive and nurturing classroom environment; maintaining student safety and health; and providing consistent student discipline.

Teacher assistants working in an elementary and secondary school settings support the lead teacher as needed. A teacher assistant's daily duties and responsibilities include grading, photocopying, project set up and clean up, tutoring, small group instruction, homework review, displaying student work on bulletin boards and display boards, presenting prepared lectures and assignments, enforcing school policies, maintaining student records, and supervising students during lunch, recess, and field trips.

Teacher assistants offering special education support may be assigned to be the full-time instructional aide of a single student or may be assigned the job of classroom support. Special education teacher assistants help students with physical, language, mental, or behavioral challenges. Specific tasks may include feeding assistance, language instruction or translation, peer mediation, riding with students on the school bus, reviewing study habits, homework help, tutoring, and documenting student progress.

All teacher assistants are required to attend staff meetings and participate in teacher mentoring relationships. Ultimately, teacher assistants must work on a daily basis to meet the needs of all students, families, lead teachers, and school administrators.

Duties and Responsibilities

- Discussing assigned teaching area with teacher to coordinate classroom efforts
- Preparing a lesson plan and submitting it to the teacher
- Planning and developing teaching aids, such as charts, graphs and bibliographies
- Presenting subject matter to students
- Preparing, giving and grading tests
- Calling roll and keeping attendance records
- Passing out school materials
- Supervising students in the classroom, cafeteria, library, halls and on school grounds
- Setting up and operating audio-visual equipment

WORK ENVIRONMENT

Physical Instructors

A teacher assistant's physical environment is the classroom and school setting. Occasionally, teacher assistants work outdoors with students. Teacher assistants generally work when school is in session and follow an annual academic schedule with ample winter, spring, and summer vacations. Many teacher assistants work part-time. Summer teaching opportunities in summer school and summer camps are common.

Relevant Skills and Abilities

Communication Skills
- Editing written information
- Speaking effectively
- Writing concisely

Interpersonal/Social Skills
- Being patient
- Cooperating with others
- Teaching others
- Working as a member of a team

Organization & Management Skills
- Demonstrating leadership
- Making decisions
- Performing duties which change frequently
- Performing routine work

Technical Skills
- Working with data or numbers

Human Environment

Teacher assistants are in constant contact with students, student families, school administrators, and fellow teachers. Teacher assistants may work with students who are on individual education plans, have physical and mental disabilities, or who are English language learners (ELL). Teacher assistants must be comfortable working with people from a wide range of backgrounds.

Technological Environment

School classrooms increasingly include computers for student use. Teacher assistants should be comfortable using Internet communication tools and teaching students to use educational software. Teacher assistants may also use computers to perform administrative tasks and record student progress. In addition, teacher assistants offering special education support to students with physical disabilities may need to help their students with adaptive technology, such as wheel chairs and hearing aids. Teacher assistants should be comfortable with standard office and audiovisual equipment.

EDUCATION, TRAINING, AND ADVANCEMENT

High School/Secondary

High school students interested in becoming teacher assistants should develop good study habits. Interested high school students should take a broad range of courses in education, child development, science, math, history, language arts, foreign language, physical education, and the arts. Those interested in the field of education may benefit from seeking internships or part-time work with children and teachers at camps and after school programs.

Suggested High School Subjects
- Arts
- Audio-Visual
- Business & Computer Technology
- Child Care
- Child Growth & Development
- Crafts
- English
- First Aid Training
- Instrumental & Vocal Music
- Mathematics
- Science
- Speech

Famous First

The first state ban on corporal punishment in schools was instituted in New Jersey in 1867. The second such ban came over 100 years later, in 1971, in Massachusetts. Today, corporal punishment is banned by all but 19 states, most of them in the South (along with selected states in the Midwest and the Mountain West).

College/Postsecondary

College students interested in becoming teacher assistants should work towards the associate's degree or bachelor's degree in education or a related field. Coursework in psychology, child development, language arts, and foreign language may also prove useful in their future work. Prior to graduation, prospective teacher assistants should gain teaching experience, through internships or work in daycare, preschool, or camp settings.

Related College Majors
- Bilingual/Bicultural Education
- Teacher Assistant/Aide Training

Adult Job Seekers

Adults seeking employment as teacher assistants should have, at a minimum, a high school or associate's degree. Those seeking jobs as teacher assistants should research the education and certification requirements of their home states, as well of the schools where they seek employment. Adult job seekers in the education field may benefit from the employment workshops and job lists maintained by professional teaching associations, such as the American Federation of Teachers (AFT).

Professional Certification and Licensure

There are no specific professional certification and licensure requirements for teacher assistants. Some states require teacher assistants to hold state teaching licenses. Those individuals planning to advance in the teaching profession may choose to pursue teaching certification, which varies by state and specialty.

Most schools require applicants to maintain a driver's license and pass a background check.

Additional Requirements

Individuals who find satisfaction, success, and job security as teacher assistants will be knowledgeable about the profession's requirements, responsibilities, and opportunities. Teacher assistants must have integrity and be highly ethical, as these professionals interact with minors and have access to personal information of students and their families. Membership in professional teaching associations is encouraged among all educational professionals as a means of building status within a professional community and networking.

Fun Fact

In *Finding Dory*, Dory helps out as a teacher assistant at Nemo's school. When she hears a lesson about animals' instincts leading them back to their families, she realizes she must have a family and sets out to find them.
Source: http://www.hcpress.com

EARNINGS AND ADVANCEMENT

Earnings depend on the individual's education and experience and the type, size and geographic location of the school district. Median annual earnings of teacher assistants were $24,900 in 2015. The lowest ten percent earned less than $17,920, and the highest ten percent earned more than $38,000.

Full-time teacher assistants have vacation days when their school is closed, as in during the summer, over holidays and in inclement weather. They may also receive life and health insurance and retirement benefits. These benefits are usually paid by the employer.

Metropolitan Areas with the Highest
Employment Level in this Occupation

Metropolitan area	Employment	Employment per thousand jobs	Anuual mean wage
Chicago-Naperville-Arlington Heights, IL	4,780	1.34	$31,240
Austin-Round Rock, TX	4,550	4.90	$35,020
Washington-Arlington-Alexandria, DC-VA-MD-WV	4,160	1.72	$43,070
New York-Jersey City-White Plains, NY-NJ	4,030	0.62	$43,050
Ann Arbor, MI	3,950	18.85	$45,290
San Diego-Carlsbad, CA	2,970	2.19	$32,330
Minneapolis-St. Paul-Bloomington, MN-WI	2,790	1.48	$33,970
Hartford-West Hartford-East Hartford, CT	2,580	4.46	$23,190
St. Louis, MO-IL	2,370	1.79	$34,040
Houston-The Woodlands-Sugar Land, TX	1,960	0.67	$24,540

Source: Bureau of Labor Statistics

EMPLOYMENT AND OUTLOOK

There were approximately 1.3 million teacher assistants employed nationally in 2014. Employment is expected to grow about as fast as the average for all occupations through the year 2024, which means employment is projected to increase 4 percent to 8 percent. Job growth will be driven by increasing student enrollments in elementary and secondary schools in both public and private settings.

Employment Trend, Projected 2014–24

Education, training, and library occupations: 8%

Total, all occupations: 7%

Teacher assistants: 6%

Note: "All Occupations" includes all occupations in the U.S. Economy. Source: U.S. Bureau of Labor Statistics, Employment Projections Program

Related Occupations
- Childcare Worker
- Elementary School Teacher
- Preschool Worker
- Secondary School Teacher

Conversation With . . .
JULIE BONDI

Special Education Assistant Teacher
Hemenway Elementary School
Framingham, Massachusetts
Education, 4-plus yrs; assistant teacher, 2½ yrs

1. What was your individual career path in terms of education/training, entry-level job, or other significant opportunity?

I was really indecisive about choosing a career path. I didn't declare a major until my junior year at Framingham State University in Massachusetts, then rapidly went through the education classes and the student teaching requirements and the Massachusetts Tests for Educator Licensure (MTELs). The semester before I was supposed to graduate, I didn't pass my last test and had to switch my major, which kept me in school another year. I graduated in 2014 with a bachelor's in geography and a minor in psychology. I got a job as a long-term substitute one-on-one aide, then switched to a job as a long-term sub for a Grade 5 special education assistant teacher. I applied for the permanent position and got it.

In my school, special ed students in grades 3 to 5 are integrated into mainstream classrooms. Each of those grades has a licensed special ed teacher and a special ed assistant teacher. My job is to help provide services that each student with an Individualized Education Program (IEP) is legally entitled to, as well as to assist mainstream teachers with the integration of those students.

I'm now working on finishing up my teaching license. I completed the Sheltered English Immersion (SEI) program, which is a new requirement for Massachusetts teachers that basically prepares us to teach all kids, no matter what their English proficiency level is. Once I pass the last teacher test, I can do my final semester of student teaching and then I'll have my license. Hopefully within the next couple of years, I'll have my own classroom and I hope I'll be at the same school because I really like it.

2. What are the most important skills and/or qualities for someone in your profession?

The most important skills are time management and organization. For qualities, you really have to be patient and compassionate. Patience is the most important. And flexible—on a day-to-day basis, literally anything can happen. One thing I learned in my education classes that really stuck with me was "equity not equality," because everyone needs something different. So you can't just teach every student the same way; you have to be flexible and give each of them what they need.

3. What do you wish you had known going into this profession?

I didn't realize how deeply a lot of what I see would affect me. Even in the best schools, there are less fortunate children that you wish you could do more for. It can be sad.

4. Are there many job opportunities in your profession? In what specific areas?

There are usually jobs available for one-on-one aides and teacher aides, but the pay can vary greatly from district to district. My title as a "special education assistant teacher" is more prevalent in schools with a high special education population. Not all school districts hire assistant teachers.

5. How do you see your profession changing in the next five years? What role will technology play in those changes, and what skills will be required?

Technology has changed day-to-day classroom life. For example, instead of writing in their journals, students write in Google Docs and give each other feedback through Google Docs. It changes the culture and atmosphere of the classroom. They're more independent. It also creates a lot of fluidity between school and home, as the students can access almost all of their school work online. Of course, one complaint about technology is that it never works when you need it to! Technology also gives students a level of freedom that some teachers are not comfortable with.

6. What do you enjoy most about your job? What do you enjoy least about your job?

I like being in school; it's just a nice atmosphere. My hours are perfect. There's a strong bond between everybody who works here. It's great to work with kids. I get to go outside at recess. It's a nice, comfortable job. I never want to work summers!

My biggest complaint is standardized tests. From April until the end of the year, it's a blur of testing. It puts a lot of pressure on students, as well as on schools, to perform well on the tests. The amount of testing just seems unnecessary.

7. Can you suggest a valuable "try this" for students considering a career in your profession?

I tell my friends all the time, be a substitute teacher. I guarantee you'll want to come back. Every single day, you make a difference. Even if you're 15 years old, volunteer at a local school. If you're old enough, which is 18, be a substitute teacher. Or work as a camp counselor or any job where you're around and responsible for a group of children. Also, check out Future Teachers of America. (www.futureteachers.org)

MORE INFORMATION

**American Association for
Employment in Education**
3040 Riverside Drive, Suite 125
Columbus, OH 43221
614.485.1111
www.aaee.org

American Federation of Teachers
Public Affairs Department
555 New Jersey Avenue, NW
Washington, DC 20001
202.879.4400
www.aft.org

**Council for Professional
Recognition**
2460 16th Street NW
Washington, DC 20009-3547
800.424.4310
www.cdacouncil.org

National Education Association
1201 16th Street NW
Washington, DC 20036-3290
202.833.4000
www.nea.org

**National Resource Center for
Paraprofessionals**
Utah State University
6526 Old Main Hill
Logan, UT 84322-6526
435.797.7272
www.nrcpara.org

Simone Isadora Flynn/Editor

What Are Your Career Interests?

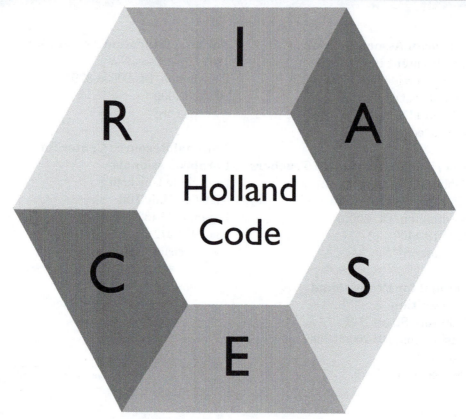

This is based on Dr. John Holland's theory that people and work environments can be loosely classified into six different groups. Each of the letters above corresponds to one of the six groups described in the following pages.

Different people's personalities may find different environments more to their liking. While you may have some interests in and similarities to several of the six groups, you may be attracted primarily to two or three of the areas. These two or three letters are your "Holland Code." For example, with a code of "RES" you would most resemble the Realistic type, somewhat less resemble the Enterprising type, and resemble the Social type even less. The types that are not in your code are the types you resemble least of all.

Most people, and most jobs, are best represented by some combination of two or three of the Holland interest areas. In addition, most people are most satisfied if there is some degree of fit between their personality and their work environment.

The rest of the pages in this booklet further explain each type and provide some examples of career possibilities, areas of study at MU, and co-curricular activities for each code. To take a more in-depth look at your Holland Code, take a self-assessment such as the SDS, Discover, or a card sort at the MU Career Center with a Career Specialist.

Realistic *(Doers)*

People who have athletic ability, prefer to work with objects, machines, tools, plants or animals, or to be outdoors.

Are you?		Can you?	Like to?
practical	independent	fix electrical things	tinker with machines/vehicles
straightforward/frank	ambitious	solve electrical problems	work outdoors
mechanically inclined	systematic	pitch a tent	be physically active
stable		play a sport	use your hands
concrete		read a blueprint	build things
reserved		plant a garden	tend/train animals
self-controlled		operate tools and machine	work on electronic equipment

**Career Possibilities
(Holland Code):**

Air Traffic Controller (SER)	Dental Technician (REI)	Laboratory Technician (RIE)	Property Manager (ESR)
Archaeologist (IRE)	Farm Manager (ESR)	Landscape Architect (AIR)	Recreation Manager (SER)
Athletic Trainer (SRE)	Fish and Game Warden (RES)	Mechanical Engineer (RIS)	Service Manager (ERS)
Cartographer (IRE)	Floral Designer (RAE)	Optician (REI)	Software Technician (RCI)
Commercial Airline Pilot (RIE)	Forester (RIS)	Petroleum Geologist (RIE)	Ultrasound Technologist (RSI)
Commercial Drafter (IRE)	Geodetic Surveyor (IRE)	Police Officer (SER)	Vocational Rehabilitation
Corrections Officer (SER)	Industrial Arts Teacher (IER)	Practical Nurse (SER)	Consultant (ESR)

Investigative *(Thinkers)*

People who like to observe, learn, investigate, analyze, evaluate, or solve problems.

Are you?		Can you?	Like to?
inquisitive	intellectually self-confident	think abstractly	explore a variety of ideas
analytical	Independent	solve math problems	work independently
scientific	logical	understand scientific theories	perform lab experiments
observant/precise	complex	do complex calculations	deal with abstractions
scholarly	Curious	use a microscope or computer	do research
cautious		interpret formulas	be challenged

**Career Possibilities
(Holland Code):**

Actuary (ISE)	Chemical Engineer (IRE)	Geologist (IRE)	Physician, General Practice (ISE)
Agronomist (IRS)	Chemist (IRE)	Horticulturist (IRS)	Psychologist (IES)
Anesthesiologist (IRS)	Computer Systems Analyst (IER)	Mathematician (IER)	Research Analyst (IRC)
Anthropologist (IRE)	Dentist (ISR)	Medical Technologist (ISA)	Statistician (IRE)
Archaeologist (IRE)	Ecologist (IRE)	Meteorologist (IRS)	Surgeon (IRA)
Biochemist (IRS)	Economist (IAS)	Nurse Practitioner (ISA)	Technical Writer (IRS)
Biologist (ISR)	Electrical Engineer (IRE)	Pharmacist (IES)	Veterinarian (IRS)

Artistic *(Creators)*

People who have artistic, innovating, or intuitional abilities and like to work in unstructured situations using their imagination and creativity.

Are you?		**Can you?**	**Like to?**
creative	original	sketch, draw, paint	attend concerts, theatre, art
imaginative	introspective	play a musical instrument	exhibits
innovative	impulsive	write stories, poetry, music	read fiction, plays, and poetry
unconventional	sensitive	sing, act, dance	work on crafts
emotional	courageous	design fashions or interiors	take photography
independent	complicated		express yourself creatively
Expressive	idealistic		deal with ambiguous ideas
	nonconforming		

Career Possibilities
(Holland Code):

Actor (AES)	Copy Writer (ASI)	Interior Designer (AES)	Medical Illustrator (AIE)
Advertising Art Director (AES)	Dance Instructor (AER)	Intelligence Research Specialist	Museum Curator (AES)
Advertising Manager (ASE)	Drama Coach (ASE)	(AEI)	Music Teacher (ASI)
Architect (AIR)	English Teacher (ASE)	Journalist/Reporter (ASE)	Photographer (AES)
Art Teacher (ASE)	Entertainer/Performer (AES)	Landscape Architect (AIR)	Writer (ASI)
Artist (ASI)	Fashion Illustrator (ASR)	Librarian (SAI)	Graphic Designer (AES)

Social *(Helpers)*

People who like to work with people to enlighten, inform, help, train, or cure them, or are skilled with words.

Are you?		**Can you?**	**Like to?**
friendly	cooperative	teach/train others	work in groups
helpful	generous	express yourself clearly	help people with problems
idealistic	responsible	lead a group discussion	do volunteer work
insightful	forgiving	mediate disputes	work with young people
outgoing	patient	plan and supervise an activity	serve others
understanding	kind	cooperate well with others	

Career Possibilities
(Holland Code):

City Manager (SEC)	Historian (SEI)	Park Naturalist (SEI)	Teacher (SAE)
Clinical Dietitian (SIE)	Hospital Administrator (SER)	Physical Therapist (SIE)	Social Worker (SEA)
College/University Faculty (SEI)	Psychologist (SEI)	Police Officer (SER)	Speech Pathologist (SAI)
Community Org. Director	Insurance Claims Examiner	Probation and Parole Officer	Vocational-Rehab. Counselor
(SEA)	(SIE)	(SEC)	(SEC)
Consumer Affairs Director	Librarian (SAI)	Real Estate Appraiser (SCE)	Volunteer Services Director
(SER)Counselor/Therapist	Medical Assistant (SCR)	Recreation Director (SER)	(SEC)
(SAE)	Minister/Priest/Rabbi (SAI)	Registered Nurse (SIA)	
	Paralegal (SCE)		

<u>E</u>nterprising *(Persuaders)*

People who like to work with people, influencing, persuading, leading or managing for organizational goals or economic gain.

Are you?
self-confident
assertive
persuasive
energetic
adventurous
popular

ambitious
agreeable
talkative
extroverted
spontaneous
optimistic

Can you?
initiate projects
convince people to do things
  your way
sell things
give talks or speeches
organize activities
lead a group
persuade others

Like to?
make decisions
be elected to office
start your own business
campaign politically
meet important people
have power or status

**Career Possibilities
(Holland Code):**

Advertising Executive (ESA)
Advertising Sales Rep (ESR)
Banker/Financial Planner (ESR)
Branch Manager (ESA)
Business Manager (ESC)
Buyer (ESA)
Chamber of Commerce Exec
  (ESA)

Credit Analyst (EAS)
Customer Service Manager
  (ESA)
Education & Training Manager
  (EIS)
Emergency Medical Technician
  (ESI)
Entrepreneur (ESA)

Foreign Service Officer (ESA)
Funeral Director (ESR)
Insurance Manager (ESC)
Interpreter (ESA)
Lawyer/Attorney (ESA)
Lobbyist (ESA)
Office Manager (ESR)
Personnel Recruiter (ESR)

Politician (ESA)
Public Relations Rep (EAS)
Retail Store Manager (ESR)
Sales Manager (ESA)
Sales Representative (ERS)
Social Service Director (ESA)
Stockbroker (ESI)
Tax Accountant (ECS)

<u>C</u>onventional *(Organizers)*

People who like to work with data, have clerical or numerical ability, carry out tasks in detail, or follow through on others' instructions.

Are you?
well-organized
accurate
numerically inclined
methodical
conscientious
efficient
conforming

practical
thrifty
systematic
structured
polite
ambitious
obedient
persistent

Can you?
work well within a system
do a lot of paper work in a short
  time
keep accurate records
use a computer terminal
write effective business letters

Like to?
follow clearly defined
  procedures
use data processing equipment
work with numbers
type or take shorthand
be responsible for details
collect or organize things

**Career Possibilities
(Holland Code):**

Abstractor (CSI)
Accountant (CSE)
Administrative Assistant (ESC)
Budget Analyst (CER)
Business Manager (ESC)
Business Programmer (CRI)
Business Teacher (CSE)
Catalog Librarian (CSE)

Claims Adjuster (SEC)
Computer Operator (CSR)
Congressional-District Aide (CES)
Cost Accountant (CES)
Court Reporter (CSE)
Credit Manager (ESC)
Customs Inspector (CEI)
Editorial Assistant (CSI)

Elementary School Teacher
  (SEC)
Financial Analyst (CSI)
Insurance Manager (ESC)
Insurance Underwriter (CSE)
Internal Auditor (ICR)
Kindergarten Teacher (ESC)

Medical Records Technician
  (CSE)
Museum Registrar (CSE)
Paralegal (SCE)
Safety Inspector (RCS)
Tax Accountant (ECS)
Tax Consultant (CES)
Travel Agent (ECS)

BIBLIOGRAPHY

General/Historical

Goldstein, Dana. *The Teacher Wars: A History of America's Most Embattled Profession*. New York: Anchor Books, 2014.

Gordon, Howard R.D. *The History and Growth of Career and Technical Education in America*, 4th ed. Long Grove, IL: Waveland Press, 2014.

Mondale, Sarah, ed. *School: The Story of American Public Education*. Boston: Beacon Press, 2002.

Ravitch, Diane. *The Death and Life of the Great American School System*, 3rd ed. New York: Basic Books, 2016.

Teaching

Anonymous. *The Secret Lives of Teachers*. Chicago: University of Chicago Press, 2015.

Armstrong, Thomas. *The Power of the Adolescent Brain: Strategies for Teaching Middle and High School Students*. Alexandria, VA: ASCD, 2016.

Bain, Ben. *What the Best College Teachers Do*. Cambridge, MA: Harvard University Press, 2004.

Baker, Nicholson. *Substitute: Going to School with a Thousand Kids*. New York: Blue Rider Press, 2016.

Brinkley, Alan, et al. *The Chicago Handbook for Teachers: A Practical Guide to the College Classroom*, 2nd ed. Chicago: University of Chicago Press, 2011.

Brown, Dave F. and Trudy Knowles. *What Every Middle School Teacher Should Know*, 3rd ed. Portsmouth, NH: Heinemann, 2014.

Green, Tena. *How to Be Successful in Your First Year of Teaching Elementary School*. Ocala, FL: Atlantic Publishing, 2010.

Gutkind, Lee, ed. *What I Didn't Know: True Stories of Becoming a Teacher*. Pittsburgh: In Fact Books, 2016.

Kellough, Richard D. and Noreen G. Kellough. *Secondary School Teaching: A Guide to Methods and Resources*, 4th ed. Upper Saddle River, NJ: Pearson, 2010.

Lortie, Dan C. *Schoolteacher: A Sociological Study*. Chicago: University of Chicago Press, 2002.

Morrison, George S. *Early Childhood Education Today*, 13th ed. Upper Saddle River, NJ: Pearson Higher Education, 2014.

Parkay, Forrest W. *Becoming a Teacher*, 10th ed. Boston: Pearson, 2015.

Smith, Deborah Deutsch and Naomi Chowdhuri Tyler. *Introduction to Special Education: Making a Difference*, 9th ed. Upper Saddle River, NJ: Pearson Higher Education, 2009.

Underwood, Joseph W., ed. *Today I Made a Difference: A Collection of Inspiring Stories from America's Top Educators*. Avon, MA: Adams Media, 2009.

Allied Areas

Fourie, Dennis and Nancy E. Loe. *Libraries in the Information Age: An Introduction and Career Exploration*. Santa Barbara, CA: Libraries Unlimited, 2016.

Littrell, John M. and Jean Sunde Peterson. *Portrait and Model of a School Counselor*. New York: Routledge, 2004.

Melber, Leah M., ed. *Teaching the Museum: Careers in Museum Education*. Washington, DC: American Alliance of Museums, 2014.

Schlatter, N. Elizabeth. *Museum Careers: A Practical Guide for Students and Novices*. New York: Routledge, 2009.

Toor, Ruth and Hilda K. Weisberg. *Being Indispensable: A School Librarian's Guide to Becoming an Invaluable Leader*. Chicago: American Library Association, 2011.

INDEX